HEALING

THE WHOLE PERSON,
THE WHOLE PLANET

Edited by Molli Nickell

Book Design and Illustrations by Gary Lund

HEALING
The Whole Person, The Whole Planet

Contributing spirit teachers include: Ramtha, Seth, Bartholomew, Hilarion, Dr. Peebles, Li Sung, John, Robbyn and His Merrye Bande, Kyros, and others.

Published by:
Beyond Words/Spirit Speaks
Route #3, Box 492 B
Hillsboro, OR 97123
503 647-5109
or call toll free
800 284-9673
Fax: 503-647-5114

First printing April, 1988

ISBN: 0-941831-14-0

Library of Congress
Catalogue Card Number: 88-70817
Copyright 2-367-824 Spirit Speaks Inc.

This book is dedicated to those whose passion for life encourages them to strive for greater understanding of it.

Dedication and passion are perfect words to describe a very special group of people who combined their efforts and talents to bring this book, and the subsequent series, to life. We wish to acknowledge and thank Glenn Nickell, Gary Lund, Richard Cohn, Bob Mason, Sharon MacDonald, Paula Nowels, Laura Spickler, Craig Jones, and all the delightful contributing spirit teachers from God's great computer room in the sky.

TABLE OF CONTENTS

EDITOR'S INTRODUCTION

Dear Reader,

Thank you for picking up this book. The material on these pages is presented to you with our best wishes for your improved or continued good health and happiness.

The healing industry has undergone some tremendous changes over the past ten years with the advent of holistic healing practices. These deal with the body, mind, *and* spirit, and are revolutionizing health care. Health practitioners are becoming more aware of the fact that human beings are indivisible, and healing must allow for all aspects, including the indefinable soul and spirit. Only by assisting the patient in understanding and dealing with all portions of themselves can the necessary harmony manifest to create a healthy body.

Understanding all aspects of the human being is also what this book is about. Those who have participated in its creation believe that both illness and healing are deeply rooted in the foundations of our being, beyond the mental, beyond the physical, extending into spirit, into the very essence of who and what we are.

What you are, what I am, what all living beings are, is energy, spirit energy. We are fragments of a universal God, expressing ourselves in physical form for the purpose of experience. We have chosen life here, on this planet, as a grand school to assist us in further understanding various aspects of life as human beings. It's that simple, and also that complicated.

Once you come to understand *why* you have made the choice to experience physical life, you can then also come to understand yourself in terms of healing what ails you. This is truly the only way that healing is accomplished.

As you grow in increased understanding of self, you will also be helping the planet to heal as well. How? Well, Mother Earth is a living being, just like you. And just as you are connected, via spirit, to all living beings, you are also connected to Earth. And she is affected by all the combined attitudes, beliefs, and behaviors of those who live on her surface.

This book is not only about healing, it's about life. You can't separate one from the other. The points of view presented here will assist you in learning more about who and what you really are. It will help you to loosen up, lighten up and love yourself more. You'll come to see yourself for the brave and courageous being you are to have chosen life on this planet at this challenging time.

As your self-awareness expands, you will feel increased peace within yourself--which ultimately leads to healing. You will also begin to feel increased peace and kinship with all other beings on the planet. You will become a ripple in the stream of ever-changing consciousness. And those around you will be affected by your changing attitudes. They will begin to change . . . and so on and so on. Get the picture?

Planetary healing, governmental changes, world peace, etc. are up to you and me and everybody else, first on an individual basis. Nobody or no "thing" is going to repair the muck-ups we have created, a planet at war--between countries, between states, between philosophies, between people, within ourselves. The groundswell of healing attitudes and healing bodies on this planet begins where it started, at home; and that's within each one of us. Let's face it, we are all in life together, *it's all of us or none.*

This book is the first of the *Gathering of Friends* series, in which many different points of view are offered from a variety of loving and wise beings called spirit teachers. The spiritual psychology they share helps us to understand more about all aspects of life as viewed from their expanded perspectives. Some of the material has been previously published in the bi-monthly *Spirit Speaks,* which is now called *CHANNELING* magazine.

The process of communication with the spirit teachers you are about to meet is called "channeling." It refers to an ancient means of communication, newly revived. Channeling is a communication process that brings helpful information forth from the collective consciousness, which might be perceived as an endless pool of energy and knowledge.

You and every living thing in the universe are composed of energy. Scientists and philosophers, from Socrates to Einstein, have acknowledged the existence of other dimensions of intelligent energy surrounding us, even though we may not be able to see, touch, hear, or smell them. For example, you cannot *see* the energy that fuses through an electrical cord to light your lamp. You just know the energy is there as light floods the room when you turn on the lamp switch. In a similar way, we are able to tune in to energies from another dimension--the spirit plane.

Communication with beings (we call them spirit teachers) on the spirit plane is accomplished through the process of channeling. Channels, frequently called trance mediums, are people with the ability to step aside from their normal state of consciousness, allowing spirit teachers to speak through them. An example of a channel/medium is Edgar Cayce, whose books of channeled teachings have been sold worldwide since the 1950's.

Spirit teachers who speak via the channeling process are compassionate beings, eager to help us more fully understand our relationship to daily trials and tribulations. Most spirit teachers have occupied physical bodies themselves and are acutely aware of the frustrations and fears that we experience. They desire to communicate with us because they wish to assist us in remembering more about who we are and why we have elected to experience physical life.

Because they are not (at the moment) in physical form, they see life from a broader perspective than we do as we struggle with the complexities of daily living. They desire to offer a helping hand to better prepare us for continuing social, economic, physical and environmental changes.

There are hundreds and thousands of different groups of spirit teachers devoting their energy and their love toward the upliftment of all humanity and the healing of the planet earth. However, for purposes of clear communication, only one spirit teacher represents each group; you might see this being as a "spokes-spirit." Many spirit teachers refer to themselves as "we" because they are speaking for the collective group.

The most important message that *all* spirit teachers have for us is that we have *chosen* to be physical human beings. They teach that in life there are no victims, there are only creators. They stress that we have chosen to be physical for the express purpose of gaining *greater understanding* of all aspects of life.

You will find that there will be statements from some spirit teachers which seemingly contradict statements made by others. All spirit teachers have experienced widely different life situations. This great variety in experience creates multiple points of view. Therefore, some of their statements, at least on the surface, may appear to be contradictory.

Consider this: if you asked eleven people to study the rose, then describe it, you would receive eleven different responses. One person would comment on the thorns, another on the stem, yet another on the aroma. All would see aspects of the whole flower from different perspectives. When you put these aspects together, they complement each other rather than contradict.

So, as you read this book and come across some of what you see as possibly conflicting passages, please remember the rose. Then listen to that still, small voice within your heart to find the truths which are perfect for your unique and special level of understanding.

Also, you may find some of the information a little difficult to understand the first time you read it, particularly if you are not familiar with spiritual or metaphysical concepts. You might look at it this way; gaining new knowledge about life (and everything else) is a little like going to tennis camp. Really!

The first time my husband and I attended a Vic Braden adult tennis camp, we were lost when he spoke about strategy. His lecture about ball placement and on-court movement went right over our heads. As beginners, all we could focus on was trying to hit the ball over the net without falling down or looking foolish in the process. One year later, after having hit thousands of tennis balls and with some playing experience under our belts, we went through the program again. This time, the strategy talk made sense to us.

So, instead of getting stuck or feeling frustrated in trying to figure out some of the more esoteric passages, just glide over them, knowing that at a later time you can re-read them and they'll make perfect sense to you.

In the words of one of our spirit contributors, Dong How Li, "Please remember, take what resonates with you, what assists, what nourishes, what feeds you; above all, what inspires you to do what you have come to do. The rest, please leave by the wayside."

All of us from Spirit Speaks Inc. and Beyond Words send you light, love, laughter, and encouragement. May God bless you.

Molli Nickell
Publisher/Editor-in-Chief
Spirit Speaks Inc.
Los Angeles, California
April, 1988

GREETINGS
FROM THE CONTRIBUTORS

"This book of channeling is a banquet for you, our friends. May you all be nourished, enriched, enlivened, and refreshed. We thank you for letting us share with you." ... Robbyn and His Merrye Bande.

Robbyn and His Merrye Bande: This is a book of "channeling." Channeling is a process which occurs as planet earth grows to new levels of wisdom and understanding, providing new information enabling the consciousness of the planet to rise. The information is provided from the world of spirit to your world through what are sometimes called "instruments," but who are people we prefer to call our special *friends.*

Who are these special friends, channels, or instruments? They are people who are able to relate to the new information and knowledge before the rest of the planet. They lend us (those of us on the spirit side) their minds to understand new concepts, their vocal chords and hands to speak to and write to you, and if we get *especially* lucky, occasionally they'll lend us their computers.

Channeling is very common on your planet.

Many of you are probably familiar with channelings and channelers from other times and places in history. There is the *Bible,* the *Bhagavad-Gita,* the *Koran,* Stonehenge, the Pyramids, and later, Shakespeare, Mozart, Bach, Beethoven, Galileo, da Vinci, Einstein, and many other artists, musicians, scientists, religious leaders, and politicians. Some were known to be inspired and some were recognized clearly as prophets.

Channeling now, as always, is a sacred trust.

It is sacred because it not only involves the spiritual lives of you, the reader, but also those friends who have so graciously given of their time to produce this material, as well as we of the spirit world.

It is sacred because each of you who read some, or all, of this book is being spoken to directly, and is in our vision as we channel on what may seem to be rather general subjects in advance of your reading this. If you were here in the flesh, we would ask for permission to enter your spiritual lives to speak to you of issues in your soul that manifest in the outer world in

ways you do not always understand. We ask you now, in spirit. If some or all of our energy and love is right for you, please read on.

We speak the truth as clearly, nobly, and honorably as the discrepancies of spirit the world communicating to the flesh and limits of language will allow. If you are not familiar with channeling, and even if you are, you may wonder why there are so many of us, and that we speak in so many, sometimes seemingly contradictory ways.

Well, it's like this. Souls on planet earth originated from many different places, and are at many different stages of evolution.

There are many ways of being in this circle we call life.

So many things must be said to many people. What is appropriate as a message to one may not be an appropriate message to all.

Remember this: as you read, do so as if you were at a banquet. You may wish to skip the turnips while others skip the beets. Or, you may skip the meats and eat mostly broccoli. Others may just eat salad and ice cream. But there is agreement on the good fortune to be invited to partake of such a lovely banquet.

This book of channeling is a banquet for our friends, that you may all go away nourished, enriched, enlivened, and refreshed. Thank you for letting us share with you.

We are all aspects of the collective consciousness

Kyros: You are all aspects of the collective consciousness. Each of you are individual droplets of water in the vast ocean of Universal Mind. You have access to all information stored there, you only need to learn how to *tune in and listen.* All that pours forth from Universal Mind is pure and designed for the highest good of all creation. A Universal Thought, however, loses *some* of its purity as it moves through the levels of human consciousness.

You must remember that universal thought is an energy which can never be accurately deciphered and interpreted by the human brain computer. You must also remember that what is verbalized by the human channel always is influenced to a degree by the channel's own programming, ego, level of awareness, and collective consciousness. There is no *pure* human channeling.

Probably the purest thoughts one has are those which cannot be verbalized, and you all have many of those.

As a human channel grows and expands in awareness and becomes more consciously aligned to the universal mind, the channel is less influenced by these things.

I want you to understand that channeling is not a unique phenomenon.

Everyone channels whether they call it that or not.

So, when someone says this or that was channeled, it does not necessarily mean it is to be *your* truth. All you have on planet earth is *relative* truth, and what is true for one may not be so for another. You must test all input from your external world against your own inner sense of truth. The human entity should still learn to test another's truth against his own and to become connected to his own higher guidance.

Some entities depend on channels to tell them what to do in their lives or to tell them what will happen in the future. Some channels do have the awareness to give such answers to you, and sometimes they can predict the future with great accuracy. Most, however, are adept at reading probabilities based on an awareness of a present state of consciousness.

You are ever-changing, and with a mere shift in consciousness, can alter your life course. Remember, your highest guidance is unique for you and it is the only guidance you should ever trust completely. You have *all* your own answers. Although your answers may help others, they are still exclusively *yours*.

About the spirit guides and teachers who have contributed to this book

Soli: My friends, spirit teachers and spirit guides are just that. They come in various shapes and forms. Some of them are from groups of entities that you choose to incarnate with. Some of these friends stay behind in the spirit realm to help guide you. Many of you have been guides and teachers for others on the earth plane while you were within the spirit dimension. You simply reverse the roles.

It is as if God has split Himself up into many small parts (smaller Gods) in order to experience the power of His own creation. You are one of those parts. Therefore, there is no one higher or lower than you or any other part of God. All creation and those in it are parts of God. There are, however, entities on different levels of evolution. Some are on a higher level because they have lived more lives and have attained more wisdom and understanding. These entities, called spirit guides, can assist you through their deeper understanding. My friends, we, in spirit, do not have *all* the answers and we do not pretend to have them. We simply bring you our perspective from a different point of view.

It is rather like we are standing on a mountain top and you are standing only halfway up. We can see more of the valley below than you can. Our vision is more far-reaching. And whatever we believe, that is *our* interpretation. In fact, we are being taught by entities who have even greater understanding than we do. There are some who are like birds flying above the mountain tops. They have an even *greater* vision. What we are trying to do is to bring vast knowledge of certain subjects and a greater vision and understanding to you in a form that your minds can accept, understand, and work with subconsciously.

Also, there are very evolved, very high teachers who remain with you for your entire life. They work with you in enabling you to acquire an even deeper knowledge and a greater understanding in life. They guide you

rare opportunity, and one that should not be taken lightly (please pardon the pun).

Gravity, of necessity, creates the form of energy in density. Energy in a dense form creates the need for time. When there isn't gravity, the energy that is *you* can do a multiple of things at once. So gravity, through density, forces the needs for choice, since you can only do one thing at a time. When you are forced to make choices, you learn about yourself.

Now, since the system is like that, inasmuch as consciousness takes a much denser form than other channels for evolvement in the universe, and since the experiences here are so intense because density clouds other channels of knowing, it was decided that it would behoove the universe to give a little assistance. And so, on this planet, you have assigned guides to help you through.

Generally speaking, we who are guides have already experienced, in some form, whatever it is that you wish to learn in this lifetime. That is why we are with you, a little like a doctoral committee. We all have our areas of expertise and can advise you, even though *you* still need to do the work, read the books, etc. Our job is to point you in the right direction you *chose* for this lifetime and help in that way.

You have your very own team of guides, spirits, angels, teachers, etc. Everyone does. There are also guides who talk to lots of people. Some are free-lance, like "consultants," who channel through lots of people or help psychics.

many ways. But realize that it is only guidance. No guide will ever interfere with your life. No guide will ever do anything within your life that will change your probability pattern.

A spirit guide can lead you through a darkened room to a light switch, but cannot make you turn it on.

You will notice there are many different opinions within the spirit dimension. In this book itself, you will find different spirit communicators and teachers who are bringing forward different perspectives. They are simply perspectives--different points of view--and as such, all have validity. You make the choice of which is most appropriate for you.

Robbyn and His Merrye Bande: In order to better understand spirit guides, teachers, counselors, angels and such, you must be clear on the role of this planet, for there are different opportunities elsewhere in the universe.

Here on Earth, we have a school for the evolution of self-knowing and free-will, accomplished through the exercise of choice. It is a dynamic and popular school and not so easy to get into! So bless the Earth, for gravity is a

travel to San Francisco and needed to rent a vehicle in which to go there. You find one, rent it, and make the trip. When you come back from that journey, you return the vehicle to the rental agency. If you decide on another trip, you again go through that same process: you choose a destination and the vehicle in which to travel. There are infinite destinations, just as well as infinite vehicles.

We are all spirit

Soli: You are not your physical bodies. You are not your emotions. You are not your intellects. You are your Higher Selves. You are spirit. You are a spirit experiencing the physical dimension through the vehicle of a physical body. It is as though you were planning to

It is in much the same way that you arrived on the earth plane. Obviously, it is not quite as simple as this, but you do choose your physical vehicle, you use it for the extent of this life, and then you leave it behind when you go. You also choose a particular time, place, and family for a particular experience needed by your higher self in order to evolve.

This, my friends, is not your only existence. You have had countless lives because as a living spirit, your higher self is experiencing through you endlessly. It is the subconscious mind and its belief systems that tries to tell you

19

that you are the isolated individual that you think you are, that what is all around you is *all that there is*, and that what you have within your physical body is *all there is of you*. In truth, your reality is that of an unlimited, infinite, and indestructible spirit with perpetual existence.

In one sense, you might say that there really is no purpose to life apart from experiencing it. There is no purpose to anything. There is no purpose to suffering or happiness except to experience it. It just is. But there is cause and effect. If you have a certain belief system or do a certain act, then there is an effect from that. But there is no purpose within any act or its effect, except to give you the experience of that act, by simply showing you what the act is. Therein you experience the power of your own creativity through thought within the physical dimension. Therefore, you can see that nothing is more important than anything else. Everything is infinite. There is no time and space. If you don't do it in this lifetime, you will do it in the next.

There is only one belief to hold onto, only one belief that you actually need in life.

I am that I am. I am God. I am everything. I am already perfection.

Now, if you hold these thoughts constantly in your consciousness, all else falls into place automatically. You do not need to do anything else at all, for then you know your God-Self, and you allow that energy to come forward in life. It is very simple. Simplicity is the key to evolution and understanding. Yet human beings want to complicate the simplest of things. This is what logic and intellect do. This is the role they play, believing, "If it is simple, it is obviously wrong. It is too easy. There must be a more complicated answer."

Yet, what you are learning to do is to let go of concepts and belief systems. You are learning to go beyond the subconscious projections through meditation and by communicating

directly with your higher self. Talk to your higher self. Feel the energy of your higher self. Know that this is truly you and also is truly God. Know that you and God are the *same* thing.

Lights - camera - action

Soli: We suggest that you view your lives as if they were movies, yes movies! We are aware that you might not see it quite that way. However, your higher self has written the overall plot of this movie that it wants to play and you are the actor. Now most of you, as actors, get so caught up in the acting role that you begin to believe in the part, instead of seeing it as just a *part* within the movie. You get so caught up within it that you see it very intensely within your being.

There are no accidents

Hilarion: When you agreed to serve as a unit aboard the great classroom called planet earth, certain conditions are accepted in contract with the Karmic Board of the Planetary Hierarchy. The lessons to be learned may include facing a specific disease if it is believed that this course of action will produce the most beneficial results. As you live with these conditions of disease and learn to accept and to be thankful for them, the character, or soul, will undergo permanent change for the better. Thus, from our perspective, disease is simply an opportunity to rise above a given situation, and to learn and grow from the experiencing of it.

We are aware that some of you have difficulty accepting that you enter life having agreed to meet specified conditions, and that *any* of the conditions commonly referred to as disease could possibly be considered beneficial. Nevertheless, that is exactly the scenario in the majority of cases.

Allow us to provide you with an example. Suppose a certain soul had experienced a number of lifetimes in an environment where there had been a chronic shortage of food. Having become adjusted to these circumstances, a subsequently more normal life might find the soul tending to overcompensate, through fear of continuing lack, by overindulging themselves. To correct this trend, another lifetime might be arranged in which the probability of excessive behavior would likely be encountered throughout childhood, leading eventually to addictive behavior in the same areas where the difficulty had been experienced before as an adult. In this way the guides and teachers assigned to work with this soul would focus attention upon the matter, and by exaggerating it to the point where it creates a serious situation in the human life, force the issue to be addressed and rectified, and thus the lesson to be learned.

This technique of releasing patterns from the past is very common these days, and we predict that addictions will grow more prevalent in the future. As returning souls seek the most effective way to encourage spiritual growth in themselves, they take on characteristics which will, through trauma, induce them to look within to remove qualities standing in the way of strength and balance. It may be correctly assumed from our statements that every circumstance of a lifetime spent in this most excellent classroom should be considered a great blessing, for every situation is precisely arranged for the greatest benefit of all who participate in it. For example, those who aspire to help their brethren are allowed an opportunity to play the supporting role to the diseased person, and thus each person finds the perfect part to play on the stage of life. As the saying goes, "There are no accidents on this planet, only opportunities."

A foot in both worlds

Bartholomew: The New Age is a very blase subject now, but if you will contemplate deeply what *new* means, you will realize we are talking about changing the old to receive the new. The difficulty with the reception of the new lies within the physical body itself. New inroads need to be *consciously* created. You cannot remain unconscious about the process and have this new, wondrous energy come pouring through your physical being as fast as you would wish it to.

Many of the difficulties you are experiencing in the physical, emotional, and even the mental sense, come from the inability of your body to truly receive and move with what is now happening in your life. When the movement through the physical is difficult, it can be jarring. Relationships that once were pleasing no longer fill you, jobs that were satisfying are harder to move through, and inner clarity still eludes you. Things like these are simply signals to tell you that *now* is the time to consider how to make these inroads so that all the clarity, wisdom, and health you seek will be yours.

If you wish to be a receiver and holder of this energy, please understand your end of the commitment. It is simply this: to watch yourself constantly, with detached observation--to see what illumines and ignites you, and to see what deadens you. You have been running on past information for many years. You can no longer do things by rote. To say that you've always done things a certain way and so proceed with your life is no longer applicable. What is called for now is a *total action*. You can enlighten yourself with the awareness that the new is ever present by keeping watch in your own physical, mental, emotional, and spiritual laboratory.

For example, if you find yourself going daily to a job that deadens you, you might consider changing it. If you find yourself with people that you resist being with, instead of continually adjusting to those relationships, you might consider it time to weed them out of your life. And when you do, my friends, please *do not fill those places until you know you are filling them with the power of the new* instead of with the repetition of the old. The human psyche is afraid of emptiness. You are *afraid* of the vast wonder that opens you to your being, so you fill your days and nights with outside events. And because of this, when the new energy caresses you, there is no room for it because you are filled with thoughts and actions that no longer bring power to your life. So when we talk about the new, you must understand to create the new, you *let go of the old*.

This new energy is pouring into the Earth and far past it. It is not just this little planet that is going to be engulfed with wonder. There is a vast area in this part of the universe that is going to be lifted and *is* being lifted into another state of understanding. Change is upon the face of this Earth. The outward manifestations of physical change mirror the inner changes that are occurring and will occur in the psyche and the physical body. With this mirror, you are presented with a very basic, helpful tool that can change your life. You have the opportunity of using yourself as an ongoing, *conscious* receptor of this power. You can be the receptor by constantly sending out the call, "Fill me, make me whole. Do whatever transmutation this body needs to have done to make me alive and aware. Help me." Or you can

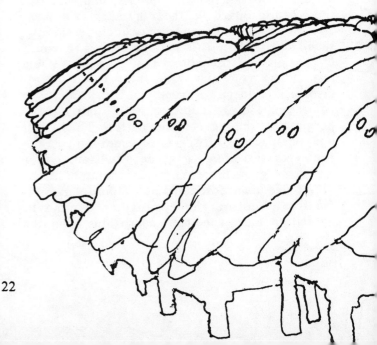

keep on stumbling through your life, trying to fix those areas that are constantly falling apart.

Each one of you has deeply recorded in your psyche an incredibly empowered statement of desire, *"I want to be! I want to be free. I want to be one with God. I want to feel total compassion. I want to be loving." You know* what to ask for. And if you can clarify what you really want for yourself once and for all, and keep that desire as a constant focus, *you will receive what you seek.*

You cannot submerge yourself in the mundane world, becoming transfixed by the manipulations of the earth plane, and at the same time be receptive to this power. *Now is the time of choice*, and the choices you make are important. By the power of your psyche's deepest desire, you will be changed. That has always been the promise. Seek you first the kingdom, and the rest will come. Please understand my desperation, because those of you who are caught, who are not willing to take your attention off the mundane life, are going to find yourselves in difficulty. Your bodies will be in trauma and your minds in confusion.

Many of you are tired of changing the surface of your life and want changes to come from the depths of your being. You have tried all the worldly ways, have you not? You have meditated in a hundred positions, gone to a hundred therapists, and although some changes have taken place, inside yourself you feel incomplete. Your life has still not been ignited. What, then, to do?

If you are ready and committed to giving the attention and awareness necessary, you can begin to change to your psyche's deepest desire. You can be open and alive to it or become closed and fight it. The power is coming and the leading edge is here! You cannot put rules on energy.

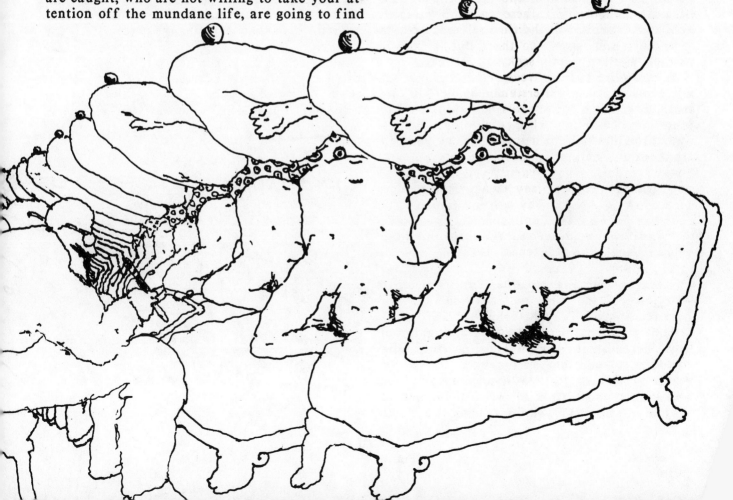

Each of you has the ability to empower the psychic field around you by putting out the call that will *draw* the energy to you.

You have asked for change, so do not try to negotiate your way through it. As the energy enters, outer forms will begin to fall away. Things that seemed very permanent will be eased from your life, and out of fear you may try to resist them, replace them, or substitute other things for them.

Instead of succumbing to fear, may I suggest an alternative, a shift in awareness? There is a part in all of you that few of you have taken the time to develop because it is not lucrative to do so. But in the last rounds of the incarnative cycle, the main commitment is not in working the material plane. The commitment is to yourself, to be aware and alive to yourself every day, and to bring into form, *your inner truth*. YOUR inner truth. You have been a nation, indeed a planet, that spends a lot of time listening to the opinions of others. And what is necessary is to spend time listening to yourself. *You* know what makes you sing, what makes you dance and laugh and love. But if you do not ask yourself what it is that you know, you will go on listening to others, and change will not come because you will not hear your own truth. Every day you spend time taking care of other people, and who is the one that is ignored? Your "self!" Sit down and ask yourself what would delight *you*. These next several years are going to be wonderful for those of you who want the movement that changes bring.

It is the creative side of you that makes your life worth living!

That outreaching, creative side is the part that inspires you, that explodes you into your own truth day by day. So spend time every day listening to what your muse is trying to tell you. There are artists of one kind or another inside *all* of you, but because you have had to focus on making the world sensible, practical and usable, those abilities are just orphans sitting in the back of your life. Understand that

24

you are wondrously complex beings. And when you live on the earth plane, you have to focus to get things done. Please consider widening the focus. Listen with your whole being, and the more you listen, the more you will trust. The more you trust, the more you will expand. And the more you expand, the happier you will be and around it will go.

Over two thousand years ago the world was in a position similar to the one it is in today. The polarities were there, the differences were there, the belief structures were firmly in place, and everyone knew just what to do in order to be *right*. If you believed in yourself enough to listen to yourself, you would realize that now is the time to become your own oracle. Ask yourself what you want, what you need, and then move into it and try it. It's a time of trial. You're going to fall on your face now and then, so when you do, just pick yourself up and try something else. To tune into this energy, you are going to have to develop a new set of ears. You are used to listening to the buzz of the world, but now is the time to develop the inner ear that listens to the inner world. It is time to have a foot in each world, and it can be done!

Living the life divine is learning to live with the awareness of your inner power and to translate it through the physical body and out into the earth plane. So set your goal to *listen*. To listen with more and more of your being so that you can sit in the most abysmal circumstances and feel alive and safe and well. That feeling of safety does not come from paying attention to the world. It comes from learning how to be the judge between the vastness and the mundane. It's an amazingly beautiful job, to bring the divine down to this planet and anchor it in everything you do and say and look upon. You consciously allow yourself to feel the divine and in doing so, silently remind others you and they are It!

A long, long time ago, you left the space of unity and moved into the plane of duality. That was not a voyage that you had a choice about. You did it because you needed to. The yearning inside your being for something vaster is the call from the deepest part of your soul that now wants to end this experiment in duality and move into union. But, my friends, making this a planet of unity is difficult--that is not why it was created. You are trying to do something to this wonderful planet that it doesn't need to have done. There are billions upon billions of people who are learning maximum lessons through *how* they function here. Many of you have learned that you no longer feel alive by killing, that joy comes from sharing and not from owning, that peace is found within and is not dependent on others. Do not condemn the planet for being what it is. It is a wondrous teacher. *Your* responsibility is to end the duality *in yourself*. And that end will come from the integration of all parts of you.

All around you people are yearning for change. That is the outward sign of a coming spiritual grace. Understand that you can go anywhere you want and the energy will find you. Please consider the wonder of this opportunity. You cannot miss. You were not wrong to pick this time. but *now is the time!* The longer you continue to stay focused on the world, forcing it to feed you the happiness that you are seeking, the longer you will be frustrated. The part of your soul that wants to be filled with something else is not going to be satisfied if your awareness is focused primarily *out there*. You must learn to be the interface between the worlds and have those worlds connect in your life in the most wondrous ways that you can. Ask to be filled with those things the soul longs for. Keep on asking for love, compassion, peace, and joy. *Then put your awareness in your heart center, and feel them.*

Every time you do feel a shift in the energy with your physical body, acknowledge it. Please acknowledge that something has happened. This is the time to empower your being, and the more of you that do, the greater the service you render to each other. Please think about it. You have asked to be sent an energy that will once and for all change and transmute your cloudy projections and illusions to true perception and clarity. You have asked to be in the world and carry out your duties, and at the same time to also be alive and ignited with the knowledge of your true being. The difference between twenty years ago and now is that the energy is here. And it's going to get stronger. So allow things to fall away and change before your eyes. Just keep moving. Know that whatever leaves, no matter how deeply you cared about it, how attached you were to it, or how meaningful it was, it is appropriate. The next movement will always appear.

In times past, it was possible to listen to the organizations of the world and to feel strong, but those organizations are now failing. Governments are being seen as less than perfect. Religions are unable to fill you with the power of the divine. And that is all absolutely as it should be. If life becomes chaotic, do not despair. Remember that you began this journey with the knowledge that, if you could open to the vaster self, you would have available, at every moment, the information necessary to empower your inner and outer life. The "outer" world is totally porous, and it moves through everything. Its wisdom is ever present and ever available.

When you listen to yourself and your truths begin to unfold, do not immediately present them to the world because discouragement committees will form to dissuade you. That change is exciting, uplifting and delightful is not something the world is ready to hear. So, be very gentle with those around you. Hold them in deep consideration and understanding. And if, by the power of your love through your changes, you can move those wonderful feelings out into the world, those around you will know that there is no harm in them. Change accomplished through the power of your inner being is absolutely peace-filled. It is so because it moves out of a place of knowing, not out of a place of fear. The wonderful excitement of listening to your *self* is that you know what is right when you hear it, and when your movement comes out of an inner knowing, it rings with truth, and that certainty brings peace to you, and to those around you.

OPENING COMMENTS

"The body is a wondrous machine that is wholly a product of the thought processes of the one who inhabits it." *From Ramtha, who lived on the earth plane 35,000 years ago.*

"Health, my friends, like love and like truth, is about owning more and more of you, not disowning, not separating, not disconnecting." *From Dong How Li, last incarnated as a Tibetan monk in the Nepalese Himalayas in 600 B.C.*

"Illness is not something that God levies upon you. Illness is something that God allows you to use in your soul's evolution." *From Dr. Peebles, whose last incarnation in the 1800's was spent in medical practice and research of the philosophical basis of illness and accidents.*

"There is no such thing as an incurable disease. There are only incurable people." *From Soli, an off-planet entity guiding the Earth's evolution.*

"What you have come here to understand is that you are beyond all the small, limited parameters of being *just* a body." *From Bartholomew, a being who speaks from a vaster field of awareness.*

"To understand your relationship to your experience of health, it is important for you to understand the relationship you have to yourself." *From John, who lived 2,000 years ago in the Middle East and was a friend to Jesus.*

"Each lifetime in body represents less than a heartbeat in the totality of this eternal and immortal quest toward enlightenment." *From Hilarion, a spirit being involved in various phases of Earth's development.*

"Healing is the manifested thought which erases the manifested thought of illness and disease." *From Kyros, an off-planet energy who has never experienced physical life.*

"The keys to good health are harmony with your fellow humans and all other inhabitants of Earth, a good relationship to Earth, your own higher self, the Creator, any visiting extraterrestrials, and general joy in being." *From Robbyn and his Merrye Bande, who are fostering social and political change via spiritual enlightenment.*

"Your religions often teach that passing into the next world is a thing of joy to be looked forward to. Yet, as we note, no one looks forward to it. It is very curious." *From Li Sung, who lived 1200 years ago in Northern China.*

HEALING IS
FINDING YOUR HEART

"Truly the heart is your treasure. It is the seat of all of your healing powers." ... Dong How Li

Dong How Li: All healing is *self-healing*, whether you do that with stones or with others who assist your process as priest, as healer, as therapist, or as friend. What you are attempting to do in the process of healing is to bring all the parts of you back into harmony again, to reinstitute communication that through some process of fear, self-loathing, disappointment, or loss, you have allowed to disconnect.

So, then, operating in a field where inside is outside and outside is inside, your healer becomes the part of you, the higher self, the transpersonal part projected, enabling you to then put your pieces back together.

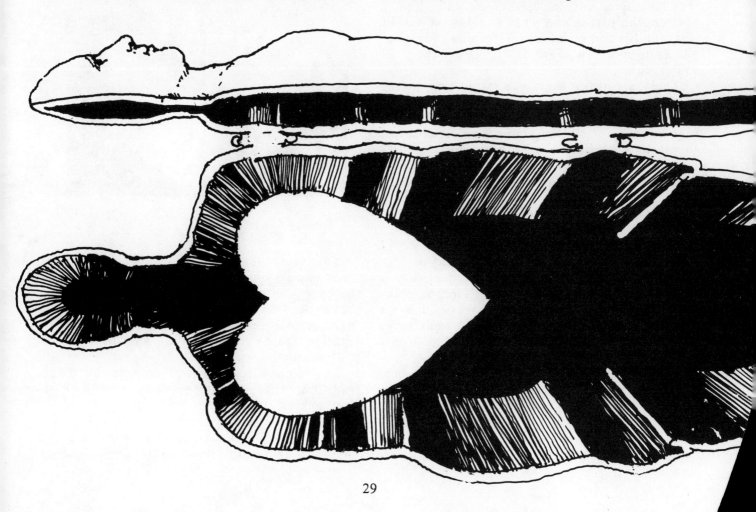

As you learn to center in the heart, it is easier to move because your heart is always with you--your center is always with you wherever you go.

Now, as you reconnect these parts of yourself, you will notice within your being and in your life, they are also reconnected. You will notice that relationships change. You will notice that you are reading the signs of life around you more clearly and better understanding their messages to you.

In the Western tradition of Judeo-Christianity, the focus has been primarily outer. Sometimes this works. But if you will notice, it is failing. More and more people are turning to more *traditional* ways of healing, more *natural* ways of healing which require they go inside. And in case you haven't already noticed, the planet and what is going on within it, around it and on it, is now forcing everyone, more and more, to go inside or "get off the pot," so to speak.

These are times for acceleration and intensification. Many, many more people will be forced, by disease (if they don't accept the messages sooner), or circumstances, or relationships, to go deeper, faster. It is not going to be so difficult as you all learn to move, especially as you all center in your hearts. As you learn to center in the heart, it is easier to move because your heart is always with you--your center is always with you wherever you go.

And no matter how topsy-turvy the world gets, or how much the ground shakes, you spin like a top from this center. So much of how I discuss healing has to do with finding your heart, and with learning what moves you, what inspires you, what recharges you, what gives you energy, as opposed to depleting you, exhausting you, or raising fear within you.

You are going to hear many spirit teachers discussing the heart for the simple reason that it is the heart that is most at stake in this time. This plague you are calling AIDS is massive broken heart. It is no mistake that in almost all of your so-called "civilized" countries, heart disease is on an incredible increase. People don't know *what* their hearts are or *where* they are, figuratively or literally. Believe me, you do not find your heart by getting a plastic one. In some ways, that is going off on the wrong track.

You must begin to find, within yourself, what moves you and what inspires you. With the energy of that, you have enough energy to move the thymus gland to reactivate and regenerate the immune system, to increase circulation inside and outside, and to improve your health.

Has it not also been said, in your Christian tradition, that the second coming will be in your hearts? This is *that* time, my friends. It is already upon you. And it is intensifying. So, how do you find your heart? How do you use medicine? How do you use the arts? How do you use stones, plants, or other people to find your heart, to heal yourself?

You must first open up to being human and feeling because only with the feeling (second chakra) and heart (fourth chakra) do you have the gateway open to the third eye (sixth chakra), which is insight. And only with feeling will you know where your heart is leading you. This is a major turnaround for this culture which would prefer to be led with its mind. But of course, it is obvious where that has led. The destruction is rampant.

Many people now are finding they have to deal with their whole emotional body, all of their feelings, and that is exactly what's going to be intensifying in the future. You will notice you will get angrier more often. You are going to notice, on the planet, many people are angry more often. This is going to be projected because they think it is easier to deal with it outside of themselves rather than inside themselves. But that only perpetuates the problem. Better they should go inside and deal with it and not have to project it outside.

There is going to be a lot of this kind of polarization. It is already starting. And you must watch for it within yourselves. You must watch your own flips in mood, in opinion, in your willingness to take responsibility and willingness not to be involved and push it away and say, "Oh that's their fault." It's going to be very challenging.

Remember that you all have chosen to be here at this time, not only for the lessons, but for the talent and the leadership you have to offer. As you know, the planet is wounded and in need of healing, and as you help yourselves, you help her and all beings upon her.

So, to encourage this healing process within yourselves, among others, and on the planet, you go inward, and work with your heart. Use whatever tools are available. But please be aware that it's easy to get hung up on the tools. Your point is to *find* your heart.

Yes, you may use red stones. Yes, you may use beautiful string music that opens up your heart. You may do improvisational movements. You may have other people, such as

psychotherapists, do work with you and so forth. There are many ways, all valid. And before you are through, you may use them all, depending on where you are at any one point and time. What you are trying to do is to open your hearts primarily to yourselves. (You know, Christianity is marvelous. It is so outer-directed, when everything Christ was doing was inner-directed.)

Now, it is no mistake that the heart is called the transformer. It is no mistake that the heart part of you is the crossroads. You draw energy up from the Earth and down from the sky. And they meet in the heart. You join energy from above and below and from all four directions around you, and they meet here in your heart. All six directions meet here.

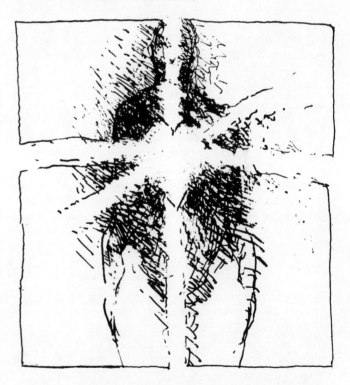

This is the cross, my friends, where you are the instrument, you are the channel for energies--upper and lower and in all directions around you. It is not a cross you carry on your back, as in Christianity. This is the cross you carry in your heart-center. Why the cross is important is because where the energies cross is where manifestation occurs and where transformation occurs. So that is why, in health and in being alive, it is so important for your heart center to be flexible, to be fluid, to be open, to be sharing.

You will notice, if you look around you at people in the streets and in different places, you will find many with hunched shoulders, hiding their hearts, protecting them, even protecting them from themselves. They are not only keeping other people out, but keeping themselves out. It is most curious.

Truly the heart is your *treasure*. It is the seat of all of your healing powers. It is the transformer. As you are finding your heart, finding what is there, where you want to go, what the blocks are that are keeping you from where you want to go, you will breathe more space, air, and allowance. You will find it easier to share.

To some degree, health is a magical act. Achieving it is a magical act. The heart is important in magic because through the heart you are connected to everything and everyone in the world and they are connected to you.

MAKING LIFE CHOICES

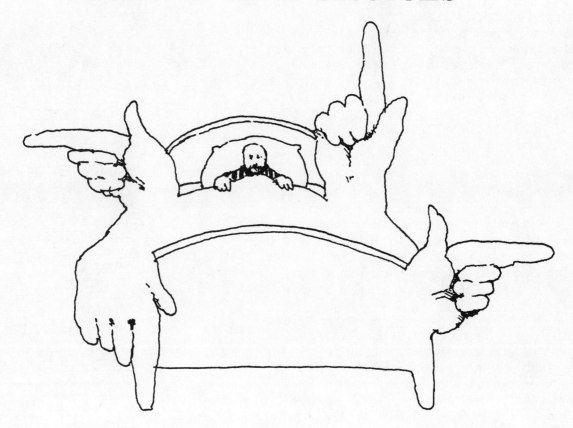

The physical body is only an instrument to gain emotional experience in mass and to fulfill certain needs for the prize of life, that which is called wisdom."... Ramtha

Soli: Health, the body, the physical dimension, how are they connected? What is disease? In order to understand this a little better, we need to speak a little of the spiritual nature of man: who and what you truly are.

The physical that you are involved in is but an illusion, is but a denseness of vibration, of energy, that you have chosen to experience within this earth plane.

You are Spirit. You are God. You are one. And yet, you find yourselves within physical bodies in the physical dimension with every *illusion* of being totally separate and isolated. Before incarnating, you review, with the help of your spirit guides and teachers, those lives that you have previously had as human beings. You then decide what would be a good life to experience upon the earth plane.

Then you view individuals of that time, you view their sexual unions, and you read the energy formed therefrom. Within that energy you read genetic patterns, you read society's attitudes, you read time and place, country, and geography. You read the psychological make-up of prospective parents. You know, therefore, the high probability of the subconscious programming that you will receive from those individuals and from the society that you will be incarnating within.

You choose, my friends, in its totality, with *full* fore-knowledge of the lives that you will most probably have. You choose your own genetic weaknesses, sometimes even to the extent of modifying the physical structure of the fetus within the body before it is born so that you will have a so-called handicap (no such thing of course, but from the point of view of the subconscious and society, that is what it is called).

And so, having viewed prospective parents and decided that they will give you a large amount of the experiences that you are wishing to have, you incarnate. Your incarnation into the body can be accomplished at any time between the actual conception itself and two or three months, approximately, after the physical birth.

Then, having chosen your body, you incarnate. You bring with you a new subconscious mind, the "tabula raza" (clean slate), a new book upon which you start to record your life experiences. Your subconscious mind records everything without censorship, all the input from the five senses, including all those things sent to you by parents, all those things you overhear when they don't think you are listening.

Everything is stored within the subconscious mind. All the belief systems so dear to the society that you have incarnated within, all the belief systems so dear to your parents and their friends, are stored within your subconscious mind. They become your personality for the rest of your life. They are your beliefs. Therefore, because they are your beliefs, they are your reality and create your reality around you.

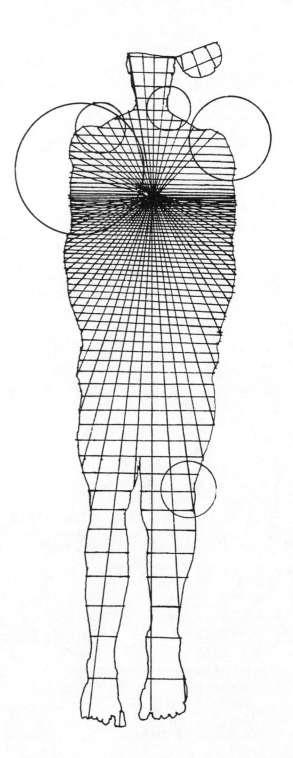

The first dis-ease that you have is incarnating within the physical body.

For example, if your momma continually says that you must not get your feet wet in the rain else you will catch a cold, guess what? For the rest of your life, you walk out in the rain, get your feet wet and catch a cold. There is absolutely no reason for it. You get your hands wet all the time, why should you get a cold getting your feet wet? And yet, it is a very dearly held belief system, and because the belief is so strong, it is the reality of a large number of people. Beliefs create your reality.

What is disease? Dis-ease, as the word implies, is a lack of ease. And the first dis-ease that you have is incarnating within the physical body.

Within the spirit dimensions you have a much higher level of vibration available to you. Your thoughts have much greater power. You have much more available to you to work with. Yet, because of karma, because of experiences that you want, you freely choose to incarnate again within the physical dimension. In doing so, there is a natural channeling down, squeezing that high energy into the lower, dense vibration of a physical body. That is the original dis-ease and it is the one that you maintain throughout your life: the feeling you have that there must be *something* more. The feeling you have that there is something missing in your life stems from what little remembrance you have of your *true* spiritual nature, of who and what you are and where you have truly come from.

Some do not pay attention to this feeling that there is something missing in their lives. For some it is so far beyond what they are dealing with, within their incarnations, that it is of no importance. For those of you who have had many lives before, you are much closer to your spiritual origin. You have chosen lives wherein you will have greater remembrance, and wherein you you will have greater motivation to remember your spiritual nature.

You do not have to strive to be spiritual because you already are spirit.

What you are seeking to do is to remember what you already are. You are already perfection. You are already God. It is the subconscious belief systems and the limitations placed therein, creating limitations of the physical body that you inhabit, that create the dis-ease, and that feeling of separateness, of aloneness, of isolation, of not knowing who you truly are. And so you go through your life always feeling as though you are, somehow, alone, always feeling that there has to be something more.

But, for those of you reading this book, the motivation is strong enough to determine what that *something* else is. The motivation leads you to begin to search, to be on the quest to understand more fully, your higher self, and to understand your true spiritual being.

Question: Why would someone choose to be born with physical or mental handicaps?

Ramtha: There are no victims in life. Entities born into bodies that are diseased or deformed or lacking in the realms of what you term "normal" are not victims, for the entity entering the body is not ignorant of the conditions he is inhabiting.

Each entity chooses his embodiment and designs it according to what he wants it to be. This is his divine right. He is the one who has dominion over that which is forming within the womb. The soul is placed within the union of the seed and the egg upon conception, but the spirit, which is the caretaker of the soul, may reject the body at any time it is forming. The spirit may even wait up to 12 months after the birth of the body before it takes hold of it. If the formation of the body within the womb is not according to the will of the entity who

35

shall be the controller of the embodiment, the spirit of its being will recall the soul from the body and allow the body to die. You call that nature, but in truth, that is free will.

What of those entities who are born, nonetheless, with bodily impairments? They have simply chosen to be this way. They have allowed this to occur because they want to experience this. The reasons are many, but in simplicity, they are always because the entity *wants* to be that way for the experience he is desiring--because it makes him happy.

Many choose impaired embodiments precisely because their happiness is to express on this plane without the function of physical beauty--for perhaps they are ready to understand and appreciate the greater beauty that lies beyond illusion of the flesh. They can simply be who they are without worrying about being accepted for their appearance or physical ability or grand intellect, whatever is esteemed here. When an entity has that burden taken from him, he can more readily experience true joy and a profound love for self in that life. And when he passes from this plane, he is beauteous in his light and he is also happy in his soul.

When you leave this plane you go to a graduated understanding where you are thought and emotion, not mass. There, you are bodiless in regard to a molecular form, but you are full-bodied in a light spectrum. There, the beauty or acceptability of the body is not measured.

The physical body is only an instrument to gain emotional experiences in mass and to fulfill certain needs for the prize of life called wisdom.

If an entity chooses a malformed embodiment, that body is in a condition of perfection for the entity inhabiting it. It is perfect for him to gain the experiences he is desiring, and he *wants* it that way. For perhaps only in that way can he learn to appreciate the body, or to humble himself enough to understand those who are the same as he. If it takes doing away

with a part of your body for you to learn to love yourself, or to experience pure joy, or to learn to have compassion and love for everyone, then let it be done.

Now, those which you call "simpletons" are very much aware of their lives. Although they may not have a great capacity for intellectual expression, they have the same capacity for thought and emotion that all do. Intellect never determined intelligence; it never determined a god.

Many of these entities are *great* masters, for they do not judge others, and they love all people, regardless of how they look or how they express. They also do not worry, they forgive continuously, and they are indeed happy. If it hurts you to look upon them, perhaps you should reassess *your* values.

What of the little bodies that have been cast aside, their bellies bloating terribly, their bones protruding through thin skin? You say to me, "How could they be happy? Why would they choose to suffer like this?"

There is an ideal on this plane of what happiness is supposed to look like.

Happiness is not only a jolly little entity with wings on its back who sits upon puffy clouds singing wonderful songs. It is whatever experience an entity creates to bring fulfillment to his being. And who are you to determine what fulfillment is for another entity?

Many choose to be born into wretched conditions for the challenge of rising above such conditions. Or they desire to come back to help and to teach entities experiencing that condition, for they have a kinship with those entities. Many do so to gain compassion for others, or a greater love for themselves or the desire to choose a better existence in their life to come. The reasons are many, and they are unique to each entity.

No one is *ever* born a victim of fate or circumstance. Entities born directly into sickness, or with bodily impairment, or in wretched conditions, have chosen that for themselves

The body is a wondrous machine that is wholly a product of the thought processes of the one who inhabits it.

fully knowing what conditions they will face. They have chosen their bodies and their parents for their own reasons, all of which equates to *want*, which equates to *happiness*. The body is a wondrous machine that is wholly a product of the thought processes of the one who inhabits it.

Every moment, the body paints the clearest, most intimate portrait of all of your feelings and attitudes. Every thought an entity has registers as an emotion within its soul, and that emotion sends to every cell within the body an electrical spark that feeds each cell. Love, freedom of expression, appreciation of unseen beauty, patience, living in the moment, allowing life to be--these are all attitudes that spark health and foreverness within the cells of the body. Self-hate, self-denial, feelings of unworthiness, insecurity, jealousy, guilt, anger, failure, sorrow--these attitudes degenerate the cells within the body to create illness and disease, for they are attitudes that alter life, that inhibit it. When your attitudes do not permit your life to be lived in freedom and in ease, the body will eventually mirror your attitudes and become dis-eased.

The body will always reflect and represent an entity's collective thinking. Those who hate themselves and despise their own bodies will often cause madness in their cells, called cancer, which will devour their embodiments. Those who are selfish will often manifest the illness termed diabetes. Those who cannot express their love will often manifest diseases of the heart. Those who have deep guilt and remorse, feeling that they must be punished and must suffer, will often manifest diseases that create great agony in their beings.

Now, everyone possesses genetic patterns within the cells of their bodies that predispose their bodies to certain diseases. Your body is prone to the same diseases that your parents manifested, for their collective attitudes were programmed into the genetic matter of the egg and sperm that came together to form the body you inhabit. That is how disease is inherited in the body. But these "chromosome patterns," as they are called, do not become activated unless you adopt the *same* attitudes that prevailed within your lineage. If you do, the chromosome structures within the DNA automatically begin to release these patterns into the body to create like diseasements. It is all very scientific and all very true.

John: In the cases whereby there is at birth a condition that has put this child at a disadvantage (for it would appear to be disadvantaged--one way or another), then immediately you want to make changes for the child. You want to make him feel that he is the same as others, in spite of what you term the irrefutable evidence of a handicapped physical form. So you support him in his handicap by giving in to the inevitable conclusion that you are being punished and the child is the vehicle of your suffering. Because the child's physical and mental attributes appear deficient in comparison to the ideal, they are often set aside and treated as abnormal. This is absolutely incorrect. They are not special nor are they different. They are manifestations of the same substance, and the same being within which all manner of physical expression shall come to be.

Karmic decisions

Dr. Peebles: There are many souls who come into bodies never to have the *need* for illness, but get caught up so much in the fears that they manifest illness. They can soul-heal themselves. Sometimes healers are able to work with them and their souls will be healed; the illness will be in remission and healing. There are

some that you can do everything for and nothing will work, for they came into that body to have that experience, which for them is a *soul experience*.

My friends, do not strive diligently to understand where an illness came from, nor where it is going. Do not attempt to justify why you or another have any illness, be it a broken bone, cancer, or AIDS. Recognize that it is an experience that is there for you at that moment or you would not be aware of it. Recognize that it is not for you to justify or to fear. It is only for you to *accept it so totally* that you are able to elevate it to its highest possible soul experience, for yourself and for others as well.

Do not even consider that you have done anything wrong nor anything that puts you aside from acceptance by the spirit guides or from God. Recognize that you, as a soul, are experiencing an event and you have a decision to make. Will you live it in the earth-binding webs and shadows or will you live it on a higher level for all to observe that there are other alternatives? Will you, by your actions, show others that they have the ability to lift their reactions to a higher level?

Those who cannot accept you for whatever illness or manifestation you have, that becomes *their* problem, not *yours*. Your only problem is to take your experience and elevate it to the highest level so that everyone around will observe your behavior and will say, "If they are able to accomplish it, then I, too, may be able to accomplish it."

Illness is not something that God levies upon you. Illness is an experience that God allows you to use in your soul's evolution.

Remember that when the soul leaves its perfect state and begins the cycles of birth and death, in its karmic interchange it develops the need for certain experiences. Illness often is little more than the tool to give the soul the opportunity to *balance* itself out. Even if you are a highly evolved vibration or soul, you still have the need to be around the environment, to see illnesses.

Frequently you will *have* an illness. You can use your illness as an opportunity to transcend, to move back onto the spirit plane. If you hold on, you will build new karma, which then creates the need for new balance. Illness, then on the higher plane, is little more than a tool to accomplish a specific goal, to return to the light. Illness is not something that God levies upon you. Illness is an experience that God allows you to use in your soul's evolution.

For example, some of you may remember the story of Miriam in the Christian Bible. Miriam was a paraplegic. She was able to physically mature, but she was still a paraplegic and she was most miserable. Her personality was critical of herself and everyone. She was what would be called a "shrew."

Now her father, hearing that the teacher Jesus was passing through the village, went to him and said, "I am a wealthy man. You and your followers are welcome to stay in my home. Those who cannot fit in my home are welcome to camp on my grounds. I will feed and clothe all of you. All I ask is that you heal my daughter."

So Jesus went to see the girl. He spoke to her, saying, "My dear, I am able to heal your soul, but I am unable to heal your body." She became enraged and screamed and cried and carried on. And so the father would not allow them to stay, for he could not accept that her body could not be healed.

Many, many months went by. Jesus returned and said once more, "I am able to heal your soul, but I cannot heal your body." For you see, hers was not a body experience. It was not a consciousness experience of free will. It was her karma, her need, to have that physical body. And so, in frustration, she gave in and Jesus was able to meditate, pray, and heal her soul.

From that point on, she was never depressed or angry again. People would come from miles around and Miriam would sing to them songs of faith, songs of encouragement. She would tell them stories of communication, telepathically, emotionally, spiritually. She spent the rest of her life as a worker for the great teacher Jesus, but as a paraplegic.

Also, my friends, realize that you each came into life to have certain experiences, and to some degree, you also came into life to allow other people to have *their* experiences. I am suggesting that there are many events in life in which you are little more than a channel for the experience. For instance, you may have a physical illness so that those 'round and about you will have the opportunity to discover their relationship to you. You become a vehicle for parents, doctors, friends to discover how to lift their reactions to you and your illness, and to transmute these reactions to a higher level. In this way, they are able to allow themselves to grow ever onward, ever upward. They become able to take on the responsibility for lifting everything to its highest possible level.

Bartholomew: As part of experiencing that you are all one, that all of life is one, there is a necessity for you to grapple with certain major *givens* the human condition has to offer. One of these is being born handicapped or becoming handicapped during your lifetime. Where I disagree with most of you is when you make this a negative condition by assuming a handicapped child or person has done something wrong in the past that it must now atone for.

It is my perception that, most of the time, the ones who come in with a handicap come with the courage and determination to bring into that situation as much love, light, power, and beauty as they can. They shine as victorious examples when they are successful. And the one thing they do not need is your pity. How dare they be given pity when they come as the warriors to show that, in the midst of incredible limitations, they can give to the world the very qualities the Christus embodied? What I think they deserve is applause.

Should you try to heal them? Absolutely. Some of you say a certain affliction has come to someone because of their karma, so there is no need for them to do anything about it. Yet, if such a one is in your life, wherein lies *your* karma? No one just drops into your life without reason. There is always a place where they fit. So when a handicapped child is present, the question arises, "What does this have to do with me?" And most of the time it has to do with your ability to take care of that being with humor, acceptance, compassion, and determination; acceptance when it's inconvenient, and humor in the face of frustration, simply allowing the wonderful feeling of rapport to continue to move between you, keeping alive all their beauty and wonder. Please understand, there is much more going on than is apparent to you. If you can remember you are more than just your body, you will remember *they* are too! Keep the vastness of your essence moving between the two of you.

No physical affliction bothers anyone as much as does the feeling of being different, separate and somehow outside of life.

That is the greatest pain. Your job, my friends, is to remove the feeling of separation by blending your awareness with theirs. Bring them into you; don't push them away by being embarrassed to look at them. Look in their faces, into their eyes, and right into their being.

And let them see you. Those are the moments to give of yourself totally. So they, in return, will know that you recognize there is only one, and that they are carrying their part of the whole while you are carrying yours.

The football game of life

Soli: Another way to understand the meaning of karma might be to compare it to a football game. You, as God, create a football game, and you sit on the sidelines watching it take place. You see the teams interacting, and you decide that yes, it is very interesting, but what does it all mean? You've created this game and

40

Although you have left the game, you are still caught up in the excitement of the game. *That* is karma. You decide all the things that you should have done differently, that you've done wrong, or that you should have done better. You decide that you're going to have another shot at it, and so you do, time and time again. You get yourself caught up into the webs and illusions of this vibration that you call reality, and they stay with you, even when you are not playing the game (when you are not in a physical body).

have written all the rules, but you're not really going to understand the game until you go into the middle of it and play it for yourself.

So you choose to be one of the players on one of the teams and you get into that game. And you decide, "This is fun. That was a wonderful run for the goal. I certainly enjoyed that!" Then, after the game, you sit in the locker room and you review the game. You say, "I shouldn't have hit that person. I shouldn't have lost my temper. I need to go back and make it up to that person. And my run for the goal was wonderful, but I could do it better. I could do it differently. I'm going to come back and have another game."

Alternative repayment plans for perceived karmic debts

Master Adalfo: Sometimes a person makes a decision to experience life in a certain way (as in illness) to deal with particular things, or to pay back some karmic debt. They can be assisted in looking at their illness and helped to make changes in their life that they need to make, helping them to know (at some appropriate time), that there are many ways in which to pay a debt. They can come to understand that, in selecting a certain illness, it was a case of making the best choice they could with the information they had available.

Later on they can say, "I have more information now, and I am going to change my mind. I don't like the decision I made. I'm going to change it." For there is the possibility of paying back a debt in some other way besides coming into life with a disease in which you have to be in a wheelchair, for example. Because that plan can, by how you deal with it, create even more karmic debts which you will then have to pay

41

again. So you all need to be aware of creativity in how you pay your debts.

Also be aware that sometimes, in the sense of paying off a debt, you bring along a disease that you may have had in a past life. This is where past-life therapy is especially helpful. You can learn when a disease is carrying over from a past life, along with the same *belief* system from that past-life experience.

Occasionally, someone will be born with a disease that is neither. It is not paying a karmic debt nor is it a pattern from past lives. So why would they choose it? Why would they create a reality that says, "You must still be born with disease."

For them it is a gift. So how does it give them a chance to look at something so that they can change it and be well? You must help them to do that by asking them those kinds of questions, but not in a rude way. A rude way is to say, "So, how is this disease a payoff for you?" Instead, encourage them to look at the aspect of how the disease is a gift.

They can look at not only what they get from this disease--in the sense of how other people are with them, or the fact that they get to lie in bed all day--but what things they are learning that people who do not have this particular disease never think of. For example, if you see with your eyes, you do not get to look at things that a blind person gets to look at. By this I mean perceive, understand, examine. The blind person gets to examine all kinds of things that the sighted person does not. And this is what I mean by gifts. You can help someone who is questioning *why* about their disease by helping them look at *how* could they have that gift in their life without the disease.

Being a part of the larger picture of life

Li Sung: You have chosen your birth, and have chosen your pattern of life. Within the *possibilities* of life, you have the ability to change your mind.

You do not exist alone in the universe. 'Tis not only *your* will that rules reality, but that of many, many others. And so there are times when your will is not *free* at all. Consider that you might be an ant, wandering through the forest, looking for a snack. Someone, setting up a picnic, puts a blanket upon you. You may not have had a plan for this. It would not have been your free will, except in choosing the time and place to look for your snack. And you might suffer death or terrible feelings as that ant, but that was *not* your desire. You see, there are many situations in life in which you choose from your free will, and once you make that choice, you must take the consequences of other peoples' choices.

So, your free will is exercised in the larger choices in life and the small as well. Sometimes, once you have agreed to the larger, then you also must agree to the smaller.

There are medical conditions which are not karmic (which your soul did not choose) but which appear in the soul's history. And these may be in response to the present environment.

Let us look at the plague. When fleas carrying this illness bite people, then people become sick and die. They have not necessarily chosen to do this, but they may have come to the *wrong place at the wrong time*. In their next lifetime they will remember this. When they have the opportunity to express themselves in health they might decide, "Oh, I must have some little illness, this will make my wife feel sorry for me." They do not choose the plague, they choose something more like poison ivy because it goes away soon.

We hope that you will choose life situations which are both fun for you and which also serve your soul.

You may decide to choose misery. Some people do. They feel their soul is served just by misery. They have no sense of humor. But wiser souls choose a path that they *enjoy* and one that also *expresses their creative abilities* and one in which they are able to be of *service* to others.

THE GREAT PLAN

"Disease provides very accurate clues to the major lessons that are available for resolution in a given lifetime." ... Hilarion

Hilarion: Before the student of this material can hope to benefit extensively from its application, it is essential that he or she believes absolutely in the previously stated concept that there are no accidents on planet earth. There must be total acceptance of the purpose of life which is to teach you the sanctity of every living thing, the reality of the interaction between all life-streams, the spiritual component which shapes all life throughout the universe, and the oneness of that spiritual force, which is sometimes called God.

Your Holy Book states that if you "Seek first the Kingdom of God, then all things shall be added unto you." This is a great truth, and an edict to be followed by any aspirant who desires to be successful in his quest. The pathway to perfect health lies in the heart, not in the head, in the practice of meditation before medicine, and in prayer before a pill. We realize that very few have arrived at a point where their faith is sufficient to allow them to live *completely* within this framework, so the physician and his treatment of the physical symptom is still required. Soon, however, there will arise a new standard of thought in which it will be acceptable to believe that new concept exists.

Total wellness depends totally upon the state of mind.

Indeed, a faction within the existing school of conventional medicine is already of this persuasion, and new proponents are marshalling every day. When these new thinkers link their energies with the many who have arrived at their conclusions based upon the spiritual teachings of the New Age, then great light will be shed throughout the world upon the practice of wellness.

The time fast approaches when this will be the norm. There has been a massive breakthrough in scientific thinking, though not all the converts are yet aware of the degree to which the new theories will affect the future of the world. Simply put, scientists have discovered that matter responds to human thought. The Edgar Cayce material taught this concept by stating "thoughts are things," which has been more generally interpreted to mean that the circumstances of life respond to a person's thinking. This is absolutely true, but so also does matter itself respond to thought processes. Using your Holy Book as an example once again, we refer you to the story of the loaves and the fishes which multiplied in response to Jesus' need to feed the multitude. In the present, many have been amazed by the feats of Sri Baba as he produces precious stones and metals from "thin air." The truth, of course, is that the air contains the substance from which is formed all matter.

Disease is no more than the cellular structure or chemical balance of the body gone awry. It manifests as the symptom of misqualified thought, and each disease points directly to some specific misconception held and practiced under the influence of the soul. Thus, every disease can be looked upon as an opportunity to change for the better. As the symptoms are analyzed and the causes at the soul level are discovered, the afflicted one need only correct the errors in his thinking to return the body to full and radiant health. The Great Master demonstrated control of matter to the ultimate degree when he restored life-force and cellular wholeness to Lazarus, and raised him from what is commonly known as the state of death. Soon, many examples of this and other similar phenomena will be seen, and these will cause a great renewal of interest in the subject throughout the scientific and spiritual communities, resulting in greater alignment of their thinking.

We assume that those who read these words believe in the immortality of the human spirit, which never dies, but moves ever onward in its journey toward enlightenment.

Each lifetime in body represents less than a heartbeat in the totality of this eternal and immortal quest toward enlightenment.

Therefore the process of leaving the body behind is regarded, from our viewpoint, as a joyous occasion. For that is when the spirit returns home to renew itself, to re-establish relationships with loved ones and eventually to prepare for the next sojourn into a learning experience in matter, if that is considered to be the wisest course of action. It is still somewhat premature, however, for most souls incarnate to accept this as truth, and so the ultimate fear that the majority hold in consciousness is of the death experience. Nothing, of course, could be farther from the truth. In fact, the transitional experience is one of loving release. It simply entails leaving behind all fear and pain, all unhappiness and disease, to return to a life filled with love and joy and peace, where great learning experiences are available in the loving presence of the Creator.

Great strides have been taken in recent years to encourage this viewpoint. New emergency techniques which deal with acute trauma in the physical body have resulted in many souls returning from what is commonly referred to as the "near death experience." This is simply the process whereby physical death is arrested before the incarnate soul has had the opportunity to completely effect the transition to spiritual form once again. The memories of those who have enjoyed these experiences are very real, far surpassing in clarity the so-called reality of everyday life. Invariably those who have returned from these adventures have found their lives radically changed forever. Indeed, the channel through which we bring you this message was provided with such an experience in 1979 during an operation. A momentary cardiac arrest allowed the soul to escape its human form, and remain on the "other side" for a protracted period. The experience continues to provide an important influence in his life to this day, manifesting as intense curiosity about all metaphysical subjects, and absolute freedom from anxiety concerning the process of physical death.

Imagine the extent to which a change of attitude is possible when the fear of death is absent. Because so many are currently coming forward via the media to testify about these experiences, great strides are being made to offset this ultimate fear in human consciousness.

Many new gifts of knowledge will be entrusted to the human race in the period preceding the turn of the century, and even more of these dispensations will be available later, as humankind demonstrates a responsible level of peaceful co-existence. Initially, these gifts will take the form of new and useful techniques to encourage all souls living in body to help one another survive the tribulations which will be so prevalent in the immediate future. The beginning of this period is being experienced, and much has already been accomplished to focus attention upon the vast numbers of people on Earth who have not the resources nor basic human skills to care for themselves. This situation is correcting itself rapidly, as the thrust of the mass media is now being directed toward the promotion of goodwill far more than in the past.

Widespread economic turmoil throughout the planet will encourage many voices to address themselves to positive change in this area of human life. It will also become known, and widely proclaimed in the media, that the unnatural manner in which agriculture is currently practiced has resulted in damaged soil and inferior crops. It will be realized that simple, natural and nutritious food, largely vegetarian in content, is the most efficient form of energy for the human body, and is the easiest to produce in quantities sufficient to meet all the world's requirements. It will become acceptable to believe in the power of the mind to heal the body. When this positive mental outlook is combined with proper physical diet and correct spiritual nutrition (currently the least understood component of total health), then enormous progress will be possible in this field.

The events which we describe are not as far off as you might suppose. Great light is currently flooding the Earth, and those who are responsible for guiding humankind in these matters are waiting for the correct moment to introduce new concepts via the many channels now open to them, and many there are, dear friends.

People who are on the so-called "spiritual path" are predisposed to believe that only those of similar persuasion are inspired by divine wisdom. Such is not the case.

Many great minds are not consciously aware of their missions, but have nevertheless come into physical form to fulfill certain important tasks agreed upon before they chose to enter. These are usually continuations of work begun in previous lives by themselves or others with whom they share their love of the truth. Many great scientists, musicians and artists fall into this category. Sometimes the work is so demanding that it could not be accomplished if

People on the so-called "spiritual path" are predisposed to believe that only those of similar persuasion are inspired by divine wisdom. Such is not the case.

the human consciousness were distracted by the dedication required by spiritual growth. The server has, in these cases, elected to devote a lifetime to the cause of humanity in sacrifice to his or her own spiritual evolvement.

Heads of state may fall into this general area, for many of these are great souls who also voluntarily devote a lifetime of service to their brethren. More and more evidence of selflessness will be observed as the Great Plan unfolds, and those who have been preparing themselves to play their vital part in it begin to make their presence felt. It is an exciting and rewarding time to be conscious of one's responsibilities and opportunities on the earth plane.

Let us return once more to our central theme. Physical health and well-being are playing an extremely important part in the Great Plan of which we speak. Many souls choose to use the physical form as the springboard to their ultimate search for God. For example, a specific physical problem may encourage the prospective seeker to alter his or her lifestyle in some positive manner, resulting in a whole new perspective on nutrition and exercise. These interests can easily become channeled into the more intimate association between body and mind, with the natural progression leading to the connection between mind and spirit, and so an essential door has been opened. Once this process is begun, the normal curiosity of the seeker's quest for the purpose of life is energized, and great spiritual growth is the usual result. Thus you see the reason behind the great interest in diet, health, and exercise that has swept the world in recent years. This is being followed closely by mass acceptance of the subsequent steps we have just described.

You may correctly conclude from what we have said that disease provides very accurate clues to the major lessons that are available for resolution in a given lifetime. Many who are taking on embodiment at this time are very strong and dedicated souls, who have elected to reincarnate in physical vehicles reflecting extremely serious and obvious disabilities. When these conditions are permanent throughout a lifetime, as more and more of them are seen to

be, then those afflicted, and their families, and the many others with whom they will be in contact, have a great opportunity to express love and caring qualities in circumstances where much personal growth is possible. While few may be able to exhibit the strength and goodness of someone like Mother Theresa, for example, many are strengthening themselves in equally important ways by caring for the chronically ill or handicapped who play such an intimate part in their lives.

Sometimes a soul is seen to recover from a given disease, only to find itself enmeshed in yet another similar or worse form of ailment. This is often looked upon as a great tragedy by those who do not understand the true purpose of life. In fact, such a circumstance is a *great blessing*, for then the lessons for all who are part of the situation may be allowed to proceed at a deeper level, and all the individual souls involved are strengthened further by undergoing the same experiences again, and perhaps again, until the lesson has been learned sufficiently by all.

Again, we digress, this time to offer a viewpoint which may be new to many of our readers. We have stated repeatedly that there are no accidents in the schoolroom called Earth. We make the point again in the following context. Imagine the case of a professional or amateur athlete, who comes into Earth having chosen a magnificent body with reflexes suitable for a career in some field of sports. On the surface it would appear that the great number who have been entering in this form recently have merely elected to follow a self-indulgent lifestyle in which few lessons are learned. The widespread interest in sports seems to provide little benefit to humankind beyond mass entertainment, exhibitionism or encouragement of violence.

Careful analysis will disclose, however, that many of the great athletes come from modest or humble backgrounds, and live lives of great dedication to their sport, where strict discipline in training and behavior is required to succeed. These souls, while appearing to enjoy circumstances which embrace only worldly success and fame, are instead providing excellent examples and role models to children and adults alike, where fitness and discipline of mind and body demonstrably lead to success. These same qualities are required to tread the straight and narrow pathway to light, and the athlete is not only preparing himself for this eventual journey, but encouraging others around him to follow his example.

Each person plays an essential part in the drama of life.

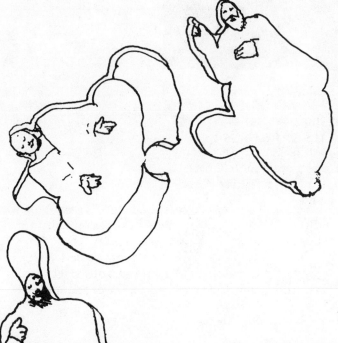

Nothing is ever wasted or lost, and each experience blends with the next to provide a mosaic rich in opportunities to experience growth. You are especially fortunate, Children of Light, to be on the planet at this profoundly important period in human history.

In much the same way have the great world servers prepared themselves for their missions. Each of these powerful souls had first to achieve mastery over the physical plane by learning to control all aspects of it. When, through study and application, the aspirant was able to set aside emotions, control the mind, and eventually to manipulate matter, even to the point of restructuring the body, then each was qualified to begin his or her most important works. Among these courageous souls are counted those who have made the most lasting impressions: Buddha, Mohammed, and all the great Biblical characters including Jesus Himself. Each one dedicated many lifetimes, subsequent to the achievement of mastery, to serving where the need was greatest. For each famous name there are a host who have served anonymously, who in their quiet way have made their important presence felt. The result has been exactly as planned, and indescribable change has resulted from this Great Plan of which we speak so often. Now there are relatively large numbers who are applying themselves to mastery. When one reflects on the truly enormous impact that a single advanced Master such as Jesus or the Buddha has made upon humankind, then it can only be imagined what the result of many avatars on the Earth at one time will be in the future. Indeed, we can only speculate on the effect ourselves, for these circumstances have never before been experienced in the physical plane.

Those who are true disciples of the New Age of love and peace are those whose goals are set on mastery, first of themselves, then of their environment. As they learn the priceless lessons which will open the way to their objective, much light is being brought into the Earth through them, to be shared with those who have yet to seek it *consciously*. The process of spiritual evolvement is exponential.

Like begets like, and though the process may seem very slow from the physical point of view, it is in fact very rapid in the cosmic scheme of things. Just now the Earth and her inhabitants are undergoing a metamorphosis, similar to the emergence of a butterfly from its chrysalis. The butterfly lives but a short few hours of earth time, but this is a lifetime to the butterfly. The coming of the New Age will be seen from the same perspective, as a beautiful golden presence arising from the dormant form of an unenlightened mass consciousness.

YOU ARE MORE THAN YOUR PHYSICAL BODY

"You are convinced that your body has a beginning (birth) and an end (death). You pretend not to know that you are a being without beginning or end, that what you are is eternal." ... John.

John: The physical body that you have is an externalization of the soul made manifest as body. The body is your intimate creation. If you maintain the point of view that your body was created exclusively through the joining of your genetic parents, then you automatically exclude any participation of the spirit in the process of creation.

From the instant of its conception, the being that you are participates in the creation of its own physical image. You are born into this world without the conscious awareness of having accepted what appears to be the predetermined state of your physical existence. Understand that what you call the personality is a self-structured blueprint of a way to be, intrinsically imbedded in your genetic coding. This genetic coding represents ideas, concepts, and principles that are in many ways unrelated to the manner through which they may manifest and express themselves in the world. Ultimately these genetic relationships are abstract, yet they are reflected unerringly in

life through practical means. The ability to remember your self-creation is within the reach of the biologically-based conscious mind.

You are the living translation of cellular genetic memory. You recreate the reality of life through the memory of each moment that you perceive yourself in it. Exactly which aspects of this cellular memory will be actualized depends greatly on your experiences in life and the beliefs that you create about it. You choose and then organize these genetic relationships in alignment with the intended purpose of this lifetime's incarnation (intended purpose meaning that which you choose to experience). All the experiences in your lifetime are but the self-realized manifestations of cellular consciousness.

When illness strikes without provocation or warning, you tend to act surprised. Are you the willing victim of a virus or bacteria that attacks the integrity of the body from the outside? Are you reacting to and being manipulated by the environment you live in?

There is some confusion surrounding the primary relationship that the individual personality has to the self-created conditions that exist in life, and that subsequently are reflected through the world condition.

You are the source through which evolves an endless cycle of self-expressive discovery and rediscovery, placing you at the dead center of your universe where the state of your personal health is absolutely and totally determined by you.

You may argue in opposition with statements such as "How could I possibly be doing this to myself? Why would I want to do this to myself? How and why would I create any condition of ill health for myself? How do I bring the flu to myself?"

Know that the physical body organism contains, within its cellular chemistry, the genetic instructions necessary for the manufacturing of virtually any disease or virus. As well, it contains, at all times, the capability of generating the cure for these conditions. What spawns this creative activity is the unconscious manifestation of self, which is your will expressing itself through the filter of your conscious beliefs about personal reality.

Health and illness can be viewed as reflections of spiritual, psychological, and physical states of being, manifested as the physical conditions through the body of the self and the world in which you live. Consciously, this relationship is seen in thoughts, ideas and beliefs you have about self. These are the tools of awareness that form the concrete framework of your personal now. From the moment that you wake up in the morning until you retire in the evening, the paradigms and patterns of your conscious experience are in a continuous state of adaptation.

Your conscious attitude can be understood as the state of evolving conscious awareness through which you will interpret and experience as the expressions of self-created personal reality. You're the observer being seen in the mirror of self-reflection, viewing your life through the opaque lens of your beliefs.

Each thought witnessed on the screen of conscious experience possesses a life energy uniquely its own. For thoughts are the culmination of a psychological process of interactive translations of unconscious knowing and awareness, converted through the deciphering of linguistic symbolism, and made manifest within the realm of the conscious mind. Here exists a porous membrane that separates the "I AM" of the conscious self from that of the unconscious self, wherein there also exists the

spiritual and ethereal planes of being. There are many complications involving what we will term the source self, which is the primary architect and cause from which the individual self emerges. It is similar to the idea of the primordial pool within which is contained all the ingredients intrinsic for the generation of physical creaturehood as you know it.

Your lives are lived for you to create the opportunity to consciously come to the realization, on your own, that you are partners with ALL THAT IS GOD. This partnership was forged and sealed through the act of your creation, established before the idea of time began, and will continue to be when time doesn't exist.

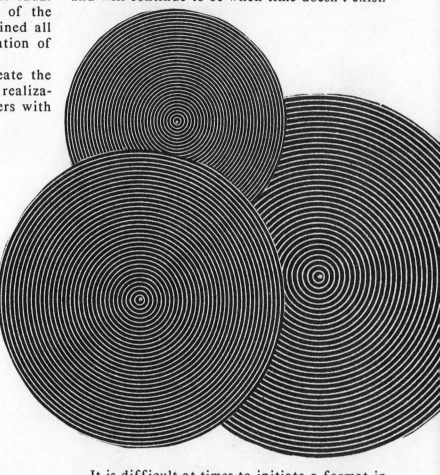

It is difficult at times to initiate a format in your mind that will answer all the questions-- why you have to experience physical illness and the resulting pain that permeates your life. You must realize that you are a multi-dimensional being, existing on many levels simultaneously, participating in the total realization of the personal self.

This relationship between you and your Source (God, All That Is) is mirrored in your world through the mind as physical, emotional, and mental aspects of personality. The relationship that you have between what you call yourself and your children will illustrate this spiritual lineage.

51

When a child is introduced through the birth experience into the world, there is a love that bonds parent and child together. The intensity and commitment to this bonding and attraction can fluctuate because your daily interaction with the world can come between you and your child. Through time, a personal history of relationship rapidly develops and is processed and screened by you in the psychological darkroom of the unconscious mind. All of the ideas and beliefs you have about your parents (and which they had about their parents) will form the primary paradigm of context and focus through which you will filter your attachment to your children.

This same relationship occurs between you and your source self, not withstanding one basic difference--you permit yourself to forget your source.

Your Source will never forget you.

Every thought you have, every emotion that you embrace, or every illness that you invite are all brought about through conscious choices. You then *exercise* your right to conscious choice through the vehicle of self-expression. You focus the light of your most inner personal ideas and beliefs and then thrust them outward onto the screen of personal self-awareness. You refer to this as consciousness realized. Because you maintain that consciousness exists within the body, you will be inclined to define consciousness in terms relative to the body.

Your experience has you convinced that the body has a beginning, defined as birth, and an end, called death, giving rise to the concept of separating what you are into the finite limitations of confined space and time. Thus you pretend not to know that you are a being *without* beginning or end, that what you are is eternal.

Each of the biological cells that unites and constitutes the image of the physical body possesses an individual consciousness and cellular awareness. Though the individual cells appear to be isolated by the apparent restrictions of form and function, indeed they are united to

one purpose. And this purpose is to recreate and externalize the multi-dimensional aspects and nature of the inner self throughout all dimensions of its being.

What you view as your conscious self, the being that you think you are, is a self-realization. Your conscious self is the fertile ground where the seeds of ego and personality are sown, with each seed containing the probable and latent characteristics of the whole self, of which you are a part.

You are the personal emissary of a vastly larger whole known as the human race. As a member in active standing, you share a common heritage with all who have come before you and all that will follow. Look around at the world and its people and you are overcome with a sense of helplessness due to the prevalence of violence, illness and death. Why? If God loves Its children, then why does It allow the pestilence of disease and long suffering to continue to punish man for his transgressions?

The conditions of illness and pain are not a punishment, for there is no punishment.

Illness is a causal attribute of your personal experience that propels you to the threshold of direct action.

When you become ill, your focus of attention is so devoted toward eliminating the pain that it literally dominates your experience. You now become the pain and there is no escape. The experience of the pain locks you into the here and now. There is no avoiding it. You must act on it now because tomorrow will not come soon enough. Yet you look for a way out of the responsibility that you have to yourself to bring about a cure for any and all conditions created within and for your own personal self. It is a method of experience through which you can discover self. So be here *now* with it because you chose it that way.

Health and illness are conditions of context that co-exist within each of you right now. You have already agreed to the conditions that will manifest in life through your being in it.

You see yourself as separate beings in the world though you are not. There is one world, one being, and this being has life through you and would do nothing that would cause permanent harm or create irreversible circumstances for itself. This would truly be self-defeating! Try to imagine yourself putting your head into the locks of a guillotine then pulling the lever, knowing full well that your actions would cause permanent damage to the body. You can't even imagine this actually occurring, however, you can easily imagine someone or something else threatening to do it for you.

In a like manner, *All That Is God* is often portrayed as a vengeful judge, presiding over the court of your life, passing sentences of cruel and unusual punishment upon you for breaking the law of God through your improper thoughts and actions which you may have expressed in life.

Take, for example, a child that is born with a physical defect. The initial reaction could be to perceive this child as an innocent victim of genetic circumstances, sentenced to a life of hardship and limitation without apparent cause or reason. In actuality, this child is a gift waiting to be unwrapped. For you cannot judge the character of the child's will to transcend the limitations of the physical package.

Realize that each and every individual has lived at least one life previous to this one. Others are more frequent visitors to this plane of being. In these lives, you have assumed a myriad of varying physical characteristics. All of this contributes to your growth and expanded awareness. Many of you at one time or another have experienced the unspeakable horrors that you see others living with today. This allows you to identify more intimately with their struggle, for the purpose of your rediscovery, that in the end it is an illusion, perceived in the mind of the beholder.

Your body holds the most direct and intimate key to your self-creation. But before you can use this key, you must stop putting the responsibility for the conditions of the body on events and circumstances that appear outside of it. Though you may not consciously perceive the mechanics of self-creation, you do experience its effects. You create your own reality. Your mind is the tool that you use to organize and interpret the experience of personal reality.

The body has a consciousness all its own, separate from that of the mind. Yet the body will respond to and interact with the conscious influence of the mind. Think of a time when you didn't want to keep a commitment you made in life, such as attending school or work. How often was sickness used as the reason to justify not keeping the commitments that you have made to yourself and others? Everyone, at one time or another, uses illness as a convenient and self-serving form of psychological self-manipulation. You understand with crystal clarity exactly *what* you are doing and *why* you are doing it. You depend on the compassion and sensitivity of others to release you from the responsibility of keeping your word, and thus you create a condition that doesn't exist to avoid a condition that does.

So it is that you have the power to create your life, and your state of well-being or lack of it. You do this to suit your own private needs and purposes.

You are the way you are because this is the way you want to be.

You may not like or even appreciate what you have in your life, but nonetheless, you are the one who put it there. Now that you are there with it, you don't want it to be the way that it is. You refuse to recognize yourself as the director of your own conscious experience. You are the actor who has temporarily forgotten that the role he portrays in life is his response to the dictates of his own inner direction.

The body has, within its structure, the capability of healing any condition of illness that it recognizes as a threat to the stability of the overall organism. But, much like the mind, the body consciousness can refuse to acknowledge the symptoms as a threat to its survival and will thus ignore them. However, medical science discovered a method to awaken the body's natural defense mechanisms with the introduction of preventive inoculation. The inoculation itself contains a strain of the viral bacteria, causing a chain reaction in the immunization system that stimulates the production of antibodies to control the spreading of the infestation. The paradox in this method of treatment is that the cure appears to come from external sources rather than internal ones.

All diseases and maladies of the body are manifested through the will of the individual themselves. How many of you are willing to accept the awesome responsibility of this self-creation?

Your medical professionals, for the most part, are dedicated and sincere in their efforts to promote the reality of health and well-being within all people. They have assumed the awesome task of being *responsible* for your health. The knowledge that they have accumulated through centuries of observation and treatment, at the same time, both liberates and confines them.

Therefore, whenever medical science is confronted with a new disease, they must first discover how it interacts within the human system, identify its basic structure, define, and label it. Once this is accomplished, they will seek to understand why the body does not react on its own to the infection. There is nothing that they put *into* the body that kills the disease. What inoculation does do is allow the body to react to the serum which is being introduced into the system. This activates the appropriate defense mechanisms that are commonly inherent within the body's system.

Instead of taking responsibility for your own body's health, you have placed the responsibility in the hands of others who are capable, but with whom it does not belong. It belongs to you, my friends. It is *your* life and *your* body. Given the state of mind and the training that you have had up to this point, you fail to recognize the relationship that you have to yourself and your physical vehicle, which is the soul made manifest in the flesh.

You must learn to heal yourself because you are the healer.

A true healer knows that it is not he that creates the healing, it is you. A healer transfers and gives back to you that which you pretend *not* to have, that being the ability to heal yourself.

Doesn't that sound like just another batch of buffalo chips? The truth can appear this way because it flies in the face of what you previously have accepted as solid evidence in your life. Somewhere along the line you forgot to take a good long hard look in the mirror and bear witness to how you screwed it up. Do not misunderstand what we say. You are not at fault and there is no blame. There is only personal accountability. Your lack of commitment and purpose in learning who and what you are, and the refusal to use the abilities and power that you have, causes both health and illness within yourself.

The mind has set up its belief structure, which has been validated by the world, to believe that when illness occurs, all you have to do is acquire the appropriate drug to eliminate the condition. The catch here is that before you can receive any relief, you must first see the physician. Remember that medicine, as it is practiced, is a business venture in which doctors are paid for practicing their craft. What they practice on is you. Why do you think they call it medical practice? We mean no disrespect nor do we harbor any ill will toward the medical profession whatsoever.

All your life you have relied on your doctors to bear the burden of keeping your body healthy. You expect them to have all the answers and cures ready when you need them. You have

Remember that you are not your body. You have a body, but it is not you.

transferred the responsibility for your health to your doctors. Remember that doctors are human beings subject to the same laws of cause and effect that you are. Their task is momentous and difficult at best. We applaud them in their endeavors to free you from the experience of illness. However, the truth is that the conditions of your life were caused by you, and not by them. Since you are experiencing life at this particular level of reality, you are somewhat confined to the physical laws as they relate to the nature of the body.

Your body is a miraculous machine and it is indeed the temple within which you reside. While within the body, you *appear* to move

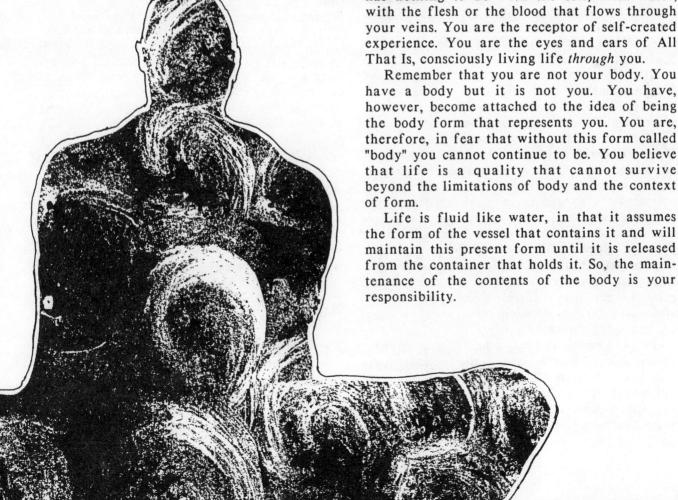

through the reality of space and time. This is an illusion. But there are considerations relative to accepting this illusion, the first of these is that you *believe* it. You believe it, and in the same instant, you are unwilling to accept it. So accept yourself as a being, whole and complete in deference to any and all abnormalities as they might manifest in you. Remember, you are only considered abnormal in relationship to the status quo that establishes the accepted norm.

You know that the quality of individual experience has changed throughout the passing of time. You also have changed in the short time span that you have been on this planet, in this world. But though you are in the world, not a single one of you is *of* the world. What you are has nothing to do with the soil, with water, with the flesh or the blood that flows through your veins. You are the receptor of self-created experience. You are the eyes and ears of All That Is, consciously living life *through* you.

Remember that you are not your body. You have a body but it is not you. You have, however, become attached to the idea of being the body form that represents you. You are, therefore, in fear that without this form called "body" you cannot continue to be. You believe that life is a quality that cannot survive beyond the limitations of body and the context of form.

Life is fluid like water, in that it assumes the form of the vessel that contains it and will maintain this present form until it is released from the container that holds it. So, the maintenance of the contents of the body is your responsibility.

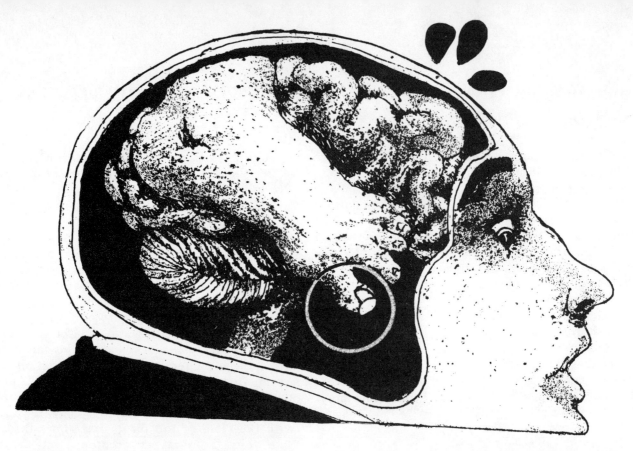

All That Is always is in a state of perfect health, so what you are is in a state of perfect health. You are not that thing that lives and breathes and moves about the room. The body is an expression of form, and what you are is an interwoven aspect of this physical expression.

Man creates in his own image and likeness. You were created in the image and likeness of All That Is God. You must realize how this relates to you in realities other than physical forms. It is expressed in your ability to experience and create. It's your ability to be *in* the world even though you are not *of* it. The physical system works with all the parts dependent on one another, though you can still function and be even if some of these parts are removed. But it is difficult to be if you remove something like a stomach, and you don't put anything back to replace it.

For example, it is extremely challenging to be in a world where sight is the primary sense and you are born blind. Though the blindness appears to be a curse, it is also a great blessing, for that individual experiences the world in ways that you cannot.

Remember that All That Is contains all that is and also all that is not. Therefore any being that you see, anything that you experience, has to occur within this All That Is. It is not as if there is any consent involved. Nor is there a superior consciousness that spends all of Its time figuring out ways of inconveniencing other portions of Itself. This would be self-defeating. All That Is knows and realizes Its own true nature, the truth of what has been done. What has been done is that you have been created to do and be as All That Is does and is.

Now, oftentimes there is short-circuiting between what you think in your mind and what your body is manifesting for you physically. When you stub your toe, you experience the pain as though it is located in your toe. Do you think nerves can feel pain? The answer is no!

The only place that the experience you call "pain" can take place is in the mind.

Pain cannot exist outside of the mind. Rather awkward of you to create the experience of pain in your mind and in the end you grab your toe. You *bought* the awesome illusion of pain.

The brain itself is incapable of feeling pain. Why is it that when you experience pain, you have this experience in and through the mind?

Where is your mind? Does it exist in the folds and convolutions of the brain? The mind organizes the sensory data and then projects the response outward into physical manifestation. And though you appear in the here and now, what you see is not what is. What your senses really tell you is how you can maintain being stuck in the illusion of space and time. It is the method that is used to support you in staying in the world to accomplish the various goals you have chosen to accomplish.

Would you believe that one of your goals as a physical being could be to realize the sufferings of the paraplegic? Yet, if you are living this life as a paraplegic, all of your time may be spent wondering, "Why me?" The reason would always be because you are the only one that it could happen to, my friend. There are no coincidences, nor any accidents. In reality, it is open-ended. You can create reality and play in it all you want, while the Source Self knows Its reasons for your being here and is going to accomplish Its goals whether you like it or not.

The truth is, in the end you will like your experience simply because it was what you were meant to do. But as always, your free will dictates and allows you to create your experience.

Naturally it's difficult to look at disease and illness and say, "How can you call what I do in my life creating?" Anything that you do to or with the body is creative, anything short of terminating the body, that is, and even this is illusion.

Concerning such areas as mental illness, whereby an individual appears to be mentally handicapped in one form or another, it is difficult for you to look at this and be with it, for what scares you most is that you could have been like that. So you will avoid contact with it. You don't want to see the suffering because in your mind, you know that the person suffering *could* be you. So, what do you do to avoid

it? You turn your head away and pretend that you do not see it.

This is exactly what you do to your body. You turn your mind away because you think that all the cures and all the illness in the world are outside of you. They're out *there* somewhere. The only thing that is out here, my friends, is the *illusion of space* and that is all-- there is nothing else.

The individual cells in your body are each equipped to recognize and send the appropriate response signals to areas of the anatomy that will trigger the release of antibodies that will defeat, neutralize, and isolate the intruder infection. When you go and receive an outside source that goes into your body and causes the body to react to it, oftentimes there can be a bio-chemical misinterpretation of the body and its signals. This will frequently create complications.

One of these areas in which this often occurs is in cancer research. Radiation does not save lives, it decays them. Yet for the purposes of short-term gain, medicine accepts its use as a retardant to progressive cancer growth. Unfortunately, it eventually incinerates the cellular bio-plasmic inner structures of the living cell, resulting in the death of the body. So they must find an alternative defense in the form of another substance which they can introduce into the body that will produce the desired reaction. That reaction is not due to the medicine so much as it is with the patient's bio-chemical molecular composition.

The individual's mental posture will directly affect the condition of health within the body. If you believe you are a victim of disease, then you may draw to yourself every cold or flu virus that comes along as you continue to be manipulated by your own beliefs. See how you set yourselves up? You are telling yourself that this is the only way that it can be. So being the God that you are (and we use the term loosely), you create it, and bring this upon yourself. On the other hand, there are those people who work with highly contagious disease conditions and never seem to be affected by the disease itself. What makes them different? How come

57

you're affected and they are not? The answer lies within trust of self.

The key is trusting yourself enough to express it through action so that eventually consciousness will acknowledge it and the ego will grow to accept it. Bear in mind that you have had a lifetime, up to this point, to practice being who you are and what you believe. So where you are now is a result of all this practicing.

When you next look into the mirror, we hope that you take the time to say to yourself, *"I've been practicing for a long time. When am I going to do something about it?"* The question is, when are you going to accept the fact that your condition, your health, and your being are your responsibility, that you have within you the ability to initiate the cure for any condition that you create?

You do not have to be consciously aware of the mechanics involved in creating it, because 99.9% of the time you are not. It seems to be something that was thrust upon you, and I must reiterate that there is *nothing* further from the truth than that. There is, however, an agreement that took place between you and yourself when you chose to come into this world. You agreed to accept and operate within the rules of this reality.

We know that you do not look upon life as a playful experience. However, it is indeed a most *magnificent playground*, but it's up to you to realize it and create it to be that way. You can treat yourself in life in any manner that you see fit. But if you accept responsibility for it, and realize that the space of your health, mentally, physically, and spiritually is up to you, then you can begin to do something about it.

You've got to get off the horse and stop the world for a moment and take a look at it. Sit down quietly with yourself and recall those times in your life when you were sick or injured. Recreate these incidents in your mind's eye as vividly as is possible. Also recreate the state of mind that you were experiencing at the time, allowing the thoughts and emotional feelings of that time to be with you in the now.

You may find this difficult at first because the state of your mind at that time was something like a nightmare that you consciously chose to forget.

Each of you have had a stomachache, and you probably can easily remember how uncomfortable and painful the experience was. The truth is that you are afraid to think about the pain because you might inadvertently create it again. So when it occurs you will do your best to avoid the issue entirely, hoping that it will disappear on its own. Quite the opposite is true, avoiding the issue does not make it go away. Your resistance to it can draw it back into your experience.

Every thought that you have had, every moment that you experience yourself, in body, will work itself out and be realized in form whether it manifests physically in this space and time or whether it is experienced by another aspect of yourself existing in another space and time.

You are at the controls of your own vehicle, your own physicalness, right down to the most minute detail. And if you don't believe this, can you tell us who is in charge?

Please don't say God *ordained* it to be this way. If this were so, you would have no free will but only fate as your destiny. Illness is not a medical thing. It is a mental/physical relationship of conscious awareness that is generated by the individual himself.

A most important aspect of being healthy is to realize that you are healthy.

You will have your problems and challenges while in the physical body relating to its state of being. Remember that you *have* a body, it is not you. If you are suffering, you are suffering in the mind because the body itself cannot physically experience pain. It is incapable of this. It is only through the magnificent alchemy of mind that all this becomes real for you and in the same way reflects the world within which you live.

DEFINITIONS OF ILLNESS

"Illness is communication from your higher self. And until you understand that communication, there cannot be healing. It is impossible because the communication is the disease." ...Soli

The fabric of illness

Enid: The very words illness, sickness, or disease tend to make us think that they represent negativity. Now, I think, personally, that this type of so-called negative experience is wonderful because it gives us such great contrast to joy. We gain by the contrast. This is not to say that we must have cloudy skies so that we can appreciate the sunshine. It's not that simplistic. But there are different fabrics, different textures to life, and believe me, illness is a texture all its own.

Sometimes, just when we're feeling our strongest, illness can really knock us down as nothing else can. It forces us to look at our own mortality on this plane and reminds us that there's such a concept of mortality in reference to this plane. But eventually we will come to realize that there is no mortality, so then we cease to be afraid of that. And at that point, illness won't be able to teach us anything more, and we won't get ill because there is nothing more it can give to us.

59

Illness as a natural state

Speaking from the Clear Light: The nature of illness is not unnatural. Now why do I say that? How can it be? How can it be that illness is not unnatural?

Understand that everything that is created is natural and normal in the immediate sense of those words. What is existing in that moment, for you, is pure and simple truth, as far as you understand it and are applying it in all levels of your understanding in that moment. So, you may believe in illness. You may believe there is a possibility that you may become ill, or you may refuse to consider that you could even have the experience of illness. You say loudly, "No, I won't even think of it. I deny such a thing." What you deny, what you are afraid of, you will draw to you because it is a lesson which you have yet to fully integrate.

Now, what is this integration that we are talking about?

Does that mean something that is fully understood at the thought level?

Does it mean something that is emotionally experienced on the emotional level?

Does it mean something that is acted out in the physical level?

Does it mean something that is inspired on the spiritual level?

Or could it perhaps mean all of these? Could integration mean the full and complete use of your total consciousness, of your total understanding, of all the tools you came here with?

Illness is an expression, albeit somewhat dramatic, of that which has not been faced on a level or many levels of your consciousness. Many who have had illness or injury seek God or seek answers from somewhere, whether they be in the form of mental or inspirational understanding. We seek because we are here to seek on all levels. That does not mean we are here to deny some levels of our consciousness while we seek for truth mentally or spiritually. We are truly here to seek on all levels of our expression: physically, emotionally, mentally, and spiritually. We are here to seek and uncover and experience our true spiritual nature and to express our true spiritual nature as our day-to-day selves. That is the simple truth. That is why we are here right now.

But how to do this? And what do I mean by "the simple truth"? Does that mean that it is easy to do? Of course not! If it were so easy to do, we all would have done it long ago. It is easy because it is a simple concept. That means a non-complicated concept. That means a concept which does not require years and years of study. Simple truths are the most practical truths, the most useful truths in your lives.

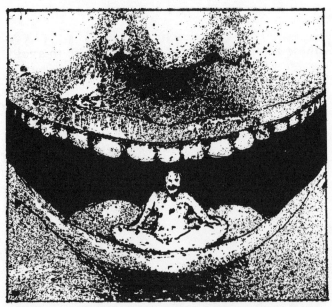

Why is it that famous gurus, famous teachers, and other famous ones who have achieved true spiritual integrity laugh so much? Why is it they are so cheerful? Is it because they have complete spiritual understanding and they are expressing it? Well, that's part of it-- but it is also because they understand that the years and years of study have brought them around in a perfect circle to their initial childhood, in which they unquestioningly accept the beauties and the wonders of life without judgment, without calculation, without analysis. They accept, just like a bird accepts that it can fly and is joyous in the act. They accept it without question. This is why gurus and famous teachers frequently will seem almost childlike at times. It is the simple truths and understandings of childhood that create complete communion with spirit on an emotional, physical, and on a mental level as well.

Illness, then, is a lack of communion with spirit or with self-understanding or with childhood. So, the nature of illness is a lack of communication with at least one portion of your expressive self.

Perhaps, for an example, there is an emotional issue which is unresolved. Perhaps it is something that you are so frightened of that the very idea of even thinking about it for a moment will bring back memories of fear, frustration, consternation, judgment, all of these feelings which you so much like to avoid.

Your emotional body is here to help you and helps you all the time, physically, by creating physical lessons in your life. You say, "You mean when I backed my car into the stop sign and put a scratch in my bumper and got a ticket by the policeman for bending the stop sign. You call that help?" Well, in a sense, it is help because it brings into your awareness the fact that there is something in your life which you have ignored. There is something that needs to be taken care of. I can assure you, my friends, that *something* will be a very simple issue. Not simple to do necessarily, but with practice something that can be done.

Perhaps you feel unworthy of a nice car. Perhaps you feel unworthy of a life unfettered by a ticket from a police officer. Perhaps that's the issue--perhaps it's another issue. But in any event, it is surely communication which has been attempted by your emotional self, by your spiritual self, by your physical self and even by your mental self which you were just not willing to listen to at that time.

Perhaps you used your will to ignore the communication, saying, "Damn the torpedoes and full speed ahead." Now, that can be useful at times. At other times, it may not be useful

because it may not resolve an issue. Some will decide to say, "Damn the torpedoes and full speed ahead," and will resolve an issue of fear. This can be good because it confronts the fear. The being has said, "I'm afraid to go through those torpedoes, but I'm going to do it. And I'm going to believe that I can do it. And if I believe that I can do it in my head and if I believe that I can do it in my heart, and my emotions, and if I act it out physically, then I will be acting out my spiritual intent on this planet. And my spiritual intent is to create safety, harmony, and comfort regardless of the physical evidence around me which I'm using to test myself."

Now, how can this be applied to illness? First, be willing to receive information from yourself. This does not always mean through your thoughts. It might be feelings. It might be information in the sense that your feelings want to express themselves and they wish to do so physically. Allow yourself to do things that might be silly.

Perhaps your body, working with your emotions, will want to do something fun. Maybe you'll want to laugh out loud. Allow yourself to laugh. What's the harm in laughing? Allow yourself to feel what happens in your body when you're laughing. Are you nervous? Are you afraid that someone will judge you harshly? If so, maybe more laughter is needed or maybe more feelings are needed or maybe thought is needed.

Do not deny the mind--the mind is here to help you. Maybe remembering is needed-- remembering who you really are in your totality. Maybe you need to be reminded to remember that you are a loving portion of the One, the all powerful, that which you might call God or the One Mind or the One Soul or the One Light.

You are not an exception. There are no exceptions. All are portions of the One. If you would see yourself as a cell in that portion of the One, then you could see how all moves together. Your Earth rotates and the animals move with a certain precision. The people all move in a certain dance together.

The nature of illness is lack of communication.

That is what illness is. It occurs because you are not listening. When you are not listening, someone will surely draw your attention. "Oh, you're not going to listen to me, 'ey? Well, you'll listen to this." So what happens is, "Oh, oh, now I am coughing and now I am sneezing. What is going on?"

Understand that illness is to catch your attention. It is to catch your attention that *you are not listening.* It is there to remind you that you do, indeed, create your reality from moment to moment by what you think and believe and also by what you feel. You create your reality by the needs that you create. And those needs will draw to you the experience you need to have to understand that you have power.

Listen, my friends. Listen. Use all your tools. Listen to your feelings. Sometimes your feelings will speak to your mind and have words to say to you. And you might hear this as inspiration.

Inspiration is the bridge that links your emotional and physical body with your mental and spiritual body.

Listen to your inspiration. It comes directly from your soul. If you feel inspired to do something silly and childlike (and that does not mean something negative, it means to do something positive), don't just say, "Well, that's only for children. I can't go outside and take a ball and throw it around up in the air all by myself. People will think I'm crazy."

Listen to yourself. Understand that if you need to express something from your childhood which was maybe nipped in the bud too soon and left unexpressed, then go ahead and express it. As long as it is positive and loving and doesn't hurt anyone, so what if it looks silly? Don't judge yourself. Let yourself be the child just as the guru or the teacher lets himself or herself be the child in the true, infinite wisdom of unquestioning, non-judgmental childhood, in its true emotionally positive, spiritually bright, loving, integral self. Let yourself be yourself. Let yourself be your total loving self, using all portions of yourself. Let your emotions speak with emotion. Let your physical body speak with physical acts. Let your mental body speak with wondrous words and thoughts. And let your spiritual body speak to you with inspiration and insights.

When you are communicating fully with yourself, illness will be a language that is no longer a part of your natural existence.

So just begin. Give yourself permission to begin by beginning. Even by beginning, you will begin to lessen the effect of illness, because by beginning, you give yourself permission to hear from all portions of yourself, to feel all portions of yourself, to act out all portions of yourself. And in this way, you will truly cure the language of illness from your reality.

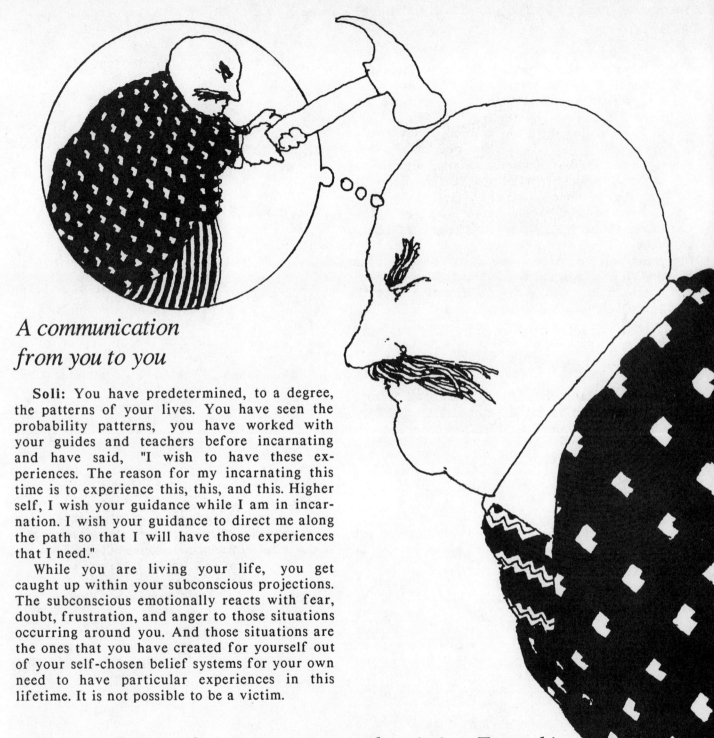

A communication from you to you

Soli: You have predetermined, to a degree, the patterns of your lives. You have seen the probability patterns, you have worked with your guides and teachers before incarnating and have said, "I wish to have these experiences. The reason for my incarnating this time is to experience this, this, and this. Higher self, I wish your guidance while I am in incarnation. I wish your guidance to direct me along the path so that I will have those experiences that I need."

While you are living your life, you get caught up within your subconscious projections. The subconscious emotionally reacts with fear, doubt, frustration, and anger to those situations occurring around you. And those situations are the ones that you have created for yourself out of your self-chosen belief systems for your own need to have particular experiences in this lifetime. It is not possible to be a victim.

You are always the creator, never the victim. Everything that happens to you upon the physical earth is of your own creation, desire, and need ... everything.

What you see around you is a reflection of yourself. Even the relationship of others to you is a reflection of how you see yourself and what you believe about yourself.

In following the path that you would wish to pursue, it would be ideal for you to go within, to be in constant contact with your higher self, to be bringing forward that guidance on the way that you need to go.

But, the subconscious mind has a few things to say about that. The subconscious mind reacts, very often, with fear and doubt regarding a course of action that you have been guided to do. You have heard the guidance, you have felt the need to go in a certain direction, but the subconscious mind comes forward with 1,001 very logical reasons why that would be a disastrous thing to do. It recalls fear and reactions to situations of similar nature that you have experienced before, and very often filters past-life experiences through into this present subconscious mind, experiences where a certain situation created great difficulty for you.

You may very well have chosen this lifetime to finally transcend the difficulties that you had that previous lifetime. And yet the feelings from that lifetime keep coming forward, giving fear and doubt about moving in the direction you are guided.

And so, the higher self, out of love for you, out of your need, out of your agreement before incarnating, must communicate with you. How can it do this? It can communicate through the physical aspects, not the spiritual. (You can communicate with your higher self through the spiritual aspects, through meditation, through understanding, through feeling.) However, your higher self must communicate with you in a way that you will take notice of. And there is challenge in that, for how can it get beyond or past the subconscious mind?

First, it brings forward an idea within the intellect that you should be doing something. If you cannot understand that communication, or if you *refuse to understand* that communication (which often happens), the higher self must then slow that vibration down a stage so you receive it within the emotional body, so that you *feel* the emotions regarding a circumstance or situation that you are in.

You begin to feel emotional. You have this emotion telling you that you need to make a change in your life. And yet, very few will understand that. Very few will take action. Most will sit back and wonder, "Why am I feeling depressed? Where is this frustration coming from? Why is that person over there doing this to me?" Always the victim, always looking for someone to blame. And so, you do not hear or understand that communication. Therefore the higher self will slow that vibration further until it manifests within the physical body.

There are very few individuals who can ignore totally a physical communication, a physical disease, an accident or some physical disability. Very often, you'll find yourself lying flat on your back in bed for a few days. You will ask yourself, "What is this communication?"

Until you understand the communication from your higher self, there cannot be healing. It is impossible because the communication is the disease.

It is a combination of your subconscious mind driving you in one direction, and your guidance and feeling wishing to take you in another. It is resistance from the subconscious that causes the disease. Pain and suffering exist *only* within the subconscious mind. They are not of spiritual origin. They are the *reaction* of the subconscious that refuses to follow that guidance, to follow that path. That is what causes disease, pain, and suffering.

And so, disease, pain, and suffering are also matters of choice. Individuals can choose to have them or choose not to by changing their lives, the path they're walking on, or the job that they're involved in and have been bored with for so long--whatever it might be.

My friends, those things which you find yourself fighting, those diseases within the body, the microbes, bacteria, viruses, they are in service to you. You do not fight them. You understand *your need for them.* You have created the circumstances whereby they have been able to multiply.

64

My friends, every single illness, every microbe imaginable, and many are imaginable at this time, are already within your physical bodies. You have every illness possible. Every molecule that exists within the earth plane exists within your physical bodies. That is why some consider the human the microcosm of the macrocosmic Earth. Every atom and molecule exists within your physical body.

How then do these molecules expand and create illness? Why is it that when two individuals are exposed to a disease, perhaps of epidemic proportions--one succumbs and the other does not? It is out of choice and need. One individual requires that communication in order to make him or her change, the other does not.

So, those "bugs" are in service to you. Once you have understood the communication behind them and have changed your life, taken action upon that communication, you simply bless and release the disease. Bless the microbes, thank them for having given you that service and they will disappear very rapidly for they know they are not needed anymore. They, too, are conscious beings because everything is life, everything has consciousness. They respond to your thoughtforms.

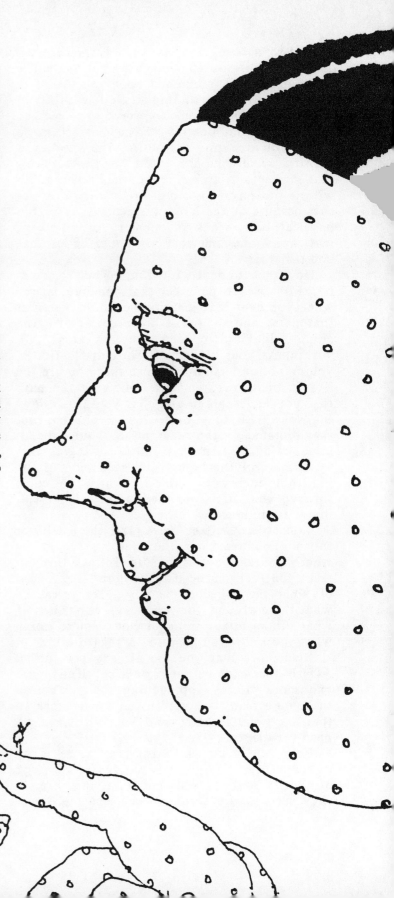

And so it is my friends, with every form of disability that you can imagine upon the earth plane, none of it is imposed upon you. All of it comes from your own higher self wishing to communicate with you. You have to have that increased communication. It becomes necessary when you are not following the guidance within, when you are not doing those things that you set up and created before you came within the physical body. Frequently this occurs because of the lack of memory within the physical body, lack of memory of who you truly are, lack of memory of the perfection that you truly are.

How then to deal with illness when it comes by? First, when you feel that communication, when you hear that idea in your mind, listen at that point and then it is not necessary for the communication to reach the physical. Go within, ask your higher self for clarification if you do not understand. Affirm that you are the living spirit, that you are following the path that you have chosen and that you are following your path to your highest evolution, not that dictated by the reactions of your subconscious mind. Affirm that you are bringing forward more of the higher self each day, allowing that energy to shine forward, to come through your life. And then, as you do so, follow that guidance.

True, there will be fears, and there will be subconscious reactions. But that, my friends, is where courage comes in, to follow through what you feel you need to be doing, regardless of what the subconscious says, regardless of what those around you might say, regardless of what others might think of you. You're doing what you know you have to do, regardless.

Remember that you are already perfection. Affirm that each day your physical life is more and more closely approaching the perfection that you already are within the spirit. Work in that way, my friends, and you will have no need for disease of any kind.

But, let it be said also that there is no punishment with this. It is not for you to look at another and say, "My goodness, they are ill, they have obviously not been hearing some-thing." Understand that you would not be upon the physical earth plane within the physical body if you did not still have things to learn. When you fully understand the workings of the subconscious mind, fully understand the power of thought, at that point, you will have no further need to be within the earth plane, and so you will move on.

The communication of pain

Master Adalfo: Pain is a warning. It is the smoke alarm going off before the fire saying, "Pay attention to me. There is something not right here." That is why, when it is ignored, pain gets worse. It says, "I said to pay attention, (slap, slap, slap), PAY ATTENTION!!" It becomes louder and louder in its request for attention.

What happens in the society in which you live though, is that you *take* something so that you do not have to feel pain. It is as though you are giving yourself the message of not having to feel. And that message sometimes carries over into the rest of your life. You wish that you could just find the aspirin for everything in your life you didn't want to feel, not just pain.

Pain sometimes is about being aware of a feeling, knowing what your feelings are and being able to examine the difference between when you have pain and when you don't. And it is important for people who have pain to learn to rate their pain. Everyone in your society believes that you either have pain or you don't. You don't think about people who go around in constant pain, but at a level at which they can function. It is important to be able to rate your pain on a level of 1 to 10. "This is a '1' headache; I hardly feel it. This is a '10' headache; I go to bed."

It is as though you had a stick. One end of the stick is pain and the other end of the stick is no pain. There are many levels of pain and many levels of no pain along that stick--like a thermometer. You can learn to look at pain like that. You can learn to see pain as an alarm, a warning. It is like the yellow caution light you have on your street traffic signals which tell you that you need to pay attention because the signal is going to change. "Pay attention, this is going to turn red." And if you do not pay attention, it does!

Soli: Pain is a resistance from the subconscious. It is most easily understood if you look at the emotional pain that so many go through; that is somewhat more easily understood.

For example, if you have a certain course of action that you need to take and you do not take it, you start to feel an emotional reaction, frustration perhaps, that is pain. Where does that come from? It comes from the fact that the subconscious mind is resisting the course of action that you need to take. And so it is that the resistance is reflected in the physical body.

If you find yourself moving along a path that will not lead to the evolution that you want because the subconscious mind is strongly resisting, then the higher self will apply the brakes to your careening along. And so the pain comes from the subconscious mind which is strenuously resisting having those brakes put upon it.

Pain is created from the thoughtform also. It has amply been demonstrated many times that by self-thought, by affirmation, by relaxation, and self-hypnosis, you can completely eliminate pain. But remember, it most likely will be tem-

porary until you understand the communication and then follow it. To do that you must work through and understand the beliefs within your subconscious mind that are creating the difficulties, that are creating the resistance to change.

In its most simple definition, my friends, pain is a resistance to change.

Enid: We encourage beings to leave behind this idea of *no pain, no gain*, of having to grow through pain. Beings get so enamored with growing through pain that they begin to think this is the only way to do it. We're trying to remind you that, "Hey, hey, you don't have to." But if you're in the middle of it, you're going to have to go out the other side before you can change your mind. Once you're through it, you can say, "Never again, that's it!" This is where you can use your scissors to cut it off.

Group decisions - 'tis the season for the flu

Enid: We have what we call "epidemics." This is when a whole army of beings decide to experience something together. So they all have the flu and then visit with one another, saying, "Did you get that, too?" It becomes a point of connection.

Just as when there are wars, sometimes they cause a point of connection. People say, "Are you afraid? I am too. Let's talk about it, let's get together."

Have you ever had the flu, and when you got through, you felt so clean? You felt as though you'd been just reamed out by a roto-rooter. Sometimes an illness helps you start over in some way, to cleanse you. You get rid of many toxins. Your body just flushes itself out because you're drinking so many liquids. And when it's over you feel so clean inside. And frequently society seems to come up a bit after one of these "group" experiences. And that good feeling flows to and through all those who had the same experience.

If you'll notice, something good happens after epidemics. For example, look at the plagues. In those early times there was so much crowding and excrement in the streets. Everything was so very dirty, unclean. And when it was over, it lead to a long cleansing period. There always are good reasons for everything that happens, even if it seems dreadful and terrible when you're going through it.

A test or a gift

Master Adalfo: Many people perceive illness or pain as a *test* of their spirituality. I do not like that thought. If someone gives you a test, the first thing that implies is that somehow you should *know* the knowledge enough to pass it. You should have the information that will be on the test; you've been exposed to it, at least. So if we say disease is a test of spirituality, it is as if all of us spirits up here in God say, "Well, he should have learned all this about spirituality. We will test him now. We will give him a disease, and we will see what he does with it." That is not how we operate up here.

When you are ill, it is more difficult to continue to communicate with spirit, or to be in touch with your own higher self because all of your energy goes toward staying alive or being without pain. When we talk about good things coming from experiencing a disease, we are meaning that it is a gift you give yourself so

that you can begin to examine things more closely, so that you can begin to feel. So, when you are ill, this is an ideal time to continue your connection with spirit so that we can help you.

It is true that often the energy simply is not there for that spiritual conection when you are really sick. That is when we most especially need the help of others who can keep us connected with spirit by giving us enough energy to maintain even a small connection with spirit, with our higher self. That connection will help you to begin to know what is going on with you and the disease.

So I will not call illness a test of spirituality. That brings with it the idea of punishment. I do not like to think of disease as punishment we inflict upon ourselves because that is not what it really is. It is a way of getting us to pay attention. So in that sense, it is not a punishment. It is a gift--even though you might have been able to think up a better one, had you known.

With the information that you had available, illness was the best gift you could come up with to make you more aware. Next time you might come up with a better present for yourself.

Why you might choose a "dreadful" illness

Enid: The whole idea of a *dreadful* illness is a very exciting thing. Remember that there are no good or bad experiences. Everything is *just* experience. Some we enjoy more than others. When we leave this plane of existence and are back home with our spirit family, we look back and say, "You know, that dreadful time after I broke my hip, I look back and I see so many glories there, so many things I learned to understand."

There are things that cannot be understood with sweetness and light because that dimension of energy is *outside* of this physical universe. So we come here and grit our teeth and say, "Okay, sock it to me. I'll take it. I will take whatever it is you want to dish out because I want to experience it."

Where else can you experience getting robbed if you don't invite a robber in? Where else can you experience an automobile wreck unless you're driving in an automobile? Things of this nature create all kinds of excitement. So, try to look at these experiences with a broader perspective, seeing them as not being negative. They may hurt and you may experience pain, but these are only societal terms which we have learned to perceive as being negative.

Sometimes these "dreadful" experiences are the best things that happen to you. Sometimes, when you have a cataclysmic thing happen to you, it wakes up all kinds of things in your psyche and in your mind that have been dormant--that you haven't paid attention to.

69

The Response of the Created

By Ebban

The Interested One
Creates
By pulling Himself
Within his personal
Vacuum

Boundaries are set
And
Experience begins

The Interested One
Expands
By pushing Himself
Through the knothole
Of his personal
Choice

Boundaries are flexed
and
Expanded Experience Continues

The punctures
The wounds
The mishaps
Cry for explanation

The Places
That won't budge
Now
Sit and smile and
Beg
For understanding

The Sensations
Trickle
Through the nerves of consciousness
And nervousness
Excites concentration

The glow of trouble
Hints once again
At the
Bliss of delight

Perfection
Sings
Eternally

Invitations float
From one realm to another
Until
All levels
Are integrated
Into desired chants
and endless
Life moments

The latest floatation
The latest invitation
and
The latest tension
Involve Inner Workings
Which act as
Private Gardeners
Playing with the soil
and hoping for rain
While constantly
Breathing the fresh new air
of a Special Scene

The Visualized Visualizes

When the scene is fulfilled
The links of the chain
Which lifted the harvest into domain
Are viewed with gratitude

And from gratitude arises newer ability

The past tension of the chains
Is seen from a new perspective

Perspective heals

New perspective
New mind
New body

The Gardener
And the Interested One
know that
Responsibility directs perspective

Responsibility heals

To respond
Is the natural profession
Of the created

To create
Is the natural response
Of the created

To heal
is
To create

To have a vision
Is to transform

Where are you?

MENTAL ILLNESS

"No one consciously invites mental or physical illness. But, if you listen to your words and the words of others, you will hear yourselves unconsciously inviting sickness all the time." ... Dong How Li

Depression

Soli: Depression very often has a very deep-seated cause far beyond your current lifetime, going right back to your first individual experience as a separate entity. While you are in Earth density, while you are in the ego personality and in the belief systems of the Earth, you feel your individuality, you feel your separateness. In fact, you are taught that you are separate.

You are taught, from childhood, that everything lies *outside* of you. You are taught that, if you are ill, you must go outside of yourself for someone to heal you or for medicine that will cure you. You are taught that if you are unhappy, you must go outside of yourself and be entertained to cheer you up. You are taught that if you are lonely, you must go outside of yourself and bring in a lover to cure that loneliness, not recognizing that everything (without exception) you see around you is a reflection of your inner being, is a reflection of what you believe about yourself, is a reflection of your relationship to your own higher self.

As you are growing up in childhood, you are taught to *judge* everything. Everything is good or bad, right or wrong, good or evil, light or dark, positive or negative. You have an arbitrary standard of judgment for absolutely every single attribute of human beingness in your lives. There is a standard of body, of

goodness, of badness. There is a standard of how much money you should have.

Also, you are brought up through your childhood, through the subconscious programming, to have *expectations* in every single area of your lives. You are taught that what a human being is, is this, this, this and that and the other thing. So you have these fixed ideas within your subconscious belief systems about what it is to be human.

And, of course, you can see very clearly that if you go to another society, a tribal society in Africa, for example, you have a totally different set of beliefs as to what is good and what is bad, what is beautiful, what is ugly. All these standards are totally arbitrary. They are man-made and man-imposed.

God does not impose morality on human beings or on anything else. The All That Is simply is. The All That Is experiences. It is man and thought that creates laws and rules that say you must do this, that, and the other thing. And each thing, each attribute, has its own arbitrary standard. And you are taught, from childhood onward, to judge everything according to these arbitrary standards.

Your lives, therefore, are a constant area of expectation. You see that life *should* be a certain way. You are seeing that humanity *should* live a certain way. You believe that your life *should* be a certain pattern, for this is what you have been taught. You have to have a certain amount of money, otherwise you are unhappy. But why are you unhappy? It is not, my friends, that poverty makes people unhappy. It is the expectation that is not being met that makes people unhappy.

When you have an expectation in your life that life should be a certain way, and the events around you don't match that expectation, what happens? You become unhappy. And if you maintain the thoughtform that things aren't working out the way they are supposed to work, your thought increases that creation of reality around you. And if you *constantly* see things not working out the way you expected them to, that becomes your reality. And so you feed into that depression, you feed that negativity.

Your subconscious mind and beliefs, my dear friends, will always do whatever is necessary to prove yourself right. In other words, if you have a belief within your subconscious mind, *all* of your experience in life will serve to substantiate that belief. If, as a child, you are taught that you are ugly and you are never going to have a love relationship of any consequence, that belief is deep down in your subconscious mind.

Later on in life you move into a relationship and deep down your subconscious is saying, "Oh yes, but this is never going to last because nobody could love an ugly person like me." And that very thought creates the reality that you see around you, it creates the reality that the loved one sees within you. It is the expression of yourself that others pick up from you. And if you do not believe yourself to be beautiful, others around you will not see you as beautiful.

And so, a relationship will come into your life and will last for a few weeks, maybe, and then it will fall away. You will say, "Oh, yes, exactly what I expected. Just goes to show what I've always known. My relationships aren't going to last." It is a vicious circle. What is in your subconscious creates your reality. What you see is your reality. And how you react and respond to that reality serves to substantiate the beliefs that were already in the subconscious mind.

My friends, depression and unhappiness are never imposed upon you.

You are never a victim of anything within your lives.

You, as spiritual beings, chose what (in some cases) would seem to be a totally negative life. But nothing is by accident. Those that seemingly live very negative lives have *chosen* those lives for the experiences thereof. You, as a higher being, as a higher power, as the higher self, as God, are experiencing your own creativity.

You are creator and creation both, and there is no separation. And you are here to experience your own creation. You can experience all aspects of it, positive and negative. It does not matter. Spirit does not judge. Your higher self does not judge. Your higher self does not care how you *handle* your life. Your higher self does not care whether you go through life kicking and screaming in pain and suffering, or whether you go through your life in joy and happiness and delight.

There are no problems. There are only events. It is your mind that turns the event into a problem.

You are never a victim of circumstance, dear friends. You draw yourselves into circumstances because you want to experience those circumstances. It is your mind that turns that experience into a depressive event or a problem.

Depression comes about when your mindset will not allow you to accept what is happening in your life with equanimity. If you could accept every change that came into your life, dear friends--every change, however small or large--with total equanimity, and look at it and say, "Well, how very interesting that this is happening in my life now, I wonder what I can do with this," at that point, you would never have a moment of disease in your life. Your body would not age. It is only your mind resisting the changes that are coming into your

being. When you resist, resist, resist what your higher self is bringing you into, that causes you to suffer. Suffering is always a creation of your mind.

Dong How Li: Imagine that each time you are dealing with your depression that it is a line. You only let yourself go so far into the pain and then you kind of eject into freak-out or panic. So, you don't quite get to look at what's under the pain. Each time you are willing to go a little further into the pain to see what the gift is that is there, you extend the line toward the exit.

But you still remember that before, there were limits to what you thought you could experience, to how much pain you could take. So

now what you are doing is gradually extending your capacity to experience the pain and remain alive. And gradually, the longer you are

75

alive, the more you are able to see, until eventually you are all the way through it. Then you know this the next time you start sinking and you get into this depression. You know that you can be in it longer and longer and survive it. And eventually you also will know that you can come back up out of it. Only at that point will the need to get depressed be gone.

Depression is layer and layer upon layer and only when you get through to the bottom layer, to the end of the cycle, and have gone through the whole cycle of the depression can you come up on the other side. By then you will have explored the fears that are under it and you won't have the need to experience it anymore. What keeps the depressive in that state is the fear of the pain. "I can't take so much. I'm going to die. I'm going to kill myself." That stops the movement; that stops the cycle so it doesn't continue and you never come out to the other side.

What's required is a willingness actually to be there with your depression and to experience it until it is through. If you identify with the pain, you can't get through it because the pain is not going through. But when you allow yourself to experience the pain going through you, what is moving through you is an energy that is kind of like a rush of water that carries the pain and your attachment out with it.

Suppose you were in a maze, but it was a linear maze. At different places in the maze you had obstacles of various sizes, like walls. You start pushing water through the maze and in certain places the water will stop. It thinks that it can't go beyond the obstacle. But if you push more water through, it will have enough force to go around the obstacle or break the obstacle and go until it is out of the maze. But every time the water comes to one of the obstacles, the conflict is intense once again. You then have the water pushing against the wall and the wall is not letting it through. So,

in other words, you must get to the place where you are able to take an intensification of the pain to dissolve the block.

You can't be very objective when you are in great pain of any kind. If you do it, you go into a split like being schizoid. You have to be *with* the pain. You need to be *in* the pain to know you can move *through* it. Objectivity comes afterwards.

Soli: Coming out of depression is like lifting yourself up by your own bootstraps. You can choose to *allow* depression to run its fullest extent, which we would advocate. So often, when you have a depression, you try to "cure" it. You go out and buy yourself an ice cream to cheer yourself up. You go out to see a movie, or do something to cheer yourself up and try to forget about what was making you depressed. It doesn't work, my friends.

All that does is repress, within your psyche, within your subconscious, the very things that are trying to come to the surface. It is as though you are putting the lid on the boiling pot. Ultimately it must explode. It is much better to let the lid off and let the steam out.

So, when you feel depressed, take a look at that depression. Allow yourself to experience it to the utmost. Within your society, you are so intellectual and so logical that you will not allow yourselves to feel. You have your feeling body closed down tight. The second chakra is screwed closed. You will not allow yourself to feel all the energy of emotion. Therefore it must manifest in the physical body because it has nowhere else to go. It can't go upwards, it must go down into the lower frequencies of the physical vibration. So you manifest a physical illness in your body.

If you are depressed, allow the emotional body its true place within your life. There is nothing wrong with emotions. There is nothing wrong with being depressed. Allow yourself to experience it. It is one of the experiences of life. And once you have experienced it to its fullest, let it go.

Cultural burnout

Dong How Li: Many times sickness is an invited condition. It is a way to force yourself to slow down, to get conscious. It is a way to attract attention. It is also a way to totally shift your inner and outer realities, particularly in some of the viral diseases and illnesses where fevers are concerned.

It's like anger. It's one of those things you use to gather enough energy to get off your present position because your culture doesn't legitimately allow you another way to do that. You are supposed to stay in your job from nine to five for fifty years and vacation two weeks a year. So how do you get out of that prison?

And there are other prisons too, prisons of consciousness. So then illness becomes a way to pressurize yourself out of them. Now, I want to say something here about pressure. You are also in a culture that is not interested in intensity. It is interested in an "even keel" with few highs and few lows. But, if you cannot experience the intensity of the pain, how can you experience the intensity of ecstatic love? If you have no peaks, your life is all plateaus.

So, you wonder why there is so much burnout in your culture? It is all too tedious. So you get sick to break out of the tedium. Of course, I speak of the unconscious intention to become ill. No one *consciously* invites disease.

But if you listen to your words and the words of others, you will hear yourselves inviting sickness all the time.

You see, there is wisdom in the depths of your being that calls forth what you need, even if you choose not to invite it. If you choose to invite it, then you have already begun the process of reconnecting with the hidden parts of yourself. You have already begun your healing. When you invite new energy into places that are not well, they begin to feel the hurt that originally drove these parts of yourself into numbness. So, sometimes, the pain is the pain of awakening, yes? It is part of the process of coming back to life, coming back into wholeness. Either way you are screaming as you are being born and dying, as you are going to sleep and awakening--moving the energy.

Alleviating stress

Kyros: Your culture seems to be greatly overstressed. This is due to the extremely high negativity which is prevalent within mass consciousness. Many methods used to relieve stress are as damaging to the physical vehicle and the mind as the stress itself. I am, of course, referring to alcohol, drugs, tranquilizers, and so on. Use of these illusionary ways of alleviating stress are not permanent. They merely blind you for the moment.

The more positive ways of alleviating stress lie in the areas of reshaping your thought processes and learning to control your mind. Such things as self-hypnosis, muscle relaxation, centering, biofeedback, and positive thinking, are but a few.

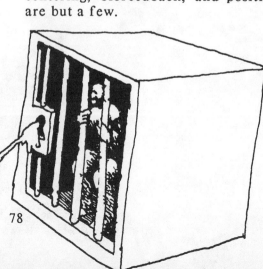

78

A certain amount of stress is good in that it triggers you into action. You would accomplish very little if there were not some degree of stress present to urge you onward. This is healthy stress.

The most damaging kind of stress, however, is the self-created kind. This is the stress which is created by the ego and its negative perceptions of the world. It is these unnatural stresses which lead entities into the use of illusionary methods of alleviation, and it is this type of stress which creates most of the illness (physical and mental) within your world. Each physical entity has a point at which, if he goes beyond, the stress factors will begin their destruction, either to the body or mind. In your culture, many entities have either gone beyond or are living right on the edge of that point.

When you feel or sense stress within, you need to analyze it. In doing so you will learn to assess whether it is natural and healthy, positive stress or whether it is manufactured stress which could lead to possible destruction.

Worry and fear are unnatural stresses, while concern and legitimate caution are healthy.

In other words, you can be concerned without worrying and you can exercise caution without experiencing fear. There's a big difference.

So, when you feel stress, think about what is causing it. Determine how important the object causing the stress is. Can you change the circumstances by either worry or fear? Will the situation drastically alter your life? As you've been told before, most things which you deem important are not that important on a cosmic level. In fact, most things will lose their importance just with the passage of a short period of time.

Too much energy is wasted in stress or worry over the future, and of fear of the future. If you take each moment as it comes to you and deal with the issues as they come to you, then let them go, you secure your future in a more positive way.

Human life moves through time and space. You cannot stop this flow. You will find your journey more enjoyable and positive if you start learning to analyze what is really important. Human entities need to learn to become more acutely aware of their present moments in order to gain the *fullness* of life. It's not that you don't make plans or prepare for future moments. In a time-space dimension, it seems that you must.

You must plant the fields in spring to prepare for the autumn harvest. But, you shouldn't *worry* about the harvest while you're planting the seeds. You enjoy and find pleasure in the present moment of planting the seeds. Then, if the locusts come and destroy the harvest, you have enjoyed the planting of the seeds.

The best way to be free of destructive stress is to live in your present moments. Let them slip to where they must go (into the past) and continue to stay in the present moment. You can't change past moments, and you can only dream and prepare for future ones. The only moment you have a guarantee of on Earth is the one you are living. Learn to relax and do the best you can with your present moments.

The past is gone, washed away by time's sea.

The future is but a dream, yet to be.

Now is your gift and your eternity.

When illness is imagined

Enid: People who appear to be hypochondriacs are no different from anyone else.

Whoever reaches for healing must be healed.

From our perspective, *all* illness is hypochondriacal in nature because we all manifest our own illnesses. If someone has one illness after another, after another, after another, that person is inviting some kind of attention that they're not getting. They say, "Well, my kidneys are hurting a little bit. They'll probably be hurting enough tomorrow to go see the doctor." So, sure enough they are, and this person goes to see the doctor and he touches them here and there. Maybe this person is Aunt Edna and she hasn't been hugged or cared about by anybody in weeks.

The person who's constantly finding one thing after another wrong with them, and it's always something different, is hurting in the heart. They're probably heartbroken.

Question: Is peace of mind possible?

Bartholomew: The only way I know for the human to feel "at peace" is to have a deep inner sense that "God's in It's heaven and all's right with *my* world." It is a feeling that everything is in harmony each moment, no matter how bad the situation looks. With this feeling comes the courage to do strange and wonderful things. For example, when the discouragement committee rises up and says, "You can't do that," you find that you can. The warrior is born within you, and you find yourself daring new ideas to fill you, new roads to call you, new responses to delight you. *You feel new.*

There is a very deep desire in the human to have other people like you. No blame. Life goes easier if people like you. But an interesting thing will happen, my friends, if you dare to be the warrior and trust what comes to you. Either your friends will respond to your deepening awareness, or think you're totally crazy and have nothing more to do with you, and they leave your life. In either case, harmony and peace are yours.

But how to get this deep feeling of "rightness," of peace? You begin as you do with any deep desire--by *stating your intention.* Tell yourself a hundred times a day, "I want peace. I want to feel it, *now*, within me. Nothing else matters as much. I don't need to be *right*, I don't need to be *heard*--I need peace. Now!" And then, withdrawing your awareness from the outer world, go inside to that place where peace abides and allow yourself to *feel it*! It is always there waiting for you to quicken it into greater and greater waves of peaceful power. It's that simple. But you must go to that inner place again and again, leaving all other desires to quiet down and dissolve. You *can* do it if you want to badly enough.

WHAT IS HEALTH

"Health is a state of balance where, within an individual body, all of the various parts, all of the cells, are resonating in harmony." ...Seth

Health is communicating
with all parts of yourself

Dong How Li: Health means taking conscious responsibility for your own creation. It means a willingness to continue to keep the parts of you (some of which you are not in such communication with) together and in communication with each other. I hesitate to say that the object is to stay physically absent of pain because the object is not to avoid pain. That's the wrong focus.

If you focus on pain, you keep creating it. The object is your own loving of your wholeness, your affirmation of your wholeness, so that whatever comes about is transformed, including the pain.

Understand that you want to encourage and continue the communication between the obvious parts of you and the not-so-obvious parts of you so there is a continual exchange going on. For many of you in this culture, that means to watch your dreams. It also means meditations and just being still, whether that's when you are asleep or awake, just to counterbalance all the activity you have around you all of the time.

Soli: When you are in the state of disease, instead of "thinking it to death," if you go within, understand the communication, talk to your higher self and make the changes in your life that are necessary to follow that guidance, you will have almost instant healing. It is not necessary for anyone ever again to have a disease. It is totally unnecessary if you choose to meditate and communicate with your higher self and then follow the guidance that you receive.

For others less evolved in their understanding, it is very different. (We do not wish to imply better or worse. There is no hierarchy. There are only degrees of evolvement, matter, or experience.) The belief systems of those less evolved are strongly ingrained within the subconscious as to the nature of healing and as to the nature of disease. They carry the thought of

It is not the traditional medical help which creates wellness, but rather the belief that wellness comes from that source.

being victims and not being responsible. It takes major shifts in thinking before the healing of any illness can take place.

The doctors in old China got paid only as long as their patients were well.

Imagine the medical profession working on those terms today! The doctors of old China understood the true nature and cause of illness. They understood that if a husband and wife were fighting constantly, sooner or later there would be a manifestation within the physical body. And so they spent their time walking around the neighborhood talking to their clients, dealing with them, listening to them, discovering what was causing difficulty in their lives and helping them to change that.

Health is a state of harmony

Seth: Health is a state of balance or harmony, a state of ease where, within an individual body, all of the various parts, all of the cells, are resonating in harmony. Health is not created by the body, but rather by the mind.

Health is a state of mental harmony where all of the thoughts are focused in the present, in the now, and are therefore harmonious.

The thoughts become inharmonious when they begin to project into the future or when they look back into the past. Then the rational mind begins to make comparisons, judgments and creates conflict.

Your mind regulates the state of your health. Your body wants to operate harmoniously. It is, however, dictated to by your mind and all your thoughts, most of which are unconscious, and many of which are very ancient, in terms of your life. You begin to think in the womb and

continue at birth and through infancy and early childhood. At those times, you think very strong thoughts as emotional responses come up in regard to what is happening to you in relation to your environment.

The thoughts in the womb, at birth and during infancy form the basis of the unconscious thought system, which regulates the state of your health. And the conscious thoughts you think, moment to moment, interact with the unconscious, oftentimes reinforcing the unconscious thoughts, and as a result, dictating the state of health of the body.

So, to maintain health, it is important to maintain harmony in all of the thoughts for they travel on air waves into the electromagnetic energy field around the body. And there they lodge. And since the field is magnetic, the thoughts indeed send out an energy of attraction which creates the state of the health. For the body mimics your beliefs about life and experience. Health is a state of perfectly harmonious thoughts about life and about experience. Health is a state of balance and of acceptance, a state of being totally immersed in the moment, in the now.

A predisposition for health comes from an harmonious adaptation to birth, to being in the body, and to early childhood experiences. Even the shape of the body is dictated by the thoughts and the emotions.

As an infant, you are responsive to your environment and create bodily responses, sometimes stiffening of the legs, locking the knee joints, curling the toes, tucking the head, pulling up the shoulders--all out of fear. Or there might be a thrusting forward of the mid-section of the body to seek balance, tightening of the buttocks as an act of resistance.

All of these responses become patterned in the consciousness and serve very greatly to dictate the shape of the body in later life. If an infant is repressed, if the infant is taught to not show any emotion, to hold in emotion it feels strongly, in spite of having no means of release, the infant actually shoves the toxicity of the emotions into the body.

Very often this situation is reflected in a body which appears bottom heavy. All of the emotion is pressed down (as it were) and coagulates in the lower body, oftentimes creating (later in life) difficulties with circulation, difficulties with the feet, difficulties with believing that you can move freely forward.

If, on the other hand, the infant has a fair amount of freedom of movement during the first year-to-year-and-a-half of life and develops some sense of self, by the time it is individually in motion, its responses to anger or to being told no generally do not lodge in the lower body, but allow for more regularity of shape. Oftentimes the infant learns to hold back feeling by repressing it in the upper body, creating distention in the abdomen, or barreling out of the chest.

These youthful adaptations to your emotional environment set up a climate for various health problems in later life. So, we must take the total picture into consideration.

There are family patterns which the growing child observes, which are fed into the computer of the mind. They also play a strong role in determining health. For if a child observes regular patterns of illness in the family, especially if that illness gets the ill family member positive attention and release from duties, then the child will come to believe in illness as a part of life from which they get some benefits.

These family patterns of behavior are stored in the subconscious computer of the mind. If health is the norm in the family, the child develops a predisposition toward health. If periodic illness is the norm, then it is likely, unless there is overcompensation of some kind, that the child ingests a belief of regular patterns of illness. A developing child, as well, knows the length of life of various family members and registers unconscious thoughts about life and health and longevity.

You have a great deal of subconscious programming which goes into determining health and even times when health is not likely to be easily maintained.

If a child has a strong belief that he must live his father's and mother's pattern, it is very likely the child will also have a belief in living their patterns in regard to health.

Oftentimes, when health is discussed, especially when it is discussed in relation to thought, the larger picture is neglected. Therefore, we wish to make very strong note of the fact that family patterns, even going back generations, are ingested into the subconscious computer of the mind of the developing child during the early years of life. These family patterns of health (or the lack of it) must be

addressed in order to promote health in the adult because the unconscious mind, indeed, rules the state of the body. And so, all of the thoughts must be examined when determining which ones are out of balance and causing disease in the body.

The subject of health is a very complex one. The thoughts you think register in the electromagnetic field around your body. They set up a field of attraction, influencing the state of the health of the body. It is true that psychics and those attuned to reading, seeing, or feeling auras can detect weaknesses in the aura, in the auric field, and in the electromagnetic field around the body, long before they actually manifest in the physical body.

The origins of the weaknesses are not only in the conscious thoughts of the thinker, but in the subconscious thoughts, and in the child's observations of the family patterns and the community patterns in regard to health. The power of suggestion operates very strongly in relation to this subject. In your media and in your society, the larger group mind's thoughts about health influence the individual's health as well.

UNDERSTANDING HEALING

"Healing is the manifested thought which erases the manifested thought of illness and disease."...Kyros

The importance of attitude

Seth: If you are born into a society--or even more intimately, into a family--which believes that the source of your health is outside of you in a doctor or a hospital, then you will have a very strong thought system or belief system in regard to seeking traditional medical help in order to promote wellness.

This belief creates temporary wellness. You get sick. You go to the doctor. You get a remedy. You get better for a time period until the disease affinity appears somewhere else in the physical body.

Remember that the true source of all disease is unbalanced thoughts. In order to achieve health it is mandatory to achieve a state of atonement with all creation, a belief in union rather than in separation, a belief in innocence rather than a belief in guilt, a belief in peace

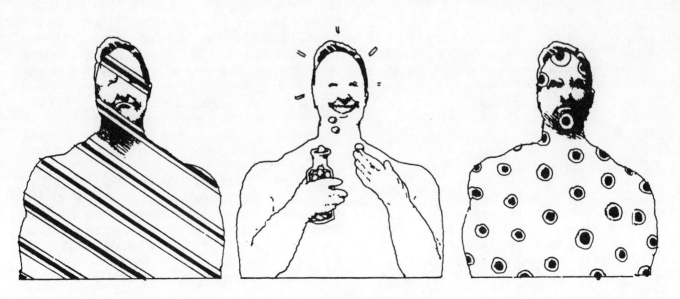

rather than a belief in war, a belief in immortality rather than a belief in death.

The evidence that you have in regard to physical illness is but data, rationally collected and arranged so as to support the beliefs of the collector of the evidence. If you review history, you see repeated instances of diseases being totally wiped out. You see increasing longevity for man on your planet. Therefore you can theorize that it is possible to wipe out disease and to wipe out death. When enough minds believe that it is possible, it is done.

It is belief that dictates the nature of your reality--belief and thoughts joined together.

If you have a belief that health is desirable and natural and that it is your right as an innocent child of the universe, then you can easily espouse health in unlimited measure. But if you have a belief in punishment, if you have a belief in guilt, if you have a belief in sin, if you have a belief in retribution, then you have a belief in disease and lack of harmony.

The rational mind has created illness as a means of bringing about death (ultimately) and also as a need of achieving certain ends. These could be, for instance, time off from work, attention from loved ones, benefits from insurance plans, justification for lawsuits, and various other secondary gains.

As you choose to believe differently, and as you work religiously with the other levels of your mind (other than conscious), you can re-work the beliefs which create illness and allow them to promote health.

Crystals, chemicals, or a beautiful blue cloth

Enid: Let's say you have a crystal. You can hold it and say, "Well, here is a little beingness and it's alive since everything in this plane is alive. And I'd like to talk to it and see if it

wouldn't help me feel better." All things are imbued by you and then transferred back to yourself as feelings. You're just magnifying the love flow from that object. There is nothing wrong with you or a healer using crystals. A healer will use the crystal to magnify the vibration. And that vibration, in being magnified, will create a good large vibration in the body and will create a feeling of well-being. And if the person being healed will accept that into himself, then he can be healed.

There are those who believe, "Crystal, you say! Oh! Take that away--I'd rather have a needle shooting some penicillin into my arm. That's more real to me." And while the doctor is shooting the liquid into the arm, he is thinking, "I sure hope this works. I would love for this person to feel better."

Realize that there's no difference between using an injection and using a crystal. It's all for the same reason and for the same intention. It totally depends upon your intention, in how you view these things.

For example, you might tend to a sick friend and say, "I'm going to get this beautiful blue velvet cloth and I'm going to put it on your chest, my dear. And you're going to hold it there for three hours. And after that, you're going to feel like a changed person." If you imbue that blue fabric with the vibration of that belief, magnify it and make it a healing thing, then it's going to work as good as the penicillin in the arm. And for the same reason.

Understand that the doctor is not shooting the penicillin into your arm and hoping it will make you die! He's hoping it will make you feel better. He has the same intention as the healer who's holding the crystal. There are lots of medicines out there that have been imbued with all the vibrations necessary to help a person feel better.

A person takes the pill and he feels better because he knows that the pill is full of the vibrations of the manufacturer of the pill who believes that symptoms are going to lessen when the pill is taken. So the person takes the pill and he gets the message of the intention from the person who made the pill. The intent is for

The only healer of illness or disease is the creator of it, which is self. Nothing can heal the body unless you first heal the attitude.

you to feel better. So understand that intent and make it work for you.

Healing the attitude

Ramtha: Attitude is the cure. *That* is what heals. When you begin to love yourself, and remove from your thought processes the attitudes that inhibit life, then peace and harmony will begin to reign within the cellular structures. But the entity must first *want* to be healed. *Want is the key.* That is the manifesting power. No one can lift illness from an entity until the entity wishes for it to be lifted and chooses to use another attitude as a tool for healing. Many are not ready to let go of their sickness--even though they say they want to be well--for in their souls, they are not complete with the purpose it is serving. Many will remain ill for their entire life, no matter what a physician or a master does for them, because the illness affords them attention, and they are afraid of losing the attention, so they will not allow the illness to be removed.

The only healer of illness or disease is the creator of it, which is self. Nothing can heal the body unless it first heals the attitude.

To help the healing occur, you can bring forth *love*--the greatest healer of all. I help to heal entities by loving them, by seeing them as perfect, regardless of why they are or how they are expressing. They relax in their beings and allow the hormones that are locked up in great glands to flow into the body, and the body begins to heal.

The greatest, most noble works you could ever accomplish will be achieved through love.

Love is the mover, and it can redesign anything. Look into the eyes of the entity and love him profoundly. When you can love a leper and hold him in your arms--even though he will not look upon your face, for he is shameful of his ugliness and stench--if you can hold him in his desperation and *love* him, and see him in perfection, that is what heals. He will look into your eyes and see no judgment there, only love and life.

Soon, he will tell the soul of his being that perhaps he is not what he has feared himself to be--that in reality he is as this wondrous entity has seen him. When an entity knows he is loved and held in esteem by another, he lifts himself to become that ideal.

If you desire to be a healing influence every moment, become a healer of the soul, a lover of all people.

There is not *one* entity not worth loving. Have compassion for all of them within your soul, and love everyone equally. If a man is deaf, his infirmity is no greater than that of the woman who suffers within her soul from feelings of inadequacy and insecurity.

Never recognize in anyone anything other than God and life. Never see imperfection. Never recognize problems. Never see a leper or a cripple as being diseased. When you see only God in others, soon that is all *they* will recognize.

Do *not* desire to go out and heal others with a touch. Do not desire to be compassionate to anyone before you have been that with yourself.

Be who you are and love yourself first, above all things.

Love your body. Honor and respect it. Give to yourself everything you would give to a great love of your life. Be so loving and compassionate with your *own* being, so pure and unlimited in your own thought processes, that you are healed in your *own* attitude and your own body. Then you become an example that motivates others to do the same, if that is their desire.

Become the Lord-God of your being. When you do, you will know that everyone is at the hands of their own creation and that love lifts them to see further. And when others say to you, "I see you have a peace about you and a light that surrounds your total being, whence come they," you can smile at them and say, "It is the Father within me that you see, from the Father that is within you." Then you are a healer of the attitude, for you give them the thought that says, "I am perfect, I am God."

Turn your eyes within, and feel the love of God that is there. Once you have done that with yourself, you will have the strength to display your love openly to everyone else, for you will know who you are and will know the depths of your love. Then you heal just by being. Become the ideal of self for self, in spite of everyone else and for everyone else.

Do not become the healer. Become God. Then you are all things to all people.

Healing is loving and healing is touching

Master Adalfo: Healing is loving and loving is healing. When we do anything which is an act of caring or an act of love, that is healing. When someone loves us, we are healed by that love. So any modality, anything that produces that loving or caring or nurtured feeling is healing. Some doctors are real healers because they have that caring, loving energy. Some are not because they do not have that energy.

There is no substitute for being touched during healing. Touching opens up parts of the body. For example, when you go to see a dentist, his assistant may help you get into the chair. And if this person is good at their job, they may take special care to arrange you nicely in the chair, to touch you.

In the society in which you live, there is very little touching of the bodies. People are not very well acquainted with their bodies. You sit in chairs. You do not sit on the floor or on the ground. You wear clothes that cover your bodies. You go to doctors and dentists to have things done that people used to take care of themselves. Most of you are not acquainted with your bodies--they are almost foreign strangers to you.

90

Massage, acupressure, rolfing--any of those ways to get more in touch and feel your physical body--are very healing. This is a culture that only feels pain and not pleasure with their physical body. Now, while some of these procedures first cause pain, that is all right because that brings your awareness to that part of the body and you feel it. Then you can move away from the pain into an enjoyment of that area as the pain goes.

These methods are very valuable. All are ways of releasing stress, of releasing toxicity, and of getting more acquainted with your body and knowing where problem areas are before they become a terrible disease to make you aware of them. If you can feel a little bit of a pinch when someone is massaging that is better than having surgery in that area so you'll *really feel it.*

Loving yourself

Master Adalfo: People are much harsher on themselves than they are on others. You cannot expect to promote healing in your own body if you don't love it, including loving the fact that it hurts. If all you want to do is quickly get rid of the pain and you are not willing to look at the part of your body that hurts, if you are not willing to say, "Oh, I love you and I am sorry you are hurting," then no healing can take place.

For most of us, it is very difficult to love ourselves. That is why it is important, and an act of loving, to go and seek help from someone else (a healer) who can love us better than we can love ourselves. That is why it is hard for people to aknowledge they need a little help be-

cause that would also be an act of loving themselves. They love themselves so little they don't even want to say, "I need help now. I need someone to love me and to help me heal."

You see, you must open the heart first so people can feel and take in the loving that healing is about.

No method of healing is effective without touching, without loving.

People need to realize that it is not necessary to rely on yourself to heal yourself, but that does not mean that you could not add to the process. As I like to say over and over, "Healing is loving and loving is healing." If you are going to heal yourself, that means you must love yourself. And there is often very little of that kind of loving.

Healing begins with believing

Kyros: Is it possible to heal yourself? The answer is yes! But, you cannot do it by yourself. You must align yourself with your own spirit, which is your own God essence.

If you have manifested illness or disease in your life experience, you must try to assess why you have done so. With the exception of prior karmic choices and decisions made before entering the physical earth plane, all illness and disease begin first as thoughts.

In fact, all manifestations and materializations of everything within your world begin first with a thought, so why should the manifestations of illness and disease be any different?

If a thought, energized and given power, can be brought into the manifested form of illness or disease, then another thought, energized and given power, can manifest into a healing.

91

it. Since man's entrance on planet earth, he has believed in it. Look at your television advertising. From it you surely must believe that in order to be human you must have flu, headaches, backaches, stomachaches, arthritis, and some even believe they are destined for heart disease, cancer, diabetes, herpes, AIDS, and on and on. With all the programming, I am sometimes surprised that man has survived as well as he has.

Oftentimes, the difficulty of creating and energizing a healing thought occurs when a human entity is feeling ill. He becomes imprisoned by the feeling of illness and lacks the will and the power to energize a new thought. Oftentimes, the pain and discomfort of a disease or illness will keep him focused on the pain and discomfort and prevent him from being able to focus on its *release*. He will then feel alone, hopeless, and helpless and the longer this condition exists, the more imprisoned by it he will become.

The spirit which resides within and without the human entity will always be working to release the healing energies which exist in all created forms. It will always be working to bring about the awareness to the entity as to why the body is diseased or ill. In other words, it will always be working to break through to the consciousness of the human entity. It usually must change the human ego and the limitations of an individual's belief system.

All illness and disease exist because you believe in illness and disease. Why do you believe in it? Because you have been programmed since your entrance to believe in

On the other side of the coin, the programming which causes man to continue his belief in illness and disease also causes him to believe in healing.

Does aspirin really make a headache go away, or does your belief that aspirin will release you from pain make it go away?

This is perhaps something that you will never be able to scientifically prove, but I will tell you that if you did not *believe* that aspirin would help, it would have no effect. Your belief system is critically important in bringing on the manifestations of *both* illness and healing. If you have an illness and you do not believe in healing, self-healing is impossible.

All healing is self-healing whether you ingest medications, undergo surgery, spend time with physicians, or offer yourself to any of the treatments within your current medical technology. To be healed you must believe in healing. You must *trust* that you can be healed. You must have *faith* in whatever method you have selected to trigger your own healing energies into action.

Self-healing begins first in your belief in healing.

Healing is the manifested thought which erases the manifested thought of illness and disease.

It involves reprogramming. Always when one desires to change how he thinks about something, there must be both the *will* and the *will-ingness* to do so. Healing has to begin in your own consciousness, and since most illness can be traced back to such negative ego vibrations and thoughts as fear, anger, hate, resentment, guilt, and so on, these must be dealt with. It is here that the real healing occurs.

What I'm trying to say is that an entity might have a properly functioning form which is seemingly disease free and yet be diseased if he harbors negative ego thoughts and vibrations. Another entity, on the other hand, may have what appears to be a diseased form and yet may not harbor negative ego vibrations and thoughts. Where it really counts, he is the one who is healed and healthy.

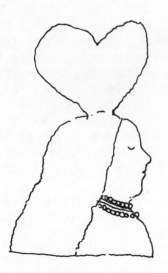

93

Love is the only energy which can create complete healing. It is the energizer needed to bring health into all areas in need of healing.

The spirit of an individual entity is always trying to create healing and health on this level. He is always trying to redirect negative ego vibrations and thoughts and transform them into positive ego vibrations and thoughts, whose energy is always love and love-borne vibrations. Love is the only energy which can create complete healing, and it is the energizer needed to bring health into all areas in need of healing.

When you are in need of healing within your own form, which I suppose would be considered self-healing, analyze your belief system about disease and wellness. Try to assess what brought the condition into manifestation. Consider the negative ego vibrations and thoughts you might be energizing to maintain the condition with. Reprogram your belief system about healing and wellness if there is a need. Release yourself from the negative ego thoughts and vibrations and feelings of non-love. Create positive vibrations and thoughts filled with love energy. Focus away from the pain and discomfort. Seek the so-called "strawberry in the patch." Always, no matter how bad something may appear to be, there is a beautiful gift waiting to be discovered. And most of all, trust in the Source of All Life. Trust in God's love is the *key to all healing.*

Remember also that upon your planet most entities *are* in need of self-healing, so be gentle with yourself and others. Do not feel that you are alone in the process of self-healing for there are many human and spiritual entities willing to help you in your process toward wholeness. Also be willing to help others in their paths toward wholeness.

As individuals are healed, so also is the planet healed.

Begin first with your own being, for as a healed or whole person you are then able to help others in their own healing processes. As it is said that "the blind cannot lead the blind," it is also true that "the sick cannot heal the sick."

Heal your mind and your form will follow.

The Greeks were not far amiss when they offered you the wisdom, "A sound mind in a sound body." Soundness means health and wholeness. Soundness is energized by Love. Soundness begins first in your own consciousness. Start there and all else will follow for your own spirit is ever working to bring your totality into balance, harmony, and wholeness.

Li Sung: The acceleration of the healing is often dependent on the situation, on the condition, and on the strength of the energies supplied to the person. There must also be a very clear basis for healing in the person's mind so that they do not resist healing but *welcome* it.

Often the conscious mind says, "I want to be healed," while the dark side of the soul says, "Oh, I want to be sick. I will prove how much pity I deserve by being sick." In such cases, there will be resistance to healing. But you here in the United States are awakening to the concept that the attitude of the mind does indeed influence and determine the body's health.

While much has been written, has been spoken, and has been taught on techniques of healing, each person prefers his or her own private assistance. But it basically is very simple.

What the mind pictures, the body commands. As the soul desires, the material body will follow the pattern.

94

Miracle healings

Soli: And so it is that each person must heal themselves. A healer cannot heal another individual without the permission of that individual's higher self. It is only at this request that you can heal. Healers can apply their arts to individuals who will stubbornly refuse to be healed. Why? Because the higher self *must communicate.* If the patient does not hear that communication, if they do not take action upon it, then there is nothing, nothing at all, of any kind, that will heal them. Nothing. No energy transference, no mechanical drug systems, nothing will heal them.

It is true that there are mechanical things which can be done that will change the balance for a time. It may appear to effect a cure for an illness. But that illness will return, and continue to return, and continue to get worse until the communication behind that disease is seen and acted upon.

What then of apparently miraculous healings, laying on of hands, energy transfers? Of course, they are real.

There are no such things as miracles, for everything is a miracle. . . or not a miracle, depending on your point of view.

There is no *one* thing that is any more special than another. Everyone has the power of energy transference, if they use it. You can transfer power from your higher self through your hands to another individual. It is up to the individual and their higher self as to whether that energy is utilized or not.

What then of the effective healers? What then of the large numbers who appear to be healed? First, ask yourself, "Why are those individuals there? Why are they there with those diseases seeking to be cured?"

It is because those individuals have a need for something within their lives to draw them out of the subconscious belief patterns that they have dealt with so strongly for so long. That something may be a healing, an apparently miraculous healing, something totally unexpected for them, something totally outside of their immediate awareness, totally outside of anything that they have dealt with before in their life to that date. Such an experience has a tremendous impact upon the subconscious and the belief systems. It blows wide open all the limiting beliefs that they have held onto so tightly for so long.

And there are some individuals who require that experience upon the earth plane. There are some whose higher selves wish them to have that sudden opening, sudden awareness, sudden expansion of their belief system into a totally new area. And so the higher self creates the circumstances where they will receive that energy, where they will receive an apparent healing. And it does, in many cases, transform the individual's life.

We are generally speaking about individuals who have dealt with a very dogmatic, very closed belief system for a long time. So-called "faith healing" works far less effectively on those individuals who are already upon the path to enlightenment and self-awareness. Why is this? Because those individuals already know that *they are responsible* for their own lives, that they must take responsibility for the creation of the disease. And since they take responsibility for the creation of the disease, they equally take responsibility for its alleviation.

And so, faith healing does not so often work in such circumstances with such individuals. What healing does work? With such individuals it is essential, first and foremost, for them to communicate with the higher self *before* the higher self has to communicate with them. It is for them, within their meditations, to work within the spiritual vibration. Communicate, open to the energy of the higher self. Follow their intuition, follow their inner guidance, and if they do that, they then have no need for the higher self to communicate with them.

Remember, the higher self has to communicate, and it can only do so in the lower vibration of intellect, emotion, and the physical. It cannot communicate with you in the spiritual aspects, but you can communicate with it in that way! The responsibility, again, is yours.

Healing as an act of separation

Dong How Li: Sometimes in physical life you need to separate from some things, from some people, from some events. That is unavoidable. But, you must remember, in that act, that truly, within the realm of creation, it is not even a separation, let alone permanent. And what you are separating from, you must own within yourselves. That is how you clear the separation in the eyes of God or the eyes of Creation.

You know how Native Americans clear an act of killing? When they go hunting, they pray to an animal to give itself up for the good of the tribe.

So, when you separate from someone, or from some illness, you also pray. You give thanks for the presence in your life. As you separate from your illness, give thanks for its presence in your life and release it. Ask that the lessons be clear so that you can *own* how you created them, how and why you *needed* them. Then you let them go in peace.

Finding safe places

Dong How Li: For those of you who want to heal yourselves, safety is very important. Western medicine thinks hospitals are the ideal safe place. I don't think so, but the *idea* is important. For healing, you do need to create a safe space because you are going to be questioning your beliefs that created the disease, and with that your fears are going to come up. You need safety, you need calmness, you need to be centered to face your own demons.

Colds

Dr. Peebles: When you have a physical cold, it is affecting various glands and organs. If it has the ability to last more than a full-day cycle, during the second day it is affecting the etheric body. By the third day it is influencing the etheric body. By the fourth day, the etheric body is cleansing it, balancing it, releasing the effects. By the fifth day, the physical body will start to carry that symptom into release.

The first twenty-four hours does not affect the etheric body. During the second twenty-four hours the cold is starting to affect the etheric body. By the third twenty-four hours, the etheric body is directly influenced. If you have worked with the healing of your philosophy, if you have been working on the acceptance of soul healing, by the fourth twenty-four hours, you are in the process of bringing that healing into the physical body from the astral forms.

I would comment that your colds, illnesses, and flus (as you know them) are part of the environmental problem. They are part of what the world needs from the cleansing process, to prepare for the major illnesses that are about to sweep the lands. Colds and illnesses are for you to balance out, to turn over to the etheric body. The etheric body is *never* totally damaged. It does, in what you would know as forty-eight hours, cleanse itself and release. If the physical human body, through lack of proper diet, through lack of proper rest, through lack of proper mental appreciation, rejects the healing from the astral, it will maintain its illness, maintain its symptom, but the etheric body goes back to its total healthful self. Your etheric bodies are aligned in perfect ways. If you are not perfectly balanced, it is because you are rejecting that from the etheric body.

Catching germs

Dr. Peebles: Dear friends, let us look at what is occurring when you have a cold, for example. Your cold is out in the room where you are.

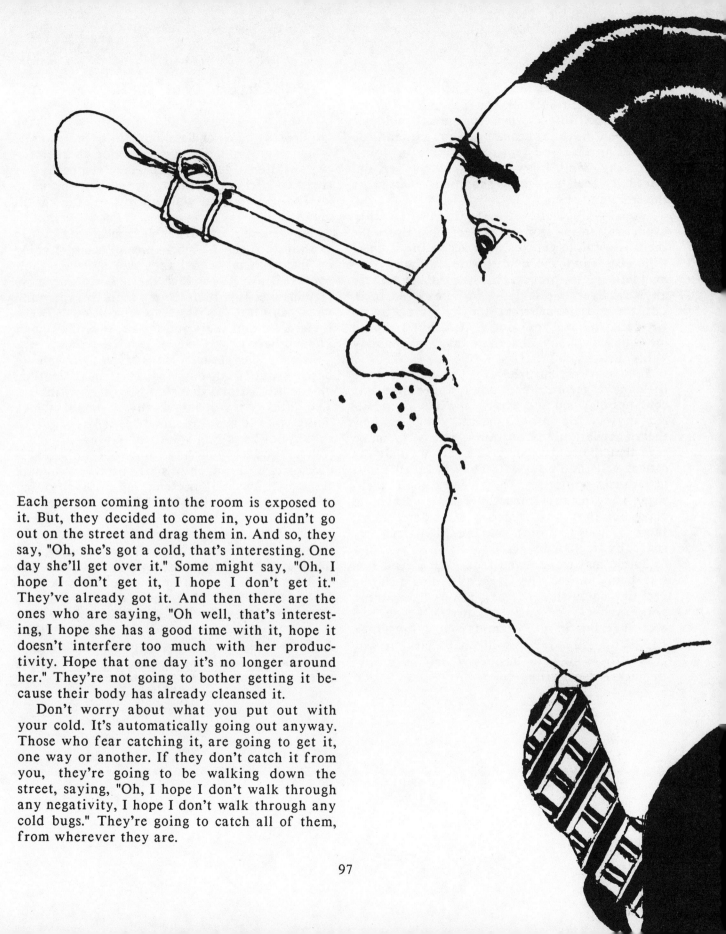

Each person coming into the room is exposed to it. But, they decided to come in, you didn't go out on the street and drag them in. And so, they say, "Oh, she's got a cold, that's interesting. One day she'll get over it." Some might say, "Oh, I hope I don't get it, I hope I don't get it." They've already got it. And then there are the ones who are saying, "Oh well, that's interesting, I hope she has a good time with it, hope it doesn't interfere too much with her productivity. Hope that one day it's no longer around her." They're not going to bother getting it because their body has already cleansed it.

Don't worry about what you put out with your cold. It's automatically going out anyway. Those who fear catching it, are going to get it, one way or another. If they don't catch it from you, they're going to be walking down the street, saying, "Oh, I hope I don't walk through any negativity, I hope I don't walk through any cold bugs." They're going to catch all of them, from wherever they are.

97

So go into your stores, go into your offices, and do everything that you feel up to. When you have an illness, when you have a cold, or when you have a headache, go out and do everything that you feel comfortable in doing. If you say, "Well, I have a cold and a fever, but I actually feel like going shopping," then go to the store and shop.

You might believe that if you do this, everybody in the store might get sick. Everyone there is going to get sick only according to their *willingness* and their ability to call upon, to magnetize, to process it. It's all out there anyway. Everyone is going to be exposed to it. Let them discover what they're going to do with it. Who are you to say, "Oh, but I should lock myself in my house, so that way nobody will get exposed."

I have a big surprise for you. All of your little cold germs, they don't understand the confines of wood and glass. They'll go out visiting anyway. Go into a laboratory and see how they have all kinds of things to try to make sure that the cold germs don't get out, that the cancer cells don't get out. They have all kinds of cleansing processes. They cleanse their scientists. They cleanse room by room by room to clear out that stuff because they don't know those viruses are not confined by time, by space, by steel, or by glass.

So, no matter how you feel, even if you feel like being in bed for five days, do it. If you feel like being sick, but being out on the street, going about your business, do it. If you feel like sneezing in public and people say, "Oh, bad, bad," you say, "Oh well, that's just the way it is." Go about your business then, that's your biggest responsibility.

Treat the children well

John: Are there any of you who have children at home or have had children at home? When your child displays behavior characteristics of illness do you experience sympathy for their condition? Naturally you wish the child well so you do what you can to treat the child's condition.

Now, if it is an infant, it is most difficult to explain to them the mechanics of what is going on inside them so that they can assist in their own healing. Know this: there is no one more responsible for themselves than infants and young children. They see no separation between themselves and their actions because they don't know otherwise.

What you eventually do is teach them how to be *irresponsible* through behavior modification, all the do this and don't do that of growing up. The child does not know why it should not be doing what it is doing, nor does it know why it should not be saying what it is saying.

The impact you have on your children is awesome. From a child's perspective, you are the omni-powerful presence of authority, imposing on their will. The child creates the idea in his mind that you do not do this or say that, based on the parent's beliefs and actions.

My friends, your children are watching you. They are watching you take drugs to alter your reality. They're watching you gobble down the prescription drugs that allow you to cope with the stress and strain of the 20th century lifestyle. They are creating in their young developing minds the belief that your way of being is the way to be and your actions express the "way that it is done" in the world today.

ABOUT HEALERS

"The function of the healer, the teacher, and the priest is to open the door. But, my friends, you must walk through it and discover what is on the other side." ...
Dong How Li

Seeking outside help is OK

Master Adalfo: You need to know that it is all right to seek help from the outside when you are ill. That is not an admission of failure. Simply accept that premise so that you can go on to other things that will, in fact, help you. And one of those things is to examine the reason for disease, to help you begin to examine why that disease is in your life. What about your life is unhappy or unpleasant that this disease fixes in some way? Because disease *does* fix something, even if it is only to make you so ill you have to stay in bed. There are many aspects to disease.

So, with the help of a healer, you look at what the disease is. You investigate what it makes you look at that you never had to look at before: what changes, what growth, what evolution you can go through to stop that process of disease.

And this process may need help from a healer. These steps could be experimentation, diet, exercise, meditation, or perhaps even taking the medications the doctor has recommended. You see, some things can be fixed and *then* talked about, then worked upon by you and your healer.

Dong How Li: When you go outside to someone to help heal you, you are already healing yourself. This is sometimes essential because it is difficult to see the overview when you are in the midst of pain. You go to a healer to have an outside part of you, a part that you are not in touch with at the time, physicalized for you, to assist you. But from my perspective, it is all your doing.

You also can accelerate the physical healing by working at other levels of yourself as well. Of course, it is at the other levels that you will learn to retrain your energy and your thoughts, so as to not recreate the problem. Sometimes people want to cure or heal or change instantly, forgetting that they may have taken a lifetime to create some of these situations. However, I'm not saying that linear time is the only time that exists, or that illness and pain can't be healed instantly, because they can, most definitely.

In order to do this, you must step out of time. You step outside of linear time to where all things are happening at once, where all parts of the being can be connected instantly-- in a moment, in a fraction. That is magic.

This is how the shamans do it. That is how the great healers in your spiritualist tradition do it, whether they are conscious of it or not. But, most of you people are bound by clocks and schedules, so it is a little harder to slip out of time.

Healing really is magic, and its companion is loving.

Psychic healers

Dr. Peebles: There is no time and there is no space. The attitude of the psychic healers, trained in recognizing and manifesting this attitude, will allow them, in fact, to go into your body, with their hands as an instrument, and go to the source of the physical problem. They will then go backwards in time. As they remove the problem, it is as if it has never even happened. As they remove the distortion, they bring it into the future, so that there is no problem there. When they are finished, as you come back to current time, you've never had surgery, you've never had illness, and you're clear in the future so there cannot even be a physical scar.

A psychic surgeon can remove an organ or remove a tumor, but if you, as a soul--a consciousness--do not acknowledge and accept this on all its levels, then within a matter of weeks, a similar affliction will present itself until you have experienced and grown through this. For you see, frequently the surgeon removes without the permission of your higher self, and so you go over and over that experience again, until you as a consciousness have grown to a point of balance with the experience.

Here I would suggest that the concept of psychic surgery cannot be taught. It cannot be learned. It is something so individualized that it is only allowed. Even if you are around it constantly, it does not mean you will learn it. You might be able to work as an associate. You might be able to work with a psychic surgeon on a close relationship level, but unless you enter this lifetime with that particular gift *in hand*, you will never learn it.

The trance level of communication to the other dimensions necessary when accomplishing psychic surgery will never happen to many. It is not yours to try to study it, or to try to practice and learn it. But just the same, it is quite possible to train yourselves to be healing channels so that the healing energy is able to come through for other people.

And here is a most important clue. If you have opened your healing channel, if you use yourself and present yourself as a healer, it is important that you acknowledge that you are being healed, that you are being strengthened each and every time you work on a subject.

Now, I hear the minds of some of you saying, "But I don't need healing." My friends, you always need the healing energies, no matter how perfect you think your lives are. You always need *that* energy. You always need to be building the foundation, building the strength that will allow you to remain above the symptoms, above the problems.

You are all existing at a time in which great illness and great disasters will sweep the land, and you will all be part of it. You will all see them. You will all be touched, you will all be affected over the next few years. You do need to learn to be on the *receiving* end of healing now, at this time. So, it is best that you discipline yourselves to recognize that you must allow yourselves to *receive* power and healing as much as you *give* it.

Revising your physical blueprint

Enid: Outside of this universe, somewhere in the fourth dimension, there is a blueprint of your body. This blueprint is of the best body that your body can be at any given time. Now, your cells go into agreement with this blueprint, and they create *that best* blueprint for you. You can change that blueprint by conscious thought, by consideration. You can alter the form of the body, the form of all its workings.

Each cell in the body contains the entire blueprint for the entire body. It's like a hologram in a sense, because each part of the body can reflect what the rest of the body is. If we didn't believe we couldn't do it, we could grow an arm back, or a finger, or a foot. But our thinking in this day and time has gone to the point where that would be just too outrageously miraculous. We couldn't have that happen and still keep our equilibrium with reality.

The telepathic agreement that keeps this world as it is, is incredibly strong. But as human beings awaken to their spiritual beingness, this agreement loosens. There will come a time when you will change your agreement to include the understanding that you can actually change your bodies.

Now, what the healer does is to come in and take a look at your blueprint, and see if the blueprint does or does not fit with what they are seeing. So the healer says, "I'm going to bring that blueprint down and remind the cells what they're supposed to be doing for good health." So, in a sense, they put that picture over the body and tell it, "Do you remember? Wake up now, wake up and remember how you're supposed to be."

All healers are in varying stages of perceptions and abilities. As long as a healer does not have feelings of being unable to heal, then they don't have to worry about the preciseness of their perception, as long as they use the intention of "I intend for your blueprint to remind these cells of how they should look, of how they should be in their *best possible way*."

Spirit doctors

Master Adalfo: Spirit healers from other dimensions can share the body of the healer, or they can just come into the room and work on their own without even using a physical body.

101

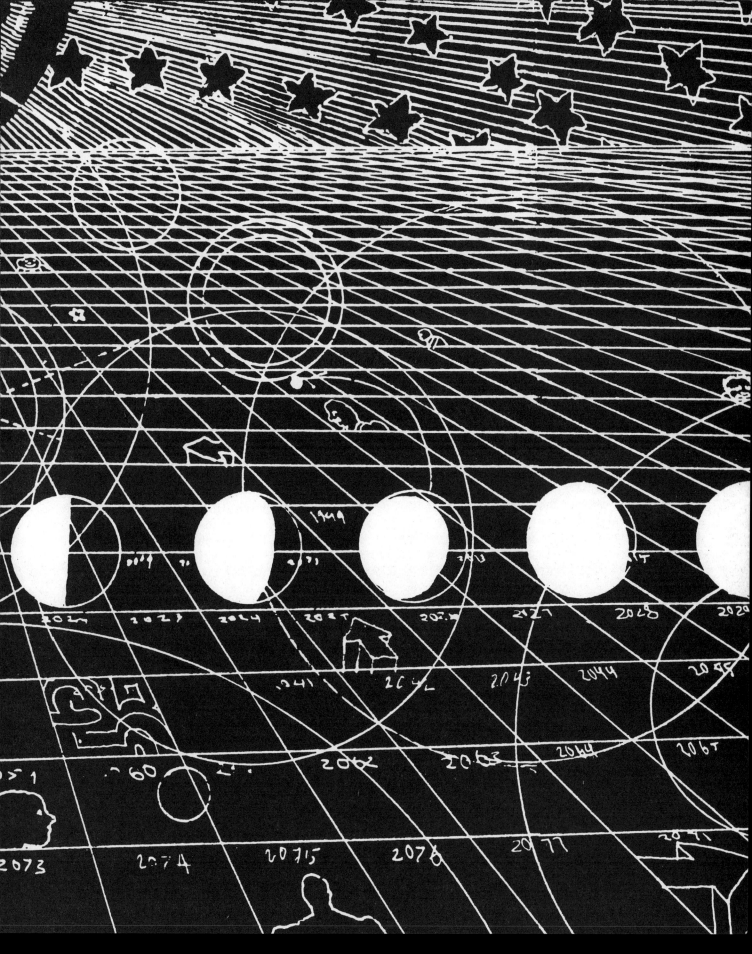

They work in various ways. One way is to use the healer's physical body, specifically, to use the healer's hands and to take over those hands in a way they wish. Or the spirit doctor can simply come in and use his "spirit hands" on the body. Sometimes there will be a whole room full of spirits working on the patient. They will all be in there doing "their thing," so to speak. They often work on the etheric plane, helping to match-up the etheric template with the physical, helping bring these into closer harmony.

Creating new diseases

Master Adalfo: People, as you know, are endlessly creative and constantly create viruses or diseases that are new. In fact, sometimes a new illness reflects the need for "newness" because people need something that will create a level of drama, something that healers aren't able to immediately "fix."

The world has often had new diseases because an established, well-known disease does not have the same symbology of what is going on, in current times, as a new disease has. To have the "black plague" now would not "fit the situation" as it did before. So now we have these relatively new diseases which are related, such as AIDS, herpes, and candida.

Working on these new diseases requires greater consciousness on the healer's part as well as on the patient's part. These diseases cannot be healed as easily as some in which the consciousness of the client doesn't have to change. These diseases require a change of consciousness--a broadening of consciousness. Those experiencing these diseases will be forced to look at what they *want* to be aware of. They will be forced to look at these issues in order to get well.

They will be forced to look at the issue of "everything is wonderful." Is it really? They will have to look at the issue of being willing to wait for what you call instant gratification.

This is the age of instant. We want instant mashed potatoes and instant this and instant

that, and people want that same thing in their lives. They want instant happiness. Utilizing new thought processes and examining beliefs deeply allows the healings (the miracles) to take place.

This all requires that the healers also change their consciousness as well. Healers cannot assist in miracles without an awareness that miracles can be produced. For example, if a healer accepts as fact that there are limitations, that AIDS is supposedly untreatable, then in helping someone with AIDS, the healer accepts that the disease will be incurable.

Sleep healing

Dr. Peebles: When you enter the period of sleep, if you have released your day and have dealt with your experiences, you blend them with all facets of yourself (physically, mentally, emotionally, and spiritually) so that your higher self is the controlling factor, as you sleep, rather than your conscious self. In this way, you blend your experiences. It is similar to being on the spirit side as you put things into their balances and their proper perspectives. And by practicing this, your higher self becomes clear and strong and will then bring about the healing of your sets of circumstances so that it will be done in one hour of sleep; at other times, this may take several nights.

You may be in a situation and know that it is not necessary, nor one that you must hold onto, yet you have not found the healing technique, or the healing energy sources on your conscious levels. You can, then, project astrally to the realm of the psychic healers and the psychic surgeons and you will have (in your sleep) psychic surgery. You will be healed.

You must have, obviously, *tremendous faith* in yourself. You must trust that your body and your mind are within your control as a total being, and that there is nothing that will obsess or possess you. In the time of sleep, if approached as a time of growth, if you prepare yourself, knowing that you will experience continued growth and balance, then healing will *automatically* take place.

Each of you always is surrounded by healing guides and teachers.

You chose, and you will choose again experiences for your own growth. Allow yourselves that right and privilege. Remember, there is no one who can heal you. There is no "thing" that can heal you if you, as a total being, are not ready for the advantages of healing.

Utilizing the Christ consciousness

Soli: Healers heal others by *assisting* them in their quest for the higher self. It is helpful to understand a little of what Jesus the Nazarene was doing and why he came upon the earth plane. He was an ordinary human being, just like you and everyone else. He was here to show that any so-called "ordinary" human being has the same power, that you can go beyond the subconscious belief systems. You can bring through the energy of the higher self, what some would call the Christ consciousness. Anyone can bring through that energy which is God.

You see, the God energy does not know negativity. Negativity exists only within the belief systems of the subconscious mind. And since the God-self, the God energy cannot know negativity, negativity does not exist around it. No one could be ill around the Nazarene when he was channeling the God energy of his higher self because that energy could not perceive negativity. And so, that form of healing, frequently brought forward by healers, helps the individual to feel the power and the knowledge of their higher selves, which they may not have been aware of before.

Beliefs influence healing

Seth: It is the *belief in healing* that heals. The person being healed accepts the surge of love that flows throughout the body in spiritual healing as it is channeled by a healer who calls upon the universe and channels the healing energy of the universe to the other. There is such a surge throughout the physical body that the afflicted one, *genuinely* seeking healing, can be moved by the healer's act of faith to release a great many negative beliefs, hitherto espoused, and to begin to change their life. Indeed, it is the *faith* that heals.

Li Sung: Similar belief systems between the healer and the one being healed are essential for healing to take place. If both believe in the same system, healing will work. If both disbelieve in the same system, it will not work. If you take a white candle to your neuropsychiatric institute and you say to the doctor, "Here, use this to heal the schizophrenic," nothing will happen. It could be you will be kicked out of the institute. But in Africa, or in other

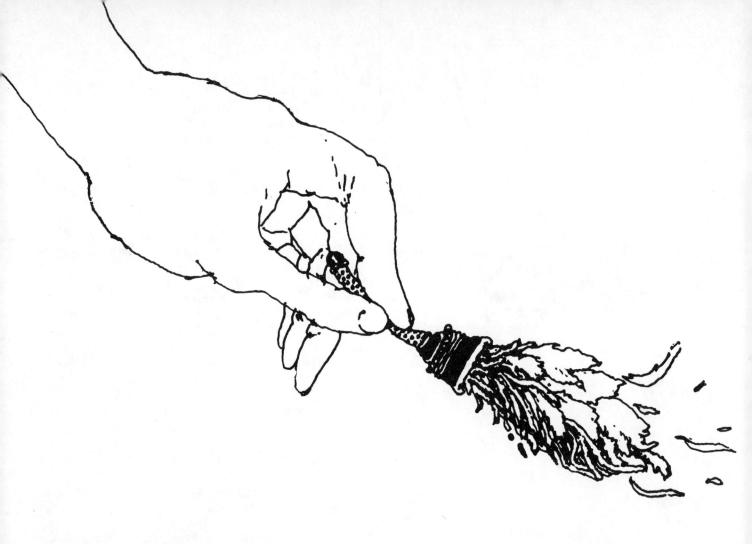

areas where people believe in this, the witch doctor will use a small amulet and a candle to achieve cures that are not possible within Western medicines. It is the combining of belief systems that makes it all possible.

Update on Kathryn Kuhlman

Li Sung: The healer you knew as Kathryn Kuhlman now is active with a group of students. She is training others to work as healing guides for those in the flesh. She does not work directly with persons in the flesh, but works as a trainer for their guides.

Very often persons, who in their physical incarnations were healers, will continue for awhile to maintain this service to others in our world. But, understand that their lives were gifted and their healing abilities were extraordinary because of karmic relations in the past. It was for them to be proof to many persons of the healing energy of the God within. That proof of the spirit was much more important than the actual healing of the disease or the body.

You all have many saints and many guides who are willing to give you assistance if you require. They will continually say to you, "You know, you can do this yourself if you only believe it." And so, as the first step, we recommend that you call on your guides, on Jesus, or on whomever you know of that brings healing help. For the second step, call on the God within yourself to achieve the healing. All things are possible for those who embrace the spirit within.

ALTERNATIVE APPROACHES TO HEALING

"One of the goals we have for the Aquarian Age is the coming together of the esoteric and the exoteric knowledges, particularly in the area of healing." . . . *Master Adalfo*

The best of both worlds

Master Adalfo: There are several ways for esoteric and exoteric knowledge to come together. We must have more doctors who are open to this. Those who are working as healers must be willing to exchange ideas with those who are in the medical profession. We can never expect doctors to be less cynical if we are overly cynical of what they do. Why should the burden be on doctors and not on those who are healers?

Healers must learn to accept what is good that medical doctors do and encourage people, when it is important, to see a medical doctor. Healers can also talk with that person's doctor. The healer can ask questions of the doctor because they (the doctor) care about the person who is in need of healing.

Doctors frequently ask questions back. Healers can learn to not be defensive, but to be direct and explain what it is they do and how. This also requires that healers become more aware of scientific language so they can actually discuss things with doctors. They cannot expect that doctors are the only ones willing to learn new terminology. As more of that happens, there will be more of an exchange of ideas and healing techniques from both sides.

Homeopathy

Soli: Any healing works if the individual believes in it strongly enough. It is the belief, not the mechanics, that creates healing. First, the individual needs to understand the communication. Secondly, the individual must believe that they can be healed.

If, for example, a person has a belief in homeopathy, that belief might be the reason for the communication because it opens up the subconscious mind of the individual. It helps the individual get away from the limited patterns and thinking of society, and from some of those thoughts that have "straight-jacketed" that individual for a number of years. The mere fact of trying homeopathy, of finding that it works, will open up a whole new area of thinking.

Understand that we are dealing with energy. All things are energy. The body that you inhabit is dense matter, is a very slow vibration, but is still energy. It has its form because that is the way your five senses perceive that particular energy and vibration. And so, all of healing is dealing with energy and vibration. Homeopathy is a very refined use of energy and vibration, going far beyond the harsh chemicals and rather "sledge-hammer" tactics of most medicine.

Herbs and crystals

Dong How Li: I rather enjoy and recommend the use of herbs for the simple reason that they stimulate your body to do what it already knows how to do but perhaps has gotten lazy about doing. Medicine comes in and takes over and does it entirely so that your body doesn't learn how to do it for itself.

Herbs help your body remember how to heal. They don't do it for you. That is an important distinction.

This is also true of crystals and ordinary rocks that you wouldn't consider so pretty. If you ask them, they are willing to take things on for you that you are finding difficulty holding and carrying for yourself. And, at the same time, some of them are very good for taking any message that you want to send, focusing it and sending it more sharply to wherever it is supposed to go.

They are like receivers and transformers and batteries. You remember the old crystal radio days? Similarily, crystals are projectors as well.

However, the way many crystals are used now is a little dangerous because people seem to be very drawn to the ones that space them out. And most of the time these people are already too spacey. What they need is something that compacts them, that solidifies them, that brings them together more, and there are stones for that too.

The lighter colored crystals, the blues, the greens especially, and the whites, the pinks, and the purples tend to elevate, tend to project, tend to radiate. The warmer colors, the blacks, the browns, the oranges, the reds, all tend to solidify, to pull in, to hold, to ground. Now, as you go within these two categories, as you feel yourself, you feel what is appropriate for you. Not all grounding energies are going to be appropriate for your special need.

Then too, there are special gems for the chakras. These also, need to be felt and communicated with silently or verbally, to find out whether they are appropriate for you. Now, I hesitate to be more specific than this. Of course, some of the most efficacious and healing of stones are not so pretty. It might be necessary to sort out effectiveness from prettiness, sometimes.

I don't want to be so specific about the

stones, to say that crystal light is good for this and turquoise is good for that. You may get that literature if you want it. But please remember, for example, just because the first chakra is traditionally red, red may not be what that chakra needs to heal itself. Blue may be what is needed because what that chakra may need is the contrast or the compliment.

So, never forget to ask yourself what you need each time you feel there is a need for healing. Don't presume. Go inward and find out what is needed. In this culture, you have a great confusion. Many of you think information is knowledge. It is not so. Knowledge you gain from experience. Knowledge is not data. Data is data, that is all. The same is true here. It is all right to know that your sixth chakra, in color, is lavender or purple. But, if you have a headache, purple may not be what you need there. So, please explore with stones, with chakras, with herbs, and with doctors.

Master Adalfo: Crystals have been used for many things in many ways by many cultures. In ancient Atlantis, they were used for many different healing purposes, and also were used to bring and enhance clearer vision, in terms of the third eye. They were implanted in foreheads of people and that had some deleterious effects. It was not one of the most wonderful things that we ever did on Atlantis, but it did have its good points. It was like many of the medical drugs you are using today, that have some side-effects. One must weigh advantages and disadvantages.

Sometimes people still have a physical memory of the crystal healing in Atlantis, and of having the crystal implanted. It is like having memories of past lives. Some people have the physical memory that the crystal is still there.

Ancient techniques of healing

Li Sung: There are special techniques, often used in the Orient and in ancient times, which are not being used yet in your time. For in-stance, the storage of energy in crystals, and indeed in whole rooms, was used so that a person who was ailing could go into that enclosure and soak up some of this energy.

The use of color healing is also an ancient healing technique. This was designed to aid the person's inner eye, to focus on the auric centers, so that the level of energy could be raised and adjusted to the proper frequency. When the appropriate color blend was applied to the patient, there was a quickening of the resonance of healing.

For many thousands of years, of course, there has been healing by laying on of hands, in which the healer projects energy which he takes from the God universe. And this often was localized in effect, so that it did alleviate pain and improve a condition for a time. But usually this did not create a permanent effect of health and well-being until it was repeated a number of times.

The most powerful type of healing has many names. Some call it prayer, and some call it channeling. Some call it absent healing. The mind of the healer first gets in touch with the God center of the universe, and then these brilliant energies can be transmitted directly to the person who requires assistance. At such times there is a radiance, a glow around the person, which you may perceive if you can see subtle energies. This healing experience can very quickly perfect the person's *natural pattern* of the body and of the life.

Very grave diseases can sometimes be instantaneously cured, although more often there is marked improvement. The healing technique which I prefer is to adjust the energies of the chakras so that a flow of energy begins to emanate through the body, generally in an upward manner, and as this happens, the subtle body becomes more healthy. It becomes more energized. Finally when the energies reach the brain, or the crown chakra, then there is a flower of beauty enclosing the person, like the petals of a flower. And when this occurs, then the person's own self-healing then begins in earnest.

Healing practices of Isis

Ting-Lao: People may be interested to realize that some of today's healing techniques have their foundation in ancient Egypt, as taught by the feminine healer Isis. Often, in those ancient times, sick people would travel to Philea and go through a process of rebirth involving gestation. It involved giving people quiet time to meditate and think and process their life. They would have special dreams about rebirthing new parts of themselves. The teachers there taught meditation and inner work as a way of inner exploration.

Also, laying on of hands healing is Isian and was done quite silently. The patient was put into an altered state of meditation, and the healer applied the laying on of hands to aid in the healing of the problem.

One of the inner practices taught there was very beneficial and is very simple to do. It is to go inside of a chakra, in your body, with your consciousness or your attention. You do this simply by sitting quietly and breathing, finding your core and pulling up energy to energize your body. This moves you out of the normal state of being and into an altered state or alpha state. Then you can focus your consciousness or

attention on a certain area of your body, a chakra or an organ. You go there and perceive, in any way that comes to you, perhaps a picture, perhaps a sound or word or phrase or a knowing, an intuition. You ask questions of that area, such as, "How are you doing now? What is going on with you now? Please give me insight as to things that I may do to help you feel better and prosper and bring me my fullest happiness." So, you communicate with that chakra or area of the body and this can aid in your healing.

The dream work at Philea and in many other cultures consisted of doing what you now call programming certain dreams, or lucid dreaming. You go into the dream world with a purpose and know that the dream world is a real place. Just as you can step into a chakra as a real place, you step into the dream world. This is the astral plane. At night, you are living there, just as you are living on the physical plane when you are awake. And it is no different, only this is now and that is then. Many people come to the point where they feel they are living 24-hours a day. They make the physical body rest at night, and then they come into the physical body in the morning. Using the dream world time to do work (just as you would do work in this world during the daylight hours) is a great opportunity to help smooth out life in a physical body.

Question: Could you share some techniques for dream programming?

Ting-Lao: If you position the head in a certain direction, it will have certain effects on the dreams. You may want to experiment with facing the head in different positions, north,

east, south, or west. Another exercise is to channel energy up through the feet before you go to sleep. First you pull the toes back toward your head, and flex the feet and pull energy into the body with your intention. Do this for four minutes, breathing energy in from the Earth. Then you massage the head to open up that energy area. Massage the head and the neck and fill the body with energy, bringing it through the legs with the breath. This opens up those areas of the brain to have conscious contact with the dream field of energy.

The next step is to program your dreams. Before you go to sleep, say, "I will dream about why my right shoulder is so painful," or "I will dream about how I can release these feelings of sadness inside." Writing it down is very good. Writing it gives you the visual reading of it, which also stimulates the dream network. You must write the dream, or dreams, down in the morning. Even though you do not understand it right then, you may understand it the next day. It is also good to read or tell your dreams to someone. As you do so, you will get realizations or insights about the symbology that is involved in the dreams.

Sound

Soli: Sound and vibration have an effect upon the subconscious mind. They help centering, especially when the individual is making the sound themselves. This allows the energy of the higher self through. That is its prime focus. Understand too, my friends, that the subconscious mind is in existence throughout the whole body, it is not just localized in the brain. In its entirety, there are areas of the brain that might be said to be its localization, but it exists throughout the body, so your whole body has memory. Sound and vibration can be working on other areas of the body and at the same time, work on the subconscious mind as well.

Master Adalfo: Sound was frequently used in healing techniques in Atlantis. Different tones, different resonating frequencies were used to treat different diseases. We would have people

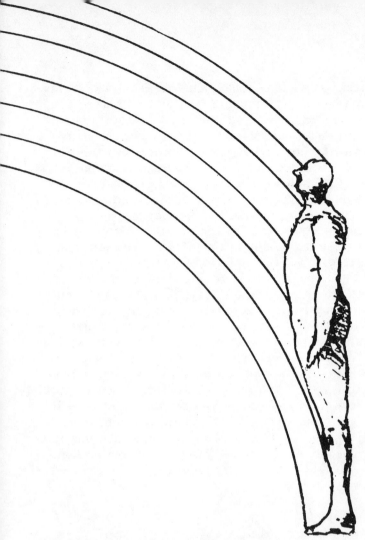

Electromagnetic healing

Li Sung: Healing that deals with magnets and magnetic fields can be very beneficial for balancing one's energy field. There is an electromagnetic component to the body that is apparent. The strengthening of it by introducing a higher vibration rate can be beneficial to a person's health if there is an initial imbalance. If the person is already at the peak of health, then there will be little difference. We do not feel that this technique is rightly employed, but it may be a developing technique in the future.

We would like to mention the idea of the electromagnetic spectrum. There a person can stand in this energy field and adjust the wave lengths of its frequency to the precise wavelengths which make him feel best, and then leave it on for a few minutes. This may be a little more complex than is presently realized. We hope that one day your researchers will be able to construct a chamber so that a person needing mental, physical, or spiritual healing can enter and be bathed in lights of the needed color frequency and also in the electromagnetic vibration that is required for greater balance. In this way, healing can be made more accessible to the many.

You people have great respect for gadgets and for machines, and yet are suspicious of persons in white robes and hands that give out energy.

So, why not invent this type of chamber so that it might become an effective electronic healing tool? We're all for it.

Showers of color

Li Sung: If you wish to make good use of colors in healing, one way would be to install a lamp or lamps which go through the colors of the rainbow. Then you stand and bathe yourself in each color. You'll find the one that makes you feel the best at that moment. And then give yourself a treatment of ten or fifteen minutes. Today, perhaps orange or yellow is good for

sit alone in chambers. The chambers were lined with organ pipes. And the specific tone or combination of tones would produce a particular frequency resonation, and the person would bask in that sound and allow it to help them heal.

You do not have quite the same thing on the planet today. But there are people who use toning, using the sound of their own voices to make specific tones that they know their bodies need. Chanting is very similar to toning, because when a specific chant is repeated over and over, it produces a specific frequency which can be used to alter physical things in the body as well as emotional, mental, and spiritual things. Tibetan gongs are a carry-over from Atlantis. They use resonation to pull specific things out from the body or to balance the sounds on a specific part of the body.

you, and perhaps the next day, blue or violet may be good. And so then you are able to complement what is required by your aura.

The way that this functions is somewhat complex and has to do with the way light is perceived by the eye and in turn, the little gland which you call the pineal. The pineal gland reacts to the light and stimulates the flow of other glandular secretions. You can trace the physiological pathway of the color through to the effect on your body. Perhaps, some day you will be taking (instead of water showers) light showers. And we would say that, of course, the rainbow effect is taken in like the white light from the sun. A short bath in the brilliant light of the sun is good for many people.

Massage

Li Sung: Many masseurs also have the spiritual intent that their patient be healed, that their patient feel better. Naturally then, the energy flows through the hands to that of the patient or the person being massaged. It can be a very powerful technique. And with a very powerful spiritual person there can even be a transformation of energies which can be channeled into the body.

A good massage will do more than make you feel better. It may even make you feel Godly.

In our world, we do not practice massage much for we have no need of bodies, but we are looking over the shoulders of those of you on the earth plane who are trying these energies. We see a whole multitude of different approaches.

We see the revered method of China, acupuncture, used in healing. And this is certainly a step forward for it aligns the energies, and if the acupuncturist is well-trained he can then use his technique to stimulate the person's spiritual enhancement as well.

It is the *intent of the healer and of the person being healed* that is important. The techniques are quite secondary. It is the force of mind and spirit that bring the desired healing about.

Understanding the chakra system

Allen Page: The word chakra comes from the Sanskrit language meaning "wheel of energy." There are seven primary wheels, and many smaller ones, of energy in the human body. Each chakra is associated with a ductless gland, a color, specific body organs and aspects of being.

Chakras have been revered and used for thousands of years in Egypt, the Orient, among native Americans, spiritualists and metaphysicians. You use the chakra system in meditation to alter your energy, to move toward wholeness and to become balanced, all of which lead to healing.

The **first chakra** - root chakra, located in the pubic area, has a color vibration of red, and is associated with the generative organs.

The **second chakra** - just below the navel, has a color vibration of orange and relates to the kidneys and digestive system.

The **third chakra** - just slightly below the diaphragm cleft, has a color vibration of yellow and is associated with the adrenals, spleen and liver.

The **fourth chakra** - heart, has a color vibration of green and is associated with the thymus gland and lungs.

The **fifth chakra** - throat, has a color vibration of blue and is associated with the thyroid gland.

The **sixth chakra** - sometimes called the "third eye," is above the eyebrows, has a color vibration of purple and is associated with the pineal gland.

The **seventh chakra** - crown chakra, is located at the top of your head. Its color vibration is white and it is associated with the pituitary gland.

Chakra meditation

Allen Page: Sit in a relaxed way. Before beginning, make an affirmation that each of your chakras will be cleansed and healed by this process, and that all blocks will be released as your chakras are put into cooperative alignment with each other, facilitating your health and well-being. Affirm that each color vibration will fill the appropriate chakra as it cleanses, heals, and transforms. Affirm also that this will be done for the organs, the aspects of your being, and the glands to which they relate, so that every part of you is filled with the appropriate vibration.

With deep breaths, draw energy up from the Earth into your feet, legs, then into your thighs and root chakra. With another deep breath, see this energy become red, vibrant fire-engine red. Sit for a few moments breathing naturally and easily. Visualize the chakra becoming more red, more and more vibrant as the wheel of red energy becomes as large as it needs to be.

Now, breathe deeply again, and draw energy from the first chakra up into the second chakra. Allow the energy to become a bright fruit orange.

Breathe deeply again, and draw energy from the second into the third chakra. Relax your breath, and sit for a few moments watching the energy become a bright lemon yellow.

When the chakra is a comfortable size and color, draw energy up with another deep breath into the fourth chakra, allowing it to become emerald green.

Draw energy up to your throat, your fifth chakra. Allow the energy to become a beautiful

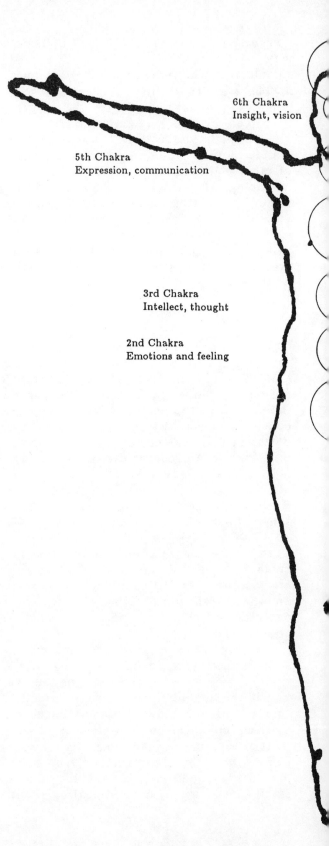

6th Chakra
Insight, vision

5th Chakra
Expression, communication

3rd Chakra
Intellect, thought

2nd Chakra
Emotions and feeling

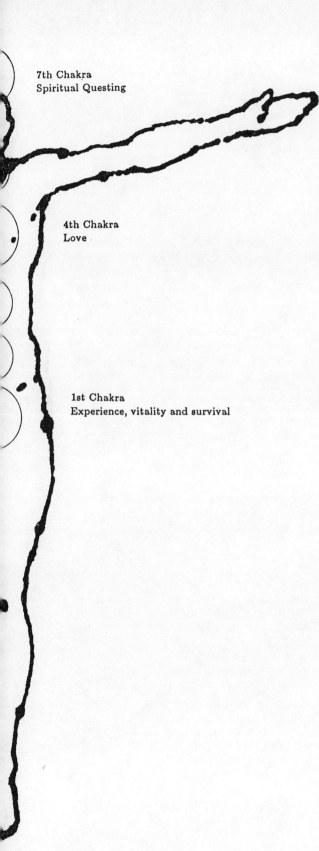

7th Chakra
Spiritual Questing

4th Chakra
Love

1st Chakra
Experience, vitality and survival

royal blue, filling your throat, the top of your chest, your mouth.

Then, draw energy up to the third eye. Relax and allow it to become a very strong and clear purple, filling your forehead and your ears and your eyes.

Again, draw energy up into the seventh chakra whose color is white. See white fleeciness (like clouds) bathing the top of your head. This fountains out from the top of your head, falling around you on all sides.

As you draw more energy up from the Earth, pull it through your body, up through each of your chakras in one continuous breath. Pull up, drawing your breath through your body and letting it flow out through the top of your head. You create a flow, a cycle of continually drawing in, using, and letting go. Drawing in, integrating, and letting go.

Now, just sit for a few moments, in stillness, with your eyes closed. And as you move through each of the chakras now, make an affirmation.

"I affirm my oneness with the Truth." In the first chakra, pray that you may always *experience* Truth. In the second, that you may always *feel* Truth. In the third, that you may always *know* Truth. In the fourth, that you may always relate to it and share it. In the fifth, that you may always *express* it appropriately. In the sixth, that you may *see* it, have insight about it, and know how to *manifest* it. And in the seventh, affirm that you *are* Truth and that you will always *enact* it.

115

STAYING HEALTHY

"Rather than an apple a day keeping the doctor away, maybe a hug & kiss will do the same thing." ... Li Sung

Communicating with your body

Robbyn and His Merrye Bande: We would like to give you some techniques which will require some attention on your part. They do work because they put you in touch with your body as never before. Your body is a good antenna--that is true, and it can give you information about how your past actions and concepts affect it long before any illness becomes apparent on the outside. Your body is good at throwing off the ill effects of your physical and mental abuse for a long time. By the time an illness has manifested, there is great discord in the temple that is your body.

117

So here's what you do. You get in touch with each bodily system. (If you don't know what they are, look them up, so you find it easier to visualize them being healthy and happy.) Then you cleanse the garbage from each, by asking each system what they like that you do, and what they'd like you to change, and what's going on with them.

For instance, start with your auditory system (ears). Relax and meditate, go deep into your subconscious and find the doorway in yourself that is marked "Hearing." Then go in and see what you find. You'll probably see old broken records and tapes that play over and over from childhood. "Do this, do that, don't do this, don't do that." Mother telling you to pick up your clothes. The Beatles from 1965. Maybe there's yelling. You'll probably have the feeling of there being lots of dust and debris. Maybe even fungus and mildew. See yourself cleaning it up, erasing the old tapes. Hear the new sounds as you program some positive tapes, "I forgive myself for believing I must. . . (fill in the blanks). I now follow my path freely and with joy."

Ask your auditory center what it would like you to do. It may say, "Quit listening to rock music," or, "Quit tuning things out." You never know. You may be doing everything just fine.

When that feels cleansed and complete, then do your eyes. Find the room that says, "Sight" and do the same cleansing process. Throw out the negative and destructive pictures of yourself and all the others that you have been hanging onto (especially the horror shows and scenes of violence, on or off the silver screen). Forgive yourself for hanging onto pictures that aren't useful to you anymore. Forgive yourself for seeing yourself as a limited being. See yourself in positive pictures doing what you need to for yourself in this lifetime. See yourself as happy.

Then go to the digestion room and clear the debris off your taste buds. Get rid of the Big Mac wrappers. Ask your stomach's forgiveness for excesses and indulgences in things that masquerade as food in this day and age. Ask what it would like to digest.

Then on to your circulatory system, your heart . . . . does it need more exercise? Does your blood need more iron? Then on to your bones. Does your skeleton need more calcium? Fewer pairs of constricting shoes? Less weight?

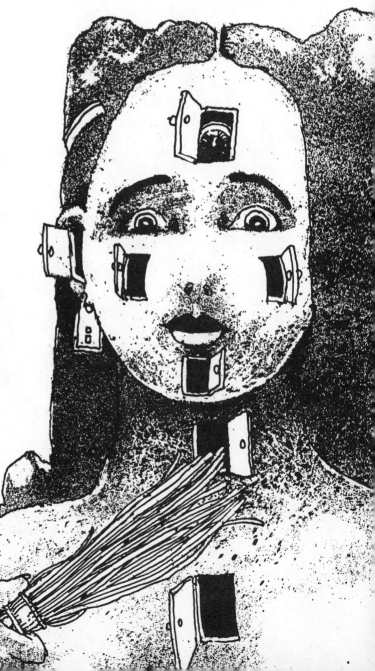

There are many who should go to doctors, for they are, in fact, guided by the Spirit. They are guided by the Universal God or they would not have gone to classes and studied to develop the ability to heal.

If you need less weight, thank the fat cells you no longer need for being of service, bless them and send their energy on its way to someone that needs it. Let it go.

Never, never criticize your body for its weight or any illness.

Too much overweight really is an illness. Any illness is just your body's way of trying to bring to your attention a disharmony between your physical self, your will, your intellect, and your spirit. So thank it for the messages.

Then, ask your lymph system what it needs, and all your organs--your liver, your pancreas, your glands, your reproductive organs. And once you've talked to every single one of them, and mentally cleansed them through their subconscious rooms, go back and consciously send white light through each system until there are no shadows or darkness anywhere.

If this process sounds easy, it's because it is. Your body is full of information that it can tell you about not being aligned with will, intellect, and spirit. If you can listen, you will be far, far ahead. But be sure that you do listen, especially if you start hearing things like, "Please don't judge anymore, it makes me sick," or, "I just can't handle all this anger you want to store!"

"You're so rigid! Quit eating all those **!!%% twinkies!!!" You may even hear red alerts like, "I'm going to quit if you don't give up this lifestyle we both hate." So be honest, just be honest because there is nothing that you cannot change for the better if you are honest and sincere. It's that easy.

Attitude

Dr. Peebles: If you are to maintain your physical health, it is important to build an attitude of healing within your own conscious mind, an attitude of acknowledgment and of acceptance for the fact that healing is individualized.

Always remember that healing is not something that you create, but that you allow.

In a way, that attitude is a creation of the *Loving Law of Allowance.*

Perhaps you do not believe in the medical profession and you do not believe in doctors. If you tell people 'round and about, "Oh, I don't believe in doctors, you shouldn't go to a doctor, you can do it this way, you can do it that way," then you are contributing to interference for them and for yourself. There are many who should go to doctors, for they are, in fact, guided by the Spirit. They are guided by the Universal God or they would not have gone to classes and studied to develop the ability to heal.

If you have put that kind of judgmental attitude about healing with doctors, eventually you will have the need for a doctor. If you then turn to the doctor and say, "Oh well, I didn't believe, but in this particular case it's my problem, my health, so I'm going to the doctor anyway," you will not be healed no matter how close to healing your soul was. Because of what you have put into motion, the healing will not work. The doctors will not be able to define a healing for you. They will not be able to find that which actually will work for you, because your aura, because your consciousness has already spent a great deal of time rejecting it. You have deluded yourself. And so you have created the opportunity for spiritual disillusionment.

Be then alert for your form of thinking. Recognize that there is nothing to avoid. There is only to transmute the vibrational interchange of energies. If you are living in a society of illness, recognize you cannot escape symptoms. You cannot escape some of the reactions simply by your diet or simply by creating your own personal environment of protection.

Live as practically in your environment as possible, carrying your attitude home to roost where it belongs. Build an attitude of willingness to be ill, willingness to be healthy, willingness to have every experience so totally, that it need not have additional karma.

Then, if you have a momentary illness, you are actually able to live it on a daily basis so totally, that if you insist on having it for a month, it is a month of new illnesses. If you are not willing and needing of it for a month, you'll release it within a day, or by the second or third day.

Learn to express perfect love

Hilarion: It is a common error among the practitioners of medicine to treat the symptom and not the disease.

Much of what causes disease has little to do with lessons applying to the physical body. Indeed, humankind has, if anything, overdeveloped this aspect of itself. The errors which are pointed out by evidence of disease are largely of the emotional and mental bodies,

primarily of the emotions. Think, if you will, about the Source of All That Is, the energy commonly referred to as God. You are reminded over and over again that God is Love. Therefore, all good or positive energies are merely variations of God's expression of love. Thus, we find the God-presence in the emotions of peace, joy, harmony, mercy, compassion, and so forth. Each of these emotions are but a form of love.

When the soul chooses to experience another lifetime in matter, it assumes certain responsibilities. It agrees to do a given amount of work, and it accepts the need to cleanse itself of certain negative traits. The latter is accomplished by manifesting specific forms of disease.

Think carefully about the use of the word as expressed in its component parts: dis-ease. Discordant human relationships are stressful, and may therefore be looked upon as dis-ease, just as are cancer or AIDS. For example, much can be learned from the experience of marriage and its responsibilities, and even more from its opposite aspect, divorce. Indeed, circumstances which jerk the soul out of its complacency and force it to take remedial action are truly the *only* lessons of value available to any human being during a given lifetime.

Each time a soul re-enters the wheel of life, it may be said to pick up where it left off in the previous lifetime. It rises quickly to the point where it understands all that it did before, and then it is automatically offered the opportunity to learn and grow beyond this level. Thus, any soul which does not make a conscious effort to remove itself from its comfortable rut may experience a very easy life right up to the point where some major lesson is introduced. The experience then encountered is often quite serious, perhaps life-threatening in nature, for the soul now has been offered a choice: leave the body at this point and return to the endless cycle of rebirth, or elect to do battle with the disease and learn from the experience.

Because the world proclaims that death is the enemy, and deep fear of this transition is

120

rooted in almost every facet of existence, the choice is almost always to fight for the preservation of the physical embodiment. The ensuing battle strengthens the soul, and is often the cause of a life-changing experience, when great personal growth can be found in the wake of a serious disease.

As we continue to look ever more deeply into the cause of physical disease, we will in fact discover that stress or conflict is at the root of it all.

Each human is primarily a divine being, an entity created of God's love in His Image. The image to which we refer has little to do with the physical form, but rather describes the energy field or spirit, which is literally at the heart of each individual. We have said, and it bears endless repetition, that God is pure love. Thus it follows that the spiritual heart of each individual is also love in its purest form. Therefore, when a human being expresses anything other than pure love, it is in conflict with its basic nature.

In the world of today, it is virtually impossible for a human being to express perfect love. The closest example of this form of expression was provided by the Great Master Jesus. His great experience as a soul, and His iron-clad discipline and will enabled Him to hold Himself firm throughout the three years of His ministry leading to His execution and victory in resurrection. His example is a great legacy from which all may benefit, and it is valuable to remember His words: "Greater things than these shall ye do," when referring to the so-called miracles He performed. These actions merely demonstrated His ability to manipulate the physical laws which control matter.

Now, when all the points we have made are taken together, we may correctly conclude that any person is able, with practice, to eliminate the stresses of mind and emotions vis-a-vis the physical plane by simply expressing pure love in every thought and deed. This is the secret of the spiritual path which has been described in metaphysical teachings throughout the ages. It is no more, nor less than the ability to control oneself perfectly, to express love for everything in the universe; thus enabling yourself to be a perfect conduit of God's perfect energy into the earth plane under every circumstance.

The degree to which this is possible is not a constant, even as God is not a constant. God, the great universal energy of Love, is continuously evolving, expanding, and embracing Itself. It must follow that the human master's task is also in a constant state of evolvement. The great souls have chosen lifetime after lifetime in service to the human race in order to grow ever closer to perfection in their expression of love. Only through this repeated selfless service can a jewel of love such as Jesus be polished to such a degree.

There is much that a person afflicted with any form of disease can do to heal himself. Only by first accepting that the disease is his own responsibility can this true form of healing begin. Practitioners of any form of physical healing can treat the symptom, and be helpful in identifying the root source of the complaint. But we repeat, only the patient can truly identify, work with, and eventually dislodge the cause of the trauma.

Incidentally, the choice of the word "patient" to represent the person under treatment is most apt, for it takes considerable perseverance and patience to get to the bottom of these matters.

If we were asked to recommend a course of treatment for any disease, we would suggest that it begin with and be centralized around a spiritual course of study such as those offered by the A.R.E. (the Edgar Cayce material) or *The Course in Miracles,* to name only two. These studies, combined with a daily regimen of meditation and prayer, added to a balanced diet that is primarily vegetarian and based on living food, must eventually produce a body free of any disease. It is indeed a patient process, but it is absolutely within the scope of anyone reading this material. One need only begin, and be determined to carry forward to success. As many who are involved in science and medicine are beginning to understand, there continues to be much to be learned about the workings of the mind.

It is the uncontrolled mind that creates all disease. A mind changed appropriately can set you free of disease forever.

Making lists

Dong How Li: The child element in all humans is essential in any act of healing. It must be engaged. What engages a child but play, humor, adventure, the unknown, assurances of love and protection and safety, beauty, color, flair, or the ongoing sense of discovery? It is all of these things you want to reawaken in yourselves for they are life giving, they are energy giving, they are healing. A very important part of the healing process is the act of discovery.

I encourage you, in your meditations, please sit and list the activities you enjoy doing, even those that you don't have the time for, that you don't have the money for, or that you can't do from where you are now. Even those. And all of them must be *affirming to your health.* (I'm not affirming cocaine habits. These days one must qualify.) Some people believe because they enjoy it, it is all right. We want what affirms *all* of you, body, emotions, mind, and spirit. Collect those, list those, and then begin to see what you can give yourself, a little at a time, then a little more and a little more and a little more.

Face life in its entirety

Soli: Most within life are so fearful of death, and therefore so fearful of life, that they cannot live. You are constantly trying to protect yourselves from the very things of existence. You lock and bolt and bar your doors and guard your person and your personality, both physically and figuratively. You guard your property and try to hold on to it as though this is the only property you are ever going to have in your life, as though you are not abundant. You try to protect yourselves from the things that are going to happen in your future, by having your insurance policies and your retirement funds.

Dear friends, if you need to experience poverty at the age of 75, if that is one of your needs in your current life, no amount of any retirement fund is going to stop that. The stock market will crash. Something will happen to allow you to have that experience, regardless. You can, of course, put it off from this life. All you are doing then is setting yourself up to come back for another lifetime and experience the things in that life.

Ultimately, the highest projection that you can have within this life, or within any other, is to transmute (lift) every experience that comes to you into its highest vibration. Not to decry it, not to bemoan it, not to sit down and say, "Oh me miserum. What has happened to me? Why are you doing this to me, God?" But rather to say, "Wow, this is an interesting experience. Now, what do I do? What challenge, what excitement, what adventure I have now! Where do I go from here?"

Bless each day

Li Sung: Each person can begin the healing with himself if he pictures the abundance of God and joy in his heart each morning, each noon and each night. Then his body will begin to follow that good feeling. Far too many people think of healing only *after* they become sick. They do not consider it while they are relatively well in body.

But if persons begin to think, "Oh, I feel pretty good today, but I bet I could feel even better," then they will attempt to show to themselves how healing can improve their well-being even beyond the level of the normal to what we call supernormal well-being.

Once that idea becomes accepted, and each day a person decides to become better than normal, disease will be vanished very much from their life. Many prefer to call on their guides and on the spirit world to assist. This is a fine idea for often those of our world are well-versed in the way that energies interplay and can be influenced. But that should be only a first step.

Health, my friends, like love, like truth, is about owning more and more of you, not disowning, not separating, not disconnecting.

The next step should be for each person to feel, within himself, the way the energies are distributed and can be influenced by his attitudes, his thoughts and his visualizations. Each person has a body, each person has a responsibility to bring that body into perfection, and he can do this only with the aid of the celestial energy.

Visualize good health

Dr. Peebles: In your daily meditations, visualize a white light flowing through your entire system. Visualize it starting at the root chakra, and moving through the entire chakra system. Visualize it flowing up tributaries into your blood stream, so that your blood stream itself is carrying particles of light, so that any darkness that it finds is gathered up and released into that light. Then visualize this process of flushing everything out of your body, everything that is not of harmony, balance, or total right action. It will help keep your physical strength in harmony. It will help you with keeping a balanced weight. It will keep you young in appearance. It will keep you in harmony with your personality, your soul, and your guides and teachers.

Now, you quite possibly might be saying, "I have a particular symptom similar to a cancerous cell." Well then, visualize the white light. And in the white light you visualize a clam, a clam that is snapping. The snapping clam goes into the light, eating and gobbling up any of the negativity. When the clam is full, you release it from your body.

You might visualize the process as being a ray gun, working within your aura, working within your body to cleanse that negativity, to cleanse out the symptoms.

Often illnesses are little more than the opportunity for you to reconnect to your lower self, reconnect to the earth-binding webs and shadows through guilts and frustrations leading to understanding of "This is below my dignity. I don't need this. I don't want it." I am suggesting then, that if you believe you are in the perfect Christ consciousness, and you are, you must live it and you must demonstrate it.

I would suggest that each of you surround yourselves with people of like thought and like vibration, so that you will be able to encourage each other. If there is one who is ill, physically or mentally, love them so much that it matters not if they are healed and it matters not that they are having a momentary, what you would call, setback. What matters is that you have been able to see the spiritual right action and now understand that no illness comes unless it was most important to the growth and evolution of the person involved.

Go with the flow

Dong How Li: Remember, health depends on flows of energy. So, emotion is energy. You go with that flow. You allow it to expand itself. And indeed, in that way, you can use it to get where you want to go.

So, my friends, crying is very important. Laughing is very important. Deep breathing is very important. Movement is very important.

Anything that encourages you to keep your energy moving. You people are so concerned about aging. Aging is an attempt to stop the flow. Aging is the accumulation of innumerable stops of the flow. What you want to do is to keep moving, keep the energy inside you moving.

Health, my friends, like love, like truth, is about owning more and more of you, not disowning, not separating, and not disconnecting.

I like to think, in my tradition, that all sin is an act of separation at any level from the rest of life, from your heart from your feet, and yourself from God.

Diet

All diets are highly individual

Dr. Peebles: Recognize also that your diets are in need of change at this time. The world that you chose to live in is changing. It is rapidly becoming incapable of feeding its vast population. And so, your diets must change to cope with the needs of others. You must find ways to keep yourselves strong and healthy by eating creative and clear foods. That might seem difficult, but it will stimulate you to the attitudes of healing.

Question: By clear diet, do you mean eating only vegetables and fruits?

Dr. Peebles: I am implying that each and every person must look within themselves to see what a clear diet means to them. People have, for instance, asked for my guidance, and for many I have said vegetarianism. For others I have included fish or fowl. Recently, and also in the distant past, I have recommended beef. It depends, of course, on how, where and why the individuals are in the place they are in. So, we must not have a philosophy that is so all-encompassing that it does not allow space for the needs of the individual.

I think the majority of vegetarians are terribly, terribly close-minded. Oh, how critical they are of all others who do not agree with them. Well, dear ones, by following a vegetarian diet they might be doing what is right for them but they won't *allow* the same space for others.

You must approach the subject of diet on the higher planes to determine that which is appropriate for your own needs. You must allow your entire body to recognize the foods that it wants and does not want, so that you automatically select, in your stores, those things that your body and your total self require. By paying attention to your body reactions, you will notice vibrations that will reject that which is less than which you wish to manifest for strength and healing of body and mind.

It is then, for each of you, to design your individualized diet. If you are to be healthy and strong, it is for you to find foods that digest, ingest and assimilate according to your own system.

All of you need cleansing fluids, so drink plenty of clear fluids such as juices, water, tea, rice-water, anything that keeps the system flushed, attracts all toxins, moves them out and through the body.

Do not wait to alter your diet until you have a symptom. Keep your body energized. Each and every morning when you awaken, check your body. Find out what it is going to need today so that you are able to constantly be preventing attachment to environmental symptoms and illnesses.

I am not overly concerned about the fact that your diet, as a nation, is abominable. I am concerned about the fact that so many of you feed into that and allow that diet to manipulate and control you. And when you eat properly, when you eat foods that are easily digested, ingested, and you still don't have the physical energy, it's high time you woke up and said, "I'm giving myself the energy to be spiritual, but this lack of physical energy is obviously another experience I also need."

So, certainly, you must work on your diet. Don't say it takes too much time and energy or say, "I'm living here where each diet is a terrible mess and that's why I'm a mess."

Remember, you chose to be in a messed-up dietary system to find out if you had the strength of character to design your own, to live in the confusion and yet become a way-shower to others.

Sugar addicts

Soli: As children, most of you have been taught that if you are unhappy, you can be cheered up by having something nice and sweet. You are taught that if you eat up all of your nasty vegetables (those things that are nutritionally good for you), you can have something really nice--that sugary stuff that, of course, is nutritionally not so good for the physical body.

Most bodies within your world are addicted to a greater or lesser degree to sugar. You become addicted within your mother's womb because she is addicted to sugar. There is a need for *sweetness* within. We need not go into the nutritional aspects of what sugar does to the physical body. It has become a major emotional need within your world when you are feeling unhappy within yourself.

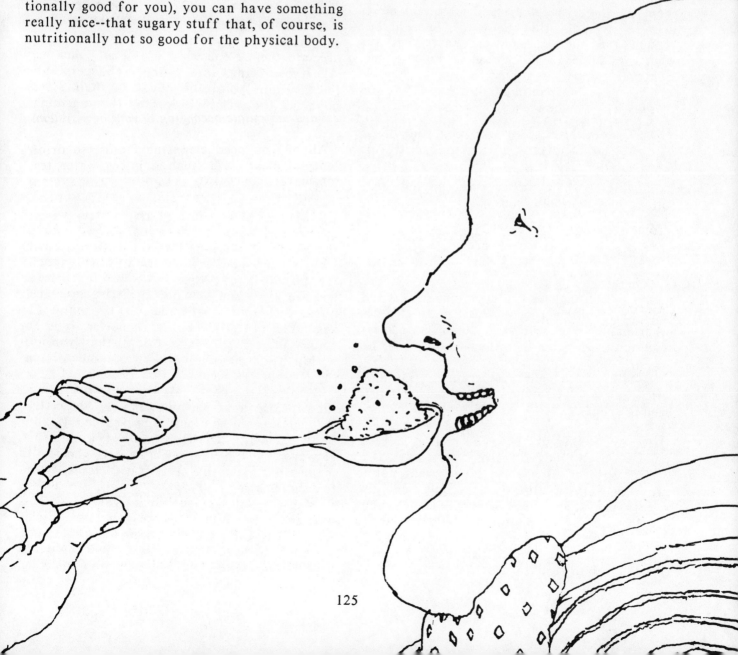

125

Question: Are artificial sweeteners more healthy for us than sugar?

Dr. Peebles: I have said for several years, that the artificial sweeteners would one day be found to be an abomination to the human body.

Vegetarianism

Enid: Vegetarianism developed through the consciousness that came from India in the twenties when diet became very much into thought. And it has developed more and more, because in India they believe, for religious reasons, that they dare not eat meat. That was what they believed was wrong to do. You see, whatever you believe is true for you.

There are no victims. And there are no reasons why you can't have your own thoughts. If you really feel, deep inside yourself that it's not right for you to do something, then you mustn't do it. But if you judge another person for doing it, then you need to look at what is happening. Perhaps you're even judging yourself, rather than being convinced.

When you believe something, you don't feel guilty about doing it.

Therefore, if someone really believes that he has to eat steak to feel good and to feel fed, then that will be good for his body. On the other hand, if everytime a person eats meat, they don't feel good, then they shouldn't eat it.

Question: Are most people enough in touch with their bodies to know if it reacts or not to certain foods?

Enid: Not yet, but they're getting more in touch with all kinds of feelings these days.

This subject of what to eat or what not to eat is a very ticklish one. People who are vegetarians have very high feelings about people who eat flesh. But understand, just as you knew what you were getting into when you came into this life, so did the cow know and so did the rabbit and so did the chicken. They knew what their service was to be. They wanted that experience or they would not have come to be that animal. Remember that nothing is ever destroyed, only converted. We live in a vast re-cycling center where *everything* is converted.

Bear Claw: Do not feel guilty for consuming the creatures who walk the Earth. They're here for you. Respect them and love them for what they have to offer to you. Learn to understand what they know. Learn to feel their love. Learn to appreciate what they give to you. Learn to respect and love them.

Should they offer their bodies for you, appreciate them. You may use them. You may take those beings into yourself and perpetuate them within yourself, honoring their selves, honoring their flesh, honoring the continuity, and the harmony of continuing life as it is on this planet.

The human digestive system

Kajuba: The human digestive system was not constructed to be carnivorous. If you look at the length of the long intestine, it is extremely long, much longer in proportion to the length of the physical body than it is within the true meat-eating animal. Your digestive system is not made to digest meat. It is made for vegetable and fruit. For that matter, it is not made for many of the things that you put within your physical bodies in your present society, not just meat.

Many of the chemicals that you put in and the processes that you put food (as you call it) through, cannot be digested by your body. Your body is made to digest plant and fruit. However, you have grown up eating meat. In many ways, your physical bodies are addicted to a meat-eating process.

Many of you, as you expand your consciousness and move into a higher understanding of self, will be falling away from eating meat; not so much because you believe you should not destroy animals, but because your physical bodies are not made for it. Eating a plant destroys the plant just as much as eating the animal destroys the animal. If you would eat totally spiritually, you would take the leaf from the plant and leave the plant in the garden. You would take the fruit from the tree and leave the tree standing. You would take those foods that are offered to you in service.

But those who do eat meat, those that find themselves incarnated in areas where there is only meat, find themselves working in harmony with nature. You will find them talking to the animal kingdom, telling them that they need a physical body in service as food for them. And the animal whose time it is to leave the earth plane will come by and offer its body in service. It is always known by the animal what it is going to be used for. And it is part of the animal's free will and choice to select that incarnation.

We do not suggest that everyone instantly stop eating meat. If you do stop, it should be a gradual process because the body will react with many toxins. The release of addictions that you call "withdrawal symptoms" is to be done carefully. Utimately, most will cease to eat meat. But while you are eating meat, do not feel guilty over it, because there are many meat-eating animals.

If you are eating meat, *bless the creature* that gave its life. Bless it. *Thank it* for the service. You will *transmute* the energy of its death, and you will *assist* the process in its evolution. You will release your guilt.

Now, fish are a different "kettle of fish" because they digest within the human body in a very different way from meat. Fish digests much more easily. It is a much better food than is meat for the human body.

Fish are rather like the plant that you take one leaf from. They are part of a *group soul* and *group spiritual beingness*. You take one fish from the school and you haven't destroyed the incarnation of that spirit. You have taken one cell from the body, as it were. It is when you, as humans, grossly misuse your *right* to such food that you create problems for yourselves.

It is one thing to fish and take one fish for

your dinner that night. It is another to send your factory ships out to sea to take vast quantities of fish which you destroy wantonly and use only a small fraction of, or turn into other things for profit. That is misuse. It is not

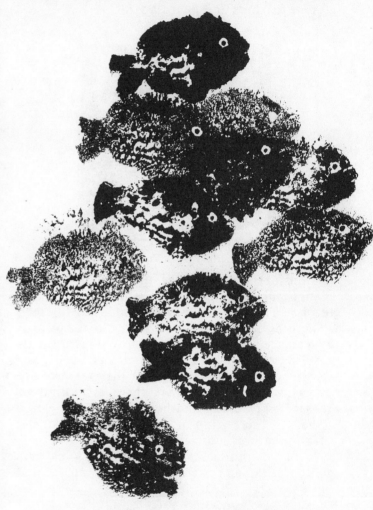

animal husbandry. It is animal abuse. It is the motivation that makes the difference. It is how you feel about it, or what you are doing it for, or what you are thinking of while you are doing it that makes the difference.

So, if you do eat meat, thank the creature. In essence, thank the vegetables that you are eating, for they also are life. They also are God, and all are in service to all.

The food and learning chain

Hilarion: It is a fact that every entity, whether expressing through the physical dimension or higher levels, has its own personal guides, teachers and guardians.

Consider the fact that the animals on this planet look to humanity as a form of composite teacher, from whom they are intended to learn something about the finer shades of emotional experience. Naturally, the individual animals also have guides and guardians at higher dimensional levels as well. But the point we are bringing out here is that there is a kind of "chain" of teaching and helping that was established in the beginning for the mutual benefit of all creatures, no matter what their level.

Thus, the animals, too, are to act as teachers to the still more elementary level represented

by the vegetal life forms on the planet. This is accomplished, interestingly enough, primarily by the act of eating the various food plants. Whenever a plant, fruit or portion of a tree is eaten by a herbivorous animal, the spiritual essence of the plant literally passes through the many sheaths of the animal during the course of ingestion. While this merging or blending is taking place, the rudimentary consciousness of the plant or fruit actually is enabled to perceive reality from the vantage point of the animal's own consciousness.

It must be understood that this represents a gigantic leap for the plant entity. Suddenly, it is given the ability to see the world through the perceptions of an entirely different creature, one of far greater complexity and advancement, in terms of spiritual cohesiveness and focusedness. This momentary glimpse of a grander vista than anything the vegetal essence had previously known provides a great impetus in the direction of further developing its own consciousness and spiritual level, in most cases.

By the same token, the plants and trees act as refiners and improvers of the mineral essence that dwells, in an almost entirely amorphous state, within the very Earth upon which the vegetal forms are growing. As the nutrients and minerals of the Earth are drawn up through the roots, stems, and trunks of the plants, bushes and trees, so is the elementary consciousness of the mineral level of being drawn through and into the life form represented by the vegetal entity. This indwelling of the mineral consciousness lasts much longer than the momentary experience of the plant or fruit when it is eaten by an animal (or a human), but such longer duration is required owing to the extreme primitiveness of the mineral essence.

There is a kind of acceleration of time which takes place as a spiritual being moves up the ladder of progress through the different levels of consciousness represented by the various life forms on the Earth. As the being becomes more and more focused and integrated, it does not require as long an exposure to the uplifting and stimulating vibrations of a higher lifeform or entity in order to be given the required impetus to improve and refine its own essence. This same apparent acceleration of time is often noted by those who are "on the path," and who are striving to improve and refine their own spiritual qualities.

We have been speaking of this chain as if the phases and levels are very clearly demarcated, with each level interacting strictly with only the levels immediately above or below it. This, however, is not the case. It will be evident, for example, that humans too, can be of benefit to plant entities by consuming them, this representing a "skipping" of one level in the chain. There is an interesting facet of this particular exception, however, namely that humans were originally meant to consume only

the fruit of the trees for sustenance. This commandment was given in the early era to which the beginning of your Bible has reference. When a human eats a fruit, an apple, an orange, or whatever, he or she is consuming a particularly sweet packet of energy provided by the tree, bush, or plant. In effect, the vegetal entity, in order to make the fruit, must gather together all of the most refined, one could say, "spiritually sweet," portions of its own being and place this in the fruit. It is from this process that the literal sweetness of the fruit arises. Hence, the human family was expected to act as refiners and teachers for a selected part of the vegetal entity, a portion more likely to benefit from the experience of momentarily merging with the far more integrated and focused consciousness of the human.

One might wonder whether the act of eating the flesh of an animal might also be of benefit to the animal consciousness. In general, this is not so. With the exception of the food chain found in the rivers, lakes, and seas of the Earth, the eating of one animal form by another does not really produce any significant benefit in terms of heightening the consciousness of the victim. This is so for several reasons. The first is the fact that the prey of a predator, for example, a rabbit being pursued, killed, and eaten by a fox, has its consciousness literally assaulted by the rush of terror and

129

desperation that occurs during the chase. Such an emotion cannot possibly be a prelude to a spiritualizing experience, even in the case where the victim is eaten whole and fresh, i.e. while the consciousness is still within the expiring body. The second reason relates to the fact that, for many carnivorous animals, only part of the kill is eaten immediately. In the case of a lion feeding on a small deer, for example, the corpse is often left in a hiding place after a first meal has been consumed, in order that the lion can return later and feast again. In the meantime, of course, the consciousness of the animal has long since departed the physical form, and would not in any sense become entrapped in or entangled with that of the lion. Indeed, the fear engendered in the prey during the chase is such as to make it practically impossible for that consciousness, once released from the dying body, to become one with the consciousness of the predator animal. The fear creates a tremendous vibrational mismatch which prevents such merging.

In the waters of the Earth, however, the consciousness of most species is too elementary to experience much in the way of fear. We speak here of the non-mammals: the fish, crustaceans, and so on. As a general rule, the larger the physical form of these creatures in the food chain, the greater is the amount of spiritual "stuff" which is experiencing reality through it. And the greater the spiritual essence, the greater is the degree of focusedness and integration. Now it is well known that the aquatic food chain proceeds in order of size: the plankton are eaten by tiny sea creatures and the smaller fishes, which are eaten by bigger fishes, which in turn are eaten by still bigger fishes, and so on.

Hence, in general, each life-form tends to be a predator of a smaller life-form and a prey to a larger one. Because of the elementary nature of the consciousness in these creatures, any chase that is preliminary to one eating another does not create the terror that occurs in a more complex (and warmblooded) land animal.

Therefore, there is little to impede the complete, though temporary, merging of the prey consciousness with that of the predator. And this, as with the eating of plants or fruit by the land animals, gives the expiring consciousness a glimpse of a higher perspective than its own, however briefly.

It will be evident that a human individual has passed beyond that primitive stage of learning wherein the only process by which to encourage development is to be eaten by some creature of greater complexity and evolvement. Indeed, when one rises to the animal level, it is a mark of retrograde spiritual movement to persist in the eating of the physical forms of other animal species.

Thus, one can say that the various natural predators of the animal kingdom, the felines, the canines and the rest, act as physical vehicles for animal souls that must learn to respect life for its own sake. The reincarnational process for such beings involves (usually) an alternation between prey and predator which continues until the consciousness acquires an empathy for its victims which is so strong that it no longer is able to kill. Thus, an animal soul may be a lion one life, a Thompson gazelle the next, and back as a lion the next, etc.

When the consciousness arrives at the point where, as a lion, the perception of the fear in its prey calls up such a strong recollection of its own fear in the previous life that it can no longer persist in the chase, its own guides may then decide to give the animal's soul a chance to improve still further by exposure to the leavening influence of humanity. The animal soul might then return as a domestic cat. The first few experiences of this smaller feline form may be in a somewhat wild setting, a barn cat, for example, but eventually, as the being became used to the human vibration, it would come as a house pet. Gradually, the love and caring that its human owners would show it would (it is hoped) prompt the animal soul to convert the fear-encouraged respect for other life forms to a genuine returned affection.

The continued eating of the cadavers of animals does place a stigma on humanity, a badge of unspirituality which we hope will be

130

eliminated over the next 50 years or so as the physical bodies of the race become more and more refined. This process will take place naturally as the racial consciousness itself rises to greater and greater heights of awareness and spiritual perspective.

An apple a day

Li Sung: We can agree that regular ingestion of fruits that provide the body and the digestive system with bulk is helpful to many. If doctors only had to see about digestive problems that could be true. But, doctors have to look at wide varieties of illnesses and conditions. So you might as well say a raisin a day or perhaps a pear or whatever.

In our view, the food that is taken by each person is not so important as the *attitude* of the person who gives the food, cooks the food, and also the one who eats it. And so you will find that food served at one house by a good woman who wishes you well will make you feel much, much better than more elaborate or much more expensive foods served by one who does not care. For the food is endowed, is imbued with energy by the person who touches it. And if there is loving intent, then the assimilation will be helpful.

We would say that rather than, an apple a day keeps the doctor away, maybe a hug and a kiss a day will keep the doctor away.

Many persons believe in saying a prayer to God before serving food. If they do it only as perfunctory ritual without meaning, then it has no consequence. But if their eyes shine with joy and gladness, if they hold up their platter of food for their family and say, "Eat, for here is the fruit provided by God who wants you to prosper," then it will bring enhancement.

Smoking/non-smoking

Dr. Peebles: If a person is a smoker, they chose it. You are free to offer your energies of healing to their higher self. If they wish to use

it to stop smoking, they will. But if they smoke, and you try to stop them by trying to make them feel guilty or uncomfortable, you are as much, at that point, out of balance as they for their smoking.

In the majority of cases, almost unanimously, the breathing in of the hot smoke, be it from any of the tobaccos, or by breathing in hot fumes or steam of almost any kind, does create a form of trauma to the mucous membranes, to the lungs themselves, and frequently stimulates an imbalance in the circulatory systems. Smoke, not tobacco, represses your ability to flow oxygen and vital life

Before enlightenment, chop wood. Afterwards, chop wood too!

forces through the blood. Goodness knows, smoking is more dangerous than most forms of alcoholic intake, unless that too is done in excess.

If your circulation is not moving, if your oxygen principles are not working, if you cannot assimilate, your chakras are going to go hysterical, close down, and go to sleep.

Now, if you are allergic to smoke, if you just prefer not to be around smoke, you must choose your environments accordingly. And in your current society, there's more cooperation in that. Make sure that you stand up and get your rightful respect. When you go into a restaurant, make sure that you sit away from smoke.

When you go to a person's home, and they are smoking, you must say, "Well I guess I wanted to be around this smoke. I, then, have to put up with it." Don't make them feel guilty. You shouldn't have accepted the invitation if you make an issue of the smoking.

When people come to your home and they say, "Oh, where's your ashtray?" you then say, "Well, I don't have smoking in my home." You don't have to explain why. "You wish to smoke, I have a lovely patio out there, or the sidewalk's right out the front door." They do not have the right to smoke in your environment. It is your environment, but when you go to theirs, and they are smoking, you must say, "Well, I guess I decided to be around all that gobbledigook today."

If you feel that you just can't go anywhere without being around smoke, know that you can. Just discipline yourself to find the right environment. And don't give in and say, "Oh well, everyone in the neighborhood smokes, I guess we'd better let smoking in the house." Not true!

Keep the purity of your environment according to that which works for you. Part of the *Loving Law of Allowance* is not just to allow everyone else their rights, but allowing yourself to live up to *your* right. That's most important, friends.

Question: What affect do marijuana, cocaine, and hallucinogens have on the body?

Dr. Peebles: Some of you go out and smoke up five, six times a day. If you do it on top of a mystical experience, for times of great celebration and communion with your higher self, there are various plants which can be of value if they are approached systemically to the higher self. You would find that the more natural the forms, the more organic of nature, if administered properly, if approached properly by the subject, can heal body/mind or open to a greater mystical understanding. If they become a *necessary* tool or element, then they are no longer a good or a valuable tool. I do not approve of the refinement, to a certain degree, that they have become chemicalized. If they are used through study, research, and proper administration in their most natural state, they can be of great value.

Exercise

Dong How Li: There are some things, traditionally in this culture, that are hard for you to deal with. Being physical is one. Some of you (especially in the New Age movement) find it easy to meditate and be spiritual and to watch beliefs, and less easy to be physical and get the exercise you need. However, that is what is required much of the time to get the energy moving again. Exercise, physical exercise keeps the energy going. It is necessary for the body.

Bear Claw: Physical exercise is the acknowledgment of the physical reality. It is an appreciation of the physical self, as an extension of the planet earth. Exercise is an honoring of the inner physical harmony and it is good. For those of you who enjoy the exercise of running or exercising in the out of doors, we suggest that you run on land rather than on pavement, or at least be near it so that your physical self can interact its cells with the cells of the harmonious beings of nature.

Saunas/sweat lodges

Bear Claw: The value which comes from the practices of using the sauna/sweat lodge is not just the sweating. It is also the passage, through the physical body, of the energy spirits that encompass you. If you take in the water while within this hot room you call a "sauna," that water filters through your physical body. Allow it to come through and as it comes through your pores and your sweat, know that it evaporates and comes out into the room.

If you choose, bring a plant that can take warmth into the room with you. Keep that heat at such a range that it will not hurt that plant. In this way, you will then have the water that you take into physical self cycling through you, supporting you, giving you nutrients. And you will sweat and your moisture will enter the air and those moistures will support the plant and allow it to grow and be harmonized. Feel the plant reaching into its source to receive its moisture and bring it up to its leaves. That evaporates and comes into your atmosphere in that little room. So you will find that the air is easier to breath, for it is moist and the inside of your body is moist.

Always remember how the harmony works. In the sweat lodge you are bringing through the spirits of yourself as well as the spirits of your ancestors in order to appreciate the continuity again and the harmony within the modern day hot room. You may not have this immediate opportunity, but should you, simply lie down and feel the spirits of your own incarnations past, allow them to come through you and allow images to flow through you as long as they are comfortable. And allow your imagination to roam and fly in all areas.

Pets: your in-house healers

Kajuba: Your pets have *chosen* to be with you just as you have *chosen* to be with them. In many ways, they provide a tremendous service to you, for they are helping you to heal. They divert from you much of the negativity that would manifest in your physical vehicle. Understand that animals in the wild do not get human illnesses, whereas animals in the home do because they are taking on the characteristics of the animals around them. They divert the energies of negativity that you humans create in your own lives. They deserve tremendous respect. They take on, many times, very heavy, onerous duties in terms of healing, in terms of deflecting negativity that you create around you.

How animals work to heal is that they take illness away, in many cases, as a diversion. Sometimes this applies to children, human children as well. Children in a family, while they are being brought up by the parents, are very much at the whim of the parental vibrations. They are part of the parental vibrations and so are animals within that family. And if there is discord within the family between husband and wife, it will manifest as illness in the children. It will manifest as illness in the animal. And, of course, sometimes it will also manifest as illness in the husband and wife as well. But it is released, to a certain extent, by any animal. The animal can help with healing.

Many times, being within the auric field of the human, the animals that would seem to be sleeping and being lazy so much of the time, are working on healing your etheric body for you.

When animals are sleeping, they actually are working in the astral planes, assisting you, and balancing emotional imbalances within you.

Because they deal so much with feeling, they can assist humans to balance their feeling bodies, and they can do this within their feeling bodies. The can also do this within the astral while they are asleep, especially your felines. They seem to like to sleep on you. When they are sleeping on you, they are very much working with you, helping to create a change of vibration and harmonization within your feeling body.

Question: Is there a particular group of animals we might observe to help us develop healing skills?

Dr. Peebles: You would, of course, not go looking for a nest of cockroaches. You would go looking for birds. You would be looking more at the birds who fly high in the sky rather than the pigeon, for there are densities and qualities within the different birds. You would not look upon the existing mutations of dogs. You would look at the more "natural" dogs, breeds that have not been manipulated or interfered with out of human efforts to control the universe.

Look, in general, at how the animals interact and often heal by taking the life of another animal. They often heal another animal or human being by first attacking it, possibly creating an antibody, possibly confronting a cellular fear for the animal to heal themselves.

Animals follow the guidance of their higher selves.

They are not controlled by sociological interference. When the higher self says, "See that person there who is all bent over and suffering? Go over to them and slap them in the mouth." You say, "Oh, I can't do that. That idea is terrible, terrible. Where did that idea come from?"

Now the animal would go over, slap them in the mouth and then lick them. And the person would find themselves standing straight because they had confronted their own fear. The animal takes the action, not because it reasons and says, "Oh, now let's do this, this, or this." It says, "There's one over there, and I just have to do this." They do it and they don't wonder what took place. They do the job and they go their way.

Change as the fountain of youth

Master Adalfo: If you were a person totally at ease with change and growth and were willing to change, there would be no aging. But I

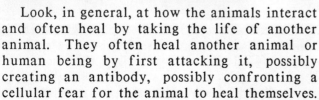

don't know of anyone here on this planet who is like that; perhaps that is why you are all still here.

If you were evolving fully and living fully in the *now* and creating a reality for yourself that was allowed to continually grow and change, then aging would not be a disease that you would have to contend with. You see, aging, in a sense, is a disease.

The question is what we can do to slow it down; to slow down the growth of that disease. You can encourage yourself to grow and change and transform. Be welcoming of new ideas, new concepts. Always express your feelings fully

and then examine them after you have expressed yourself. But first and foremost, have feelings, own your feelings. Own them in the *now*. When you do not own everything in the moment, then aging persists, you get steadily older.

One major aspect of aging is that people don't embrace new ideas. Those who do not seem to age like others do are embracing new ideas, new thoughts. They are in the *now* with them; making those new things a part of their reality. However, this alone does not keep you younger. It is the concept of new ideas and a willingness to continue to evolve and remain active. When you remain active, you are exposed to new things all the time and have to grow and change. That is why *being* active keeps you younger, because of what being active is about.

Understanding the cycles of the universe

Ting-Lao: It is quite prevalent in the consciousness of many to consult their astrologer before surgery and also to look at the phase of the moon, whether it is waxing or waning. All cycles are important in healing and they all work together: cycles of seasons, a person's astrological birth sign and astrological configuration.

Understand that healing is cyclical, and health is cyclical. Sometimes people need more sleep, otherwise they will get sick. You know

that animals follow the cycle of the seasons. In the fall and winter, it is normal and natural to slow down, and many animals sleep more, or hibernate. People seem to be needing more sleep, especially during the wintertime. It is a natural cycle. Many times people push, push, push themselves and that is why we get a cycle of flus and colds in the wintertime. People push themselves, and do not respect their natural cycle.

Many times people do not understand why they are feeling tired or fatigued or confused or, at times, even more energetic. Often it has to do with how planetary movement is affecting them. The planets, stars, and moon do affect many of the flows in the body. The most obvious and well-known cycle is the moon. It is very important because it does control the water and much of the body is made up of water. And that also influences the emotions. Most women are aware of this because of their moon-cycle time, but we also want men to be aware that their blood and their tissues are made up of primarily water, and the moon pulls and pushes and affects them also. The water in the brain centers, blood pressure--many things are related to the cycle of the moon.

Many times you hear people say that things will be better in the morning, and lots of times they are. Remember that the moon changes all the time and if you are not feeling so good one day, it is okay to rest and perhaps you will truly be better in the morning. You do not always have to worry or go to the doctor or go to a healer. Sometimes you can just rest and be with yourself and let things be better in the morning because the universe around you is constantly changing.

The harmony of nature

Bear Claw: Ancient Indian peoples experienced illness differently than people today do. Perhaps it was because we lived as the plants and animals. We lived in harmony with the land. For those of you who are experiencing disease, I would suggest that you study the harmony of nature. This may not be easy to do in a city. But, you can go to a park and study the grass, how it lives in harmony with the tree.

136

The grass grows at the root of the tree and yet the tree is not jealous of the grass who takes from it the water it needs. The tree knows that its roots go deeper and can seek out areas of water and support for itself that the grass does not need. The grass knows that it can reach water toward the surface and can feel the sun's rays that come through the leaves of the tree. They live in harmony together.

Study closely and feel the leaves of the tree. Sense yourself in the leaves and feel them being nurtured by the water from the ground and by the wind as it plays gently around the leafy edges. Feel the sun as it caresses and warms the leaves.

The more you experience the harmony that spirit Mother-Father-Earth is here to support you, the more you will be willing to receive support from your Earth and all that grows and walks upon it.

It is always good to have soil about. So, for those of you who have plants, it is good for you to touch the soil and to get close to your plants. Appreciate them. Look at them closely. See how all of their beauty is also part of their function. If you do not have plants, have a little soil around or some rocks so that you may be near land in your own way.

Go for walks in areas that are not paved so that you can be on the land, so that you can feel the land and see all around and about you the land in its natural glory and harmony. Do not separate yourself so far from the land that you forget that your physical body comes from the land and returns to it.

And all during your life cycle you must be reminded of that so that it is not lonely, so that body does not feel lonely and pine for the land. Do not deny your physical body its comforts on the land.

Ask for assistance

Hilarion: We who have been entrusted with the loving task of guiding the human lifestream along a specific path to enlightenment, are delighted to see the topics under discussion in this book assuming an evermore widespread interest in human consciousness. This is no accident. Much effort has been expended to ensure that a new level of Truth is available whenever there are sufficient numbers prepared to receive it.

At this period in the history of the human race, massive change is afoot. Millions are seeing the futility of lives wasted in mindless pursuit of war, fear, and other power-based forms of dominance; and are turning toward peace and sanity and love, the qualities that comprise their true nature. The only qualification required of anyone who wishes to follow this path is the desire to do so.

Each soul incarnate on Earth has a spiritual support group at his disposal. Commonly referred to as guides or teachers, these caring entities are alert to any indication that their charge is ready to accept a higher degree of responsibility for his life. They respond by arranging to bring circumstances across the seeker's path which, if acted upon, will help him or her to discover the required lessons. The seeker can greatly accelerate this process by consciously working with these spiritual teachers, and this has much to recommend it.

Because spiritual law dictates that any request for assistance must originate from the plane issuing the request, permission for the intervention of a spiritual guide or teacher must come from the one requiring help. The request is most usually issued in the form of prayer for advice in a certain area of the disciple's life.

For example, a seeker may feel that little progress is being made in his spiritual growth, and ask in prayer to be shown the most effective course of action to be taken next. Shortly thereafter, an unexpected telephone call might be received from an old friend who announces that she is forming a *Course in Miracles* study group, and issues the seeker an invitation to join. This may seem like pure coincidence at first, but if the suggestion thus provided is ignored, the clue will be repeated under different circumstances, until the desired results are achieved.

The value of this technique is readily apparent, and by applying it diligently you can literally chart your course through life, avoiding all the shoals and hazards normally encountered with trial and error navigation. Life becomes an exciting game as clues to the next phase are sought constantly in response to requests for advice about every new experience.

We urge those who seek enlightenment and healing to follow these guidelines, and we especially recommend the establishment of a working relationship with those in spirit who care deeply for all human development, and who have been entrusted with the responsibility of guiding their human brethren while they are undergoing the adventure of a life in body upon the Earth.

Let go and let God

Master Adalfo: I would like to mention that at any and all points of an illness, you can let go and let God. That is not to say you don't do anything--that is the misunderstanding of that saying. People say, "Now it is time for me to let go and let God," and they sit back and rest on their laurels and say, "I'm letting God do it all. I don't have to do anything." That is not true.

God will not do it all for you. That is not how God works. Since the principle of God is in you, that means that you are going to have to enact that principle by *doing*. Letting go and letting God means that you let go of the controlling aspect of things, "This is how I wanted things to turn out," that sort of obsessiveness that people get into. "This is how I want it to go. I want to do it this way--one--two--three."

If you are going to let go and let the principle of God take over, that means you are going to let your God-Self lead the way as you work with that God principle. It means that you cannot lay it all out and arrange it. You have to make a Statement of Intent and begin to follow where that leads you. And be willing to say, "I think perhaps if we did this, it would help." It may not always happen exactly as you intend, and you have to be willing to let what happens, happen. That is part of the letting go,

of surrendering, and why it is so important to know what you want--to intend properly. Some people don't intend very fully. So they get what they want and they get a few other things that they didn't actually want.

So letting go and letting God is letting go of *control*, letting the God principle take over, surrendering to the rightness of God in action, and surrendering to result.

Helping hands

Enid: If you've got a friend who is experiencing illness, you can send that person decisions for healing. You can picture them thinking, "I'm well and happy." And if it's appropriate for them, they'll start thinking, "Well, that's what I should be thinking--I'm well and happy," and they'll start thinking that. So if you feel that a being needs a little encouragement to think well of himself or think himself well, you just send it right along. He'll sign for it and then keep it, *Special Delivery*.

Ting-Lao: Many of you are members of a family with ill people. When you feel that they "should" (a non-healthy word in that often it is not the truth when you think that another should do something), it is often not so.

For example, let us take someone who is very ill with a skin disorder and this person runs from one nutritionist to another acupuncturist to a psychic to another therapist to another therapist to another psychic to another nutritionist every day. They are trying to get better but never taking time to be introspective or just to lay quietly and heal.

There are many ways to help this person who runs around and is on a treadmill expending energy. Understand that *using* energy, not *having* energy, heals.

You think this person "should" slow down and take time to heal. There is much work that can be done on the energy level. In other words, many times when we talk-talk-talk to people, they are hearing with their ears and it goes in one ear and out the other. It is very possible to do work on energy levels in situations like this

Robbyn and His Merrye Bande: And for those of you who can't or won't listen to your body, and who don't want to align your various parts of yourselves, and those of you who profess to think that this planet is the worst ever and in the worst state ever, well, we have good news! Yep, a new planet . . . a new school

where another person is not progressing to greater happiness.

The caring person, in other words we on the other side of the situation who see a "should," can use energy. Each night we can pray to the person's highest self to please awaken, please align yourselves in harmony with the rest of the bodies. We can also send much loving energy and strong energy--just send-send-send energy telepathically and with care.

As you go to sleep at night, you can go to sleep contemplating them or thinking about them. In this way you can work with them in the energy world when you are not in your body at night.

139

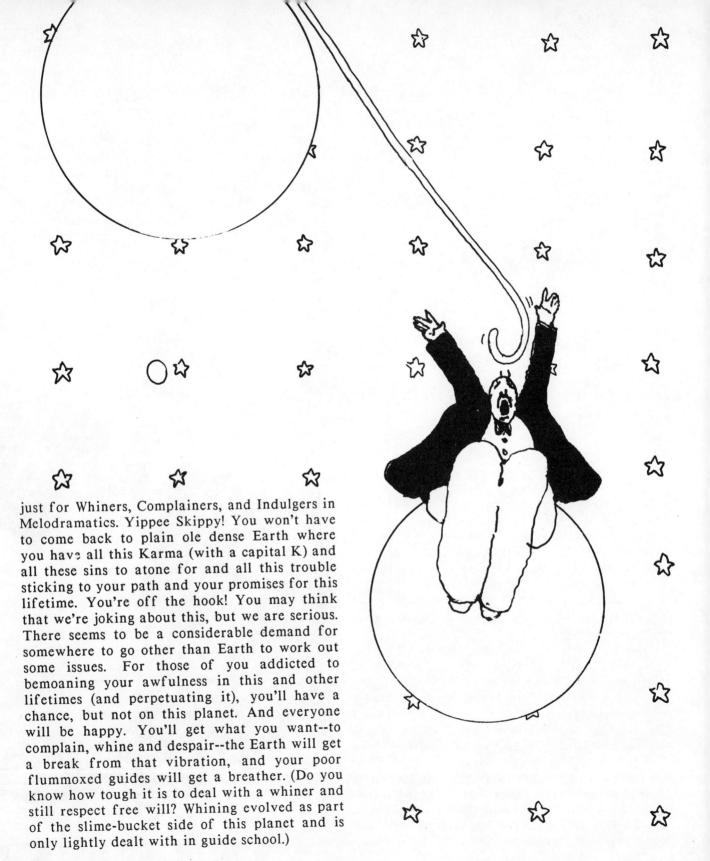

just for Whiners, Complainers, and Indulgers in
Melodramatics. Yippee Skippy! You won't have
to come back to plain ole dense Earth where
you have all this Karma (with a capital K) and
all these sins to atone for and all this trouble
sticking to your path and your promises for this
lifetime. You're off the hook! You may think
that we're joking about this, but we are serious.
There seems to be a considerable demand for
somewhere to go other than Earth to work out
some issues. For those of you addicted to
bemoaning your awfulness in this and other
lifetimes (and perpetuating it), you'll have a
chance, but not on this planet. And everyone
will be happy. You'll get what you want--to
complain, whine and despair--the Earth will get
a break from that vibration, and your poor
flummoxed guides will get a breather. (Do you
know how tough it is to deal with a whiner and
still respect free will? Whining evolved as part
of the slime-bucket side of this planet and is
only lightly dealt with in guide school.)

A GLOBAL
PERSPECTIVE ON ILLNESS

"The Earth has a karma and a path to travel in the Creation, just as you do. Earth is a free-will planet that has chosen to be in the light." ... Robbyn and His Merrye Bande

Robbyn and His Merrye Bande: Illness, especially large-scale illness, such as plague, cholera, some flu epidemics, and most recently, AIDS, cause much fear, confusion, and much pain upon death. Generally wholesale diseases (not very popular) have a very doubtful reputation among you indeed. And somewhat rightly so . . . they take everything not entirely in the light with them. They also occasionally take some things that *are* in the light. However, illnesses, even such as these, still have a purpose and can be a very powerful opportunity to learn, and a powerful incentive to change!

What is disease? Well, as you know, disease is a state of *unease* in the soul. If we look back to the last time there were large-scale plagues and pestilence on the land, we can learn something. A state of disease existed in the Dark Ages in Europe. The Dark Ages saw the destruction of communal property and living. The land, just prior to that time, was considered to belong to no one and to everyone all at once. There were many natural healers, and midwifery had a

valued, honored, and respected following. Everyone saw and spoke to the spirits, and the magical kingdoms of faeries, gnomes, and elves were far, far closer than they are today. Wizardry was an honorable calling, and seers, mystics, and white witches were perfectly respectable.

Then the darkness set in, and in the name of economy, the concept of private ownership of the Earth was born. In the name of the church, wizards, seers, mystics, and witches, and other innocents were put to death by the millions. In the name of modern medicine, midwives and natural healers were put to death or brutalized into stillness and silence. Jews and gypsies were put to death, and the Inquisition became part of everyone's lives.

The Church at Rome got "stinking rich," as you might say, taking the property and wealth of those it condemned and extracting fear money from others. Power of the most corrupt sort was put into the hands of the most evil and corrupt, and innocents suffered. The Earth and

Earth's angels wept (as they do every time the inhabitants of the planet get carried away in their unreasonableness. If you think the planet that hosts you is an unfeeling chunk of dirt, you are very wrong), and after the weeping was through, plague was set forth from organisms that are a part of the Earth, there for just such a purpose, to serve as an act of cleansing.

And for those of you thinking, "Well, that's what happened, so that's just what should have been," well, that is what happened, and that's what could have been, not what *should have* been. It was not the perfect solution for Earth at that time, just as the sinking of Atlantis and Lemuria were not perfect solutions. The Earth, like any overtaxed mother sometimes does, smacked all the fighting children instead of finding the culprits who started it and defending the innocents. Then she starts all over again to teach them better after the darkness is gone.

142

Consider how you'd feel if you were burned alive and tortured just because your eyes were green or because of some unusual birthmarks or moles on your body (presumed signs of witchcraft). You think you would have chosen it, especially knowing that the horror of the hatred and violence would shatter your soul into a thousand fragmented pieces many of which still live in a fractured and terrified agony? Think again. So what was the Dark Ages reflecting to its "victims?" Possibly that they needed to take action earlier than they did. They believed too much in the right and established way of continuing on. But then again, possibly nothing . . . we often see mirrors without our reflection.

It was not practical to sink England and Europe at that time, so the Earth's atmosphere opened up just a little to let in more ultraviolet rays, causing some peoples' immune systems to weaken, and then the organisms to cause the plague simply spread throughout the land. Soon, the negativity was gone, and special souls came to the planet to help things advance, and the Age of Enlightenment was born.

Not only did the arts flourish, but sanitation was improved, and the Earth's acres were tilled in a more humane and charitable fashion (for awhile, anyway). Burning, torturing, and maiming people fell out of vogue (for awhile, anyway). The department of the Inquisition within the Papacy of the Catholic Church in Rome was set to intensive study of the legitimacy of miracles (and, of course, true miracles are always Catholic . . . we make a little joke!).

Not all diseases, plagues, and pestilence are so far-reaching or extreme, however. The Dust Bowl and grasshoppers of the 1930's were just a hint to farmers to change their farming practices. And because each disease has different characteristics, you can count on the fact that they do not occur for the same reasons.

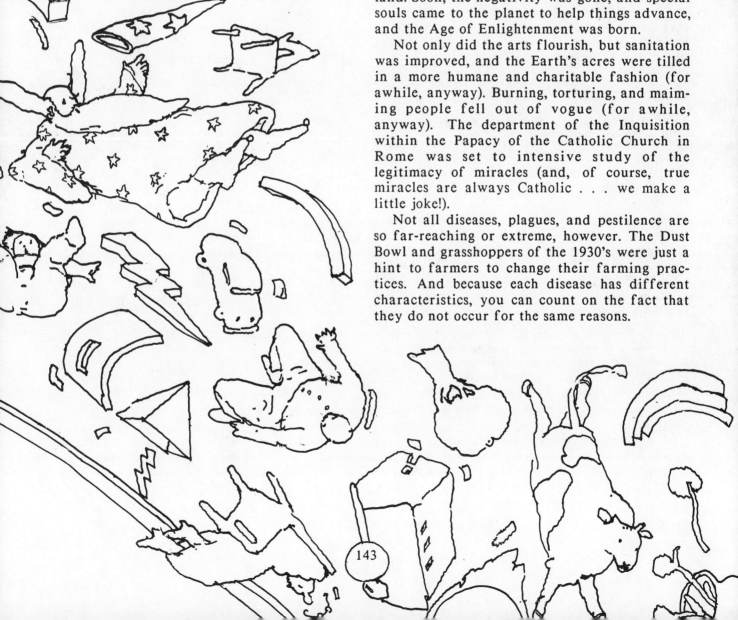

Consider the Earth's position. We know that lots of you think that the Earth is just a grody (we just love the new slang of this age!) dirt ball that you have to hang out on because of some karmic debt you owed to someone. We'd like to clear that one up. You don't get sent here because you've been bad. Rather you've been given the opportunity to be here to *learn* more about yourself. Not just any planet (as you well know if you look at the rest of your solar system) gets to have a life-form inhabit it. Many planets would just love to have visitors, but they're just not advanced enough. The Earth is very wise, patient, gracious, and beautiful. However, because it is a planet that has chosen free will as its mode of existence, that means occasionally the darkness gets out of hand. Then, as you know, Mother Earth bops everyone in the area and starts all over again.

The karmic and ultimate lesson in this sort of situation is not to go along with the crowd, and to do what you know in your own heart is right. Furthermore, in case you ever have the chance to die knowing you are right (in the light), it is far less traumatizing than to die not really knowing why this is happening to you. This doesn't happen too often, but for that rare occasion.

So what does all this business, including the Dark Ages, the Dust Bowl and such have to do with disease? Well, those souls on Earth, at that time, weren't aligned with the higher consciousness of the planet, and that caused a disharmony with the Earth, within themselves, and with each other. Hence, death, disease, and despair. And, of course, there are always floods, earthquakes, tidal waves, ice ages, shifting of the Earth's axis. Once the Earth quit having gravity for about fifteen minutes. Almost everyone drifted off a couple of miles, and when she turned it back on, SPLAT! That sure cleared the air for awhile.

Now you're probably wondering how the Earth can do all these rotten things. Well, it's like this. It is not Earth's opportunity to humor everyone and everything. The Earth has a karma and a path to travel in the Creation just as you do. The Earth is a free-will planet that has chosen the light. And with the recent shifts in energy aligning the planet to a closer harmony with others in the light, it will choose more and more carefully only to invite and retain those of you who also want to experience

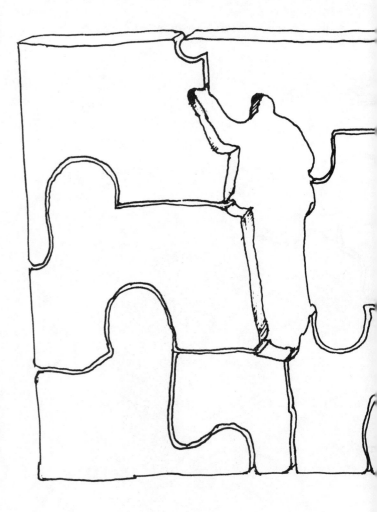

free will in the light. As we frequently say, gravity is a rare opportunity, an opportunity to experience the best that you can be out of choice, and choice only. Know, too, that if you choose not to be the best you can, you do risk the Earth evicting an ungracious tenant!

If you do want to stay, the solution is simple. Remember, you and your spirituality is a sacred trust. A Sacred Trust. *A SACRED TRUST!* We cannot say that to you and the rest of the world too often. To violate a sacred trust

is to induce illness, on a personal or large-scale social basis. To violate a sacred trust is to be less than clear and honest with yourself and others. Sometimes in history, it becomes endemic, in other words, everyone does it, like in the Dark Ages.

It is very common now, particularly in this society, to be less than clear and honest. The form that is taken now is in over-aggrandizing the ego under the guise of *identity,* or *self.* That over-aggrandizement has taken the form of guilt and suffering and their counterparts, overcoming guilt and victim-blaming. It is time to transcend both guilt and the need to release guilt, including all the victimhood/victimizer games and all the adamant insistence that *everything is perfect* in an attempt to control and confine to the comfort of your limited ego an unlimited, independent, ever-changing universe. It is your struggle to assign order to the universe that causes you such pain and suffering. Saying things are perfect is just imposing your own limited beliefs and desires on a reality that has its own right to be ... and to be free of your limitations. You may create your own reality, but you don't create reality for anyone or anything else. Just bear that in mind.

Many of you who believe in the New Age have been finding yourselves weakened and sickened and in conflict with things in your reality. And you have, in many cases, found this very disconcerting and confusing. For most, it is the over-aggrandizement of the ego in imposing your beliefs on the universe. When you can give that up, you will find that many of you with fear-related diseases (kidney diseases, some cancers, obesity) will become well. You will have more energy and more focus on the important aspects of life such as *being uniquely you.*

When you can give up your ego-involvement of wanting to force things to fit your picture, to be a certain way, and when you can listen to your higher self and the harmony of the universe, you will find yourself with a renewed vigor and energy, and you will find the planet a much more hospitable and accommodating place to live. When you do this, you will be exercising the right use of *Will,* a term you will hear more and more about as the energy continues to shift on the planet.

How to do this? Do your best and have a balanced mind and heart so that you know what you really think and feel at all times. By

The key to good health is harmony with your fellow humans and all other inhabitants of Earth, maintaining a good relationship to Earth, your higher self, the Creator, any visiting extraterrestrials, and being generally joyful in being.

best we do not mean the New Age "everything is perfect" best. That and the popular tendency to judge "victims" are not as much in the light as you think. It leads to people using those phrases in the most outrageous ways to manipulate and exploit others when they really know *all* the rest, even prayer and meditation, chanting, fasting, vegetarianism, and crystals are optional. If they make you feel good, do them. Just know that if you're not doing your very best, living in the light as best you can, and clear on what you think and feel, you are not being a gracious visitor to Earth, and she just might ask you to leave . . . rather suddenly.

But not to worry. Earth has a sense of humor (she puts up with all of us, doesn't she--you on her surface--we in her atmosphere?), and she will be patient if you stumble as long as you are earnestly trying. When you insist that everything around you is just "perfect," this means that you have become complacent, and if you won't try, Earth becomes impatient.

A final note to so many of our California friends. Please quit putting so much fearful energy into *the big one.* Your energy is giving the Earth such a cramp there that she'll have to flex her muscles in a big way to relieve it. We don't think that's what you really want!

Let us tell you a true story that happened in your time frame. In 1984 there was a rather large earthquake (in your terms) in the United States in a state not generally known for its earthquakes. (We're not going to tell you where. It's up to your geological and geographical sincerity to find out the details.) Anyway, the Earth was feeling a little cramped and had to do a few jumping jacks to feel better. And the people in that state, who were all pretty much

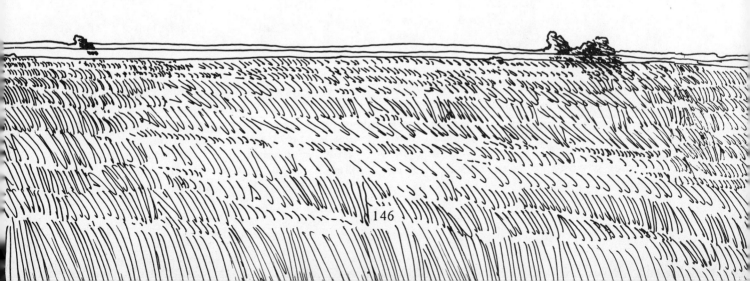

146

in tune with the Earth, did jumping jacks with the Earth. Here's what happened . . . NOTHING! The cows and other animals had noticed and said, "Gosh, isn't this exciting!!" A few people noticed their hanging plants moving, and said, "Gosh, how nice for the plants!" But that's about it. Damage? None. In fact, your earthquake enthusiasts and experts from somewhere else had to tell this little state what had happened and that they were sitting on a newly discovered major fault line. The people just said, "Oh, isn't that interesting." End of that earthquake story. You see, they like the Earth, and the Earth pretty much likes them. They try to do their best, and they're pretty clear on their thoughts and feelings. That's all it takes, you see.

The key to good health is harmony with your fellow humans and all other inhabitants of Earth: a good relationship to Earth, your higher self, the Creator, any visiting extra-terrestrials, and general joy in being.

And the rest of it? The misery, disease, death, destruction, fear, and despair? It's nothing in the face of doing your very best with a clear mind and heart. It's just that simple.

AIDS

"There will be no major cure found for AIDS because it is a soul experience, individually and collectively. It is a natural evolutionary process and will not be cured before it has gone about its natural cycle and done what it was designed to accomplish." ... Dr. Peebles

Robbyn and His Merrye Bande: AIDS is a rather simple response to a whole category of issues facing the planet right now that are causing more than their fair share of confusion. There are solutions to this confusion, and AIDS is only one (of the hardest) of them. It is one way for the planet to ease her pain. It is exactly for this reason that AIDS is occurring.

As we often say, gravity is a rare opportunity, but with it comes the potential for physical manifestation that many do not want to acknowledge including the Earth's right to fight back once in awhile by producing elements that will annihilate bodies that do not really wish to be here.

It's like this. With density, (a physical body) comes several parts (actually there are millions if you go cell for cell, but we want to talk about a more global level first). As you all know, you are a soul with a physical body; you don't *have* a soul, you *are* one. When you decided that you wanted to incarnate on Earth, you agreed to abide by the physical laws on the planet at that time, (laws of gravity, thermodynamics, vibrational blending, and so on) and that meant that if you chose to be an intelligent human life-form, you would have, roughly, two arms, two legs, two eyes, working parts, a heart, kidneys, lungs--the usual stuff. Part of the original equipment is a will, consisting of emotions and feelings, and an intellect, consisting of thoughts and intuitive abilities.

Now, put that together with a soul, moving through the cells at all times, (and no, your body is not connected to your soul by some metaphysical rubber band that hangs you out down here in the dirt. Your soul is the spark plug, the energy and the light, the twinkle in your eye.) and you've got your basic human. Your soul is here in the sand box with you, unless you're sleeping, astral traveling, or dead. So mix that up with obscure memories of previous incarnations, throw in a dash of this life's purpose, and we must admit, all you little sweethearts out there are pretty complex organizational units!

And believe us, there is nothing more delightful than a well-balanced, happy human with all parts intact and functioning. We mean this in a spiritual sense, not a physical one. A person can be handicapped or maimed (your word for their choices) and be perfectly spiritually balanced. The whole universe (and we do mean this literally) smiles on a happy well-balanced human.

So how to get all the parts happy and functioning and moving in the right direction? Anything less is disease.

Well, one thing is that human beings must have the opportunity to love. Yes, humans *need*

love. We cannot overemphasize this enough. It's part of what you agreed to experience on this planet, so you do need it--unconditional, conditional, from us (your guides), from the universe, the Creator, each other, pets, your planet, and anywhere else you can get it, but, most importantly, from yourself.

Humans also need to freely express their will, their feelings, emotions (all of which have gotten a lot of bad press in the last few centuries). And, finally, humans must exercise their intellectual faculty. They *must* think and dream. They must exercise their intuitive ability.

And that's all it takes to be human. Yup. It's as simple as that. But you see, since there are so few essential elements, they are all *very important*. If one part is even slightly off, it can create problems. And that can cause disease. And it is very popular in America (and elsewhere) today, to ignore many of these simple needs, especially expression of will (although intellect has taken quite a beating here lately, by people who want to express their will inappropriately.) And expressing will is so easy! Will is not the evil, awful, and wicked demon some have deemed it to be, but it is allowing the passion, enthusiasm and joy that is in each one of us to be expressed in the direction we have chosen for our life purpose.

For some it is printing or writing; for others it is the search for excellence in all things; for still others, it is expressing through parenthood or devotion to a spiritual purpose. And within those broader categories, it is always, always being in touch with your feelings, emotions and (and this is a very important connection) knowing what you think and what your intuitions are. Because the planet is based on density, you'd be surprised at how often you do not know what you really think and feel. It's easy for you to ignore what's *inside* because you have a body that attracts your attention *outside*.

If you don't know what is going on with you inside, you are open for negative thoughts and feelings to overwhelm you mentally and, eventually, physically. Those negative thoughts will do this by causing separation from all or some

part of yourself. And this is very, very sad. Usually, it takes the form of self-judgment, self-hate, misunderstanding self, self-ridicule or some other form of self-denial. And you can't stay immune to the cost of abusing yourself in some form, forever. And the collective mindset of the planet right now is to abuse self (and therefore others), and it is costing a lot to the Earth in general.

Whoever named it AIDS, did so on divine inspiration. "Acquired Immune Deficiency Syndrome." More and more individuals' spirits are no longer immune to the mindset of judgment and self-abuse and alienation from their parts that they have been taught and are caught up with. By the way, all disease on this planet has to do with the breakdown of the immune system for the same reasons, it's just that AIDS has confounded your abilities to fix it because AIDS is the extreme and ultimate self-denial.

People have asked, time and time again, why so many gay men have contracted the disease. That's easy. There is male energy and there is female energy. Male and female energy is like energy in magnets. The two different polarities attract their opposite energy and repel their same polarity. So it is with male and female energy. By nature, they attract. For men to love men in the male/female way or for women to love women in the male/female way is to work against their natural repulsion or tendency to draw apart. Since this, terra firma, is a planet of feminine energy, the females have less to overcome in a woman/woman bonding. For men, the extra stress is telling.

People unconsciously recognize and understand the male/female bonding principle. And because it is part of everybody's opportunity on the planet to be able to reproduce, people judge this obvious denial of this natural attraction as "unnatural." And for most people, it is. However, there are some for whom it is the chosen path. They wanted to experience the life of overcoming the male/male or female/female resistance. And they are doing fine. Even if they contract (we mean this literally) AIDS, they will do fine because they chose that coming into this life. They will re-group and go on without struggle and pain and suffering.

Now, here is where this gets very confusing. There are also others who have *chosen* a gay life-style for very unclear reasons during the course of their incarnation. Mind sets are very strong on this planet, particularly that of looking outside yourself or your spiritual team for guidance and definition. Many people who incarnated as post-war baby boomers have done this, and they are checking out before their

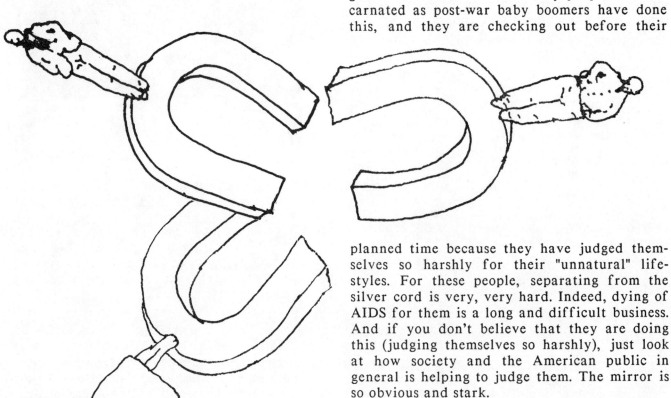

planned time because they have judged themselves so harshly for their "unnatural" life-styles. For these people, separating from the silver cord is very, very hard. Indeed, dying of AIDS for them is a long and difficult business. And if you don't believe that they are doing this (judging themselves so harshly), just look at how society and the American public in general is helping to judge them. The mirror is so obvious and stark.

And what of the heterosexuals or children with AIDS? Well, in most cases, they have judged themselves to that point or have chosen a life with a long protracted illness in order to come to a greater conscious understanding of what life is.

Again, to be clear, *whatever people do is fine*. But if people are doing things outside of their timing or outside of their life plan, they run a greater risk of confusing themselves. So, if they hadn't planned to be gay or have AIDS, and if they've acted out a gay life-style or contracted AIDS somehow, then they run a greater risk of confusing themselves because this may be at odds or taking away from what they had planned for themselves and then they'll want to come back again and do what they didn't do.

And that brings us to a very important point. You hear a lot about how things are just "perfect" as they are. And in the sense that "perfect" (for lack of a better word) means that which correlates to objective reality, in the sense that it means what you *could* do at the time, given your blocks and understanding. But in the sense that "perfect" means "ideal" or "optimum," forget it.

Many of you have interpreted this concept to mean that things are hunky-dory. That was never intended to be the case. This concept was just given to you to help alleviate the guilt and blame you put on yourself . . . to lessen the judgment. However, many of you have done yourself and others great harm by taking this concept and letting it go to the other extreme. When you do this, your body and soul find it very hard to keep up with each other, and damage is done. Sometimes you have been known to use this option that "everything is perfect" like a baseball bat against someone else's head, or against the Earth, or you say, "Well, I was inspired," or, "My guides said so," or, "In my heart, it's right. I'm at peace and clear with my decision." (Don't you wish!)

Well, we don't quite know how to break this to you, but when you do this to other people, in your perfect world, it's perfectly perfect for them to slug you right back (you do it to yourself) through a direct hit, or through their thoughts. They hit back and it will affect you because you generated it in the first place, even

if they *asked* you to hit them. In your perfect world, it is perfectly perfect for them to change their minds and retaliate. (Yes, we know this is filling some of your little hearts with dread and terror, but relax, for every problem, there is a solution.) The more serious problem, though, the real kicker is, if you didn't really

feel quite as assured of your rightness as you thought, you subconsciously attract your own violence (physical, psychic, emotional, mental, spiritual, whatever) back to you. When it hits home, it hits harder than anyone or anything else could possibly hit you. You are never, ever immune to yourself.

The more negative your outlook (to yourself and others), the more likely you are to contract AIDS. This may sound very hard, but there is a way out, should you decide not to be ill. First, here is how you get AIDS.

You get AIDS if you are denying yourself, punishing yourself, judging yourself, hating yourself, lying to yourself, and in general, negatively abusing yourself to such an extent that your body can no longer tolerate the stress of the melodramas you've created, or your soul can no longer communicate with your body or vice versa or because you are so far off your path that you're convinced that you can't get back in this lifetime. Or your will is stifled or your intellect runs rampant. (Usually, you will interpret this as the outside world being hostile to you.) So you decide to save time, check out, and try to get back to what it is that you were *really* going to do in this lifetime.

The more you struggle against it, the more you sorrow with your disease, the more you regret it, is the extent to which you are off your beaten path. Those who learn quietly and softly with the disease have probably chosen it, and it was part of their plan.

Your own behavior and acceptance of the circumstances are the key to whether now is the time for you to experience AIDS or not.

If not, there are ways, if you sincerely want to, to reverse and/or avoid this illness (and others).

Bartholomew: We cannot say there is only a single meaning for this particular situation called AIDS. One part of the answer is to say that many people need to move into a deep understanding of *their own* sexuality--what it means to them and how they can live their lives most creatively and abundantly with this energy. So in one sense, sexuality is the issue, but not in the way the negative mind would have it.

There has to be a way for mankind, *as a whole*, to look within and ask a basic question, "How do I live my sexual life most dynamically and with the most awareness and clarity?" That the issue is sexual is obvious, and it is around AIDS that it is coming into focus. It is an issue, quite frankly, that has been lying asleep for a long time. From the Victorian era, sexuality has been very regimented in this part of the world. Few people have had a chance to ask them-

selves what *they* think about it. They have had other people or organizations telling them what they *should* think.

Whenever there is a necessity to look at an area of consciousness which is buried, something like AIDS will come into creation. The physical condition know as cancer has been prevalent in recent years. Out of it has come an understanding that the medical model is not perfect, that there has to be a deep commitment on the part of each individual to decide what life is bringing to his or her body. How can you live in a way that is harmonious with your own energy field? What decisions do you need to make to keep yourself free of this condition? Until recently, the medical model was almost totally omnipotent because everyone believed in it without question. But doubt will always have to come whenever you place your power outside of yourself. *Doctors do not keep you free of cancer. You do.* On some level you all know this.

All right then, what is the lesson about AIDS? You will find out when you begin to examine your ideas about sexuality. And beyond that, decide what it means to live your life dynamically--becoming responsible for your choices and knowing there is always risk involved. Because sexuality falls into the physical arena, and because the end-product at this time is so horrendous, AIDS has gotten everybody's attention, just as cancer did when it first appeared.

I believe you have the capability to come up with a solution to the dilemma as far as the physical body is concerned. So instead of moving into fear, *watch* what is happening. People who move into fear *move into exclusion.*

Many difficult things are surfacing because of AIDS, and you are going to have to start addressing the issues beyond the sexual realm. For example: the fear of children in the schools catching AIDS from a schoolmate. Is it realistic? Is it not? There are many judgments around the segment of the population manifesting this illness. Where do you stand with *your* judgments? Many such things are being brought into question. Please do not be simplistic and say, "AIDS means so and so for this planet." The question is what does it mean for you? Ask yourself what deep fears it brings up in your psyche. Take the responsibility of asking yourself, "What do I feel? What do I intend to do in my life around this question?"

There has always been some major movement in the world that takes away life. Cancer is terrible, but the understanding of it is now different because clarification is beginning to unfold. Now, dynamic choices are being made around this disease. I am not saying it is wonderful that cancer is here. I am simply observing there are *victorious ways to deal with all the difficulties* that come into your planet. And I feel you must take the responsibility for discovering what perceptions and fears the issue of AIDS brings up for you so you can be victorious. Start dealing with them on your own. If you want to help the whole situation, you can help best by understanding what it all means to you.

There is another part of the question to bring forward here, and it is this. Why are so many alive, vital people suddenly dying? I realize, from your perception, death can be a very negative issue. But I would like to remind you of something you already know. Death can be a moment of absolute heroic wonder, beauty, and clarity *when experienced from an empowered position.*

Tasteless as it is, war is one opportunity to experience death from an empowered position. There is no overt war going on now for your country. Please understand, *as a positive statement*, there have to be ways for young people to die. There has to be a victorious way for young people to leave the earth plane. Outside of suicide and war, what is left are accidents and illnesses, which have always been here and always will be, in one form or another.

Death remains an opportunity. I understand the agony and I know how it feels, but an entity chooses to die when it realizes the maximum moment for death is *appropriate*. There is a time when all things move into equilibrium and death is best. The momentum is maximum for doing what needs to be done. The mental, the physical, and the emotional are in a state of

readiness and the necessity is there. And the willing choice is made on a deep level.

Someone walks down the street and a brick drops on his head. You wonder if it is a caprice. But no, there is an inner knowing of the appropriateness of that action. For those

Many people who are dying of AIDS are dying victoriously, with a tremendous amount of power.

left behind, it looks dismal or difficult. Nevertheless, people choose what is available out of the repertoire of choices. I don't mean to be simplistic, but there are only a certain number of choices. When the entity decides it's time to go, it looks around and picks a way. When it is not necessary to stay, staying is inappropriate. Painful, but correct.

Never say someone dies to help someone else. That is not the truth. A consciousness dies because it is time. You will know this directly when you start to die. You will say, "I am not dying so only that person can benefit. I am dying because I need to, because there are certain things in my mechanism that say it is time. The off-ramp is present and I am going."

You look around and make your choice--lightening or something equally as dramatic. You take what's there, what is available, *what will teach you.* And you pick from the choices of mankind.

Many people who are dying of AIDS are dying victoriously, with a tremendous amount of power.

There *will be a solution*, a cure, at which time the intensity of this opportunity will no longer be available.

So look at it from the positive side, you will see that people need to have creative choices on how to leave this planet. It is empowering to say, "I've got five months to live--and I am going to live like a warrior. I am going to get my life in order. I am going to be powerfully alive to the end." That is a dynamic and aware way to die. When the cure comes, people will get well and other opportunities will have to present themselves. Right now it is a victorious choice for many people.

It is fashionable today to say that AIDS is God's punishment against those practicing male homosexuality. I would present another point of view for your consideration; is it not possible that the message to the western world at large is to examine their judgments against a minority, and to ask if it might be this very *judgment* that has put the minority in a weakened state and thereby susceptible to disease? Since it is a *sexual judgment*, would it not be in the sexual arena that such disease would manifest? Is it possible this need not have happened if compassion and understanding had been present rather than isolation and condemnation? If you wish to participate in finding a "cure" for a situation whose roots involve all of mankind, consider working deeply on removing those pieces of judgment on this issue that reside in *your* mind. Such is the nature of true service to mankind.

The Black Plague

Ramtha: This pertains to your tomorrow.

There was a year in your counting; it was called 1348. And there was a place called Europe. Know you were that is? It is sort of a conglomerate of diffused boundaries. Well, there was a great war within many of these boundaries, and the war was the war of Catholicism against Judaism. Those which were Catholic did not like those which were Jew, for they blamed them for *crucifying* their Lord. And yet Yeshua ben Joseph had said, "Behold! I have come to *fulfill* the prophesy." Without what happened at Jerusalem, Yeshua *never* could have achieved that. They forgot that.

During these times, the Jews within these countries were being forced to convert to a religious belief, Christianity. Those who did not convert were hated by the people who were the "good" Christians, who then slaughtered, mutilated, maimed, burned, and destroyed

156

them. (Very "godlike," wouldn't you say?) All through this place called Europe, the air was polluted with the stench of burning carcasses and bloody, mutilated, rotting bodies on the road. (Perhaps that is where the devil was "born" and where "hell" got its deepest meaning.) Whole groups of frenzied, fickle people rioted and participated in the murder of Jews because someone told them that if they did, God would *love* them.

A most peculiar thing happened in 1348. There came on the shores of that continent a horrid thing. A disease was born. It came out of *nowhere*, and it consumed over 25 million people, one-third of the population, in just one decade. This most odious of plagues did not have religious preferences. The Church said it was a curse of God upon the heathens, but the Christians died too. It ate away at the Catholics, it ate away at the Orientals, it ate away at the Jewish people. It had no religious preferences. The only preference it had was that it devoured only those with the attitude of hatred, bigotry, and decadence.

Now, in your light, you are "known" by your attitude. And magnetically, you draw to you what you are. That is the *law*, because you are God. That is why the plague consumed only those entities.

The plague, called the Black Plague, was a reprisal from nature against those whose attitude had collapsed below the survival level. You can war against nature just so long before it declares war on you. In other words, life is going to get rid of those who do not go forward. So, the disease got rid of them, one-third of the population.

So deadly was this disease that they had to turn their attention away from their bigotry to base survival. They had to *redefine* what was important.

Now, you use barely one-third of your brain. Did you know that? And one-third mind is the lowest point man can fall to before the human race becomes extinct. In other words, you are now *below* survival. Your society is into decadence, perversion. You rape your children. You defile your women. You men molest one another. You brutalize sex, eroticize violence, and you sell fear in the marketplace--and you are *insensitive* to it! When you are insensitive to it, it means you are living in decadence, below survival.

In 1348, they too were below survival; they had slipped into decadence. What kind of entity beheads a babe because its mother will not convert? Hmmmm? That is not being concerned with *survival*; that is decadence! Well, you have slipped into decadence liken unto that of the year 1348.

You are all God. And when gods begin to have inward collapse, so comes what I call the "War of Valued Life." There are plagues now upon your land; and from those plagues are growing more plagues. They will never be cured, and they will take from the world one-third of your population before the end of your next decade. That is how it is seen at this moment in time.

These plagues aren't something that comes from outer space! *You created them!* Your body is trying desperately to keep you together, but you are tearing it apart by always criticizing it! It is either too fat or too thin or too old or the wrong sex. When you do that, what is your body going to do with you? It can only stand so much pressure. Either it's good enough or it isn't! If you don't allow it to be what it is, it's going to get rid of you. A little plant with a frog upon its leaf, the caterpillar and the butterfly, the black stallion with fiery nostrils--it is the life force within them that is declaring war on you, because you are corrupting and impeding the evolutionary process called Forever. And in that war, masters, Life will win, always.

The plagues are new here, and you created them, because you are degrading your body and spirit; you are collapsing inwardly. Thus you are going to die.

Ominous? In some ways it is, depending upon how limited you are. The plague is here, and there are many who will not escape it, because they will not get out of the boxes of social consciousness to become Life again. That is the way that you overcome it. It is the *only* way--through virtue, noble virtue.

157

This is an important topic that has been evaded by many. You have been patronized, stroked, and complemented into dying. You have not had to face history, soul memories, and your "now" in such a vivid and painful understanding.

So, that is your destiny, as it is seen at this moment. Now *what* did I just say? *As it is seen this moment.* Your destiny is seen because the shadow of it is cast by your attitudes. Everything you think manifests, and the plagues are the *result* of your thinking, of your attitudes, if you will. In the tomorrow of your time, the whole of the world *could* be lifted by a grand experience--at least up to the point of survival.

Your consciousness has fallen below survival into decadence. When you come back up to survival, the disease will go away. You have the power to change it *at any moment.*

How do you change this most ominous shadow? By *loving* what you are. Loving yourself means to hold yourself in the grandest and highest esteem. It means to *know* you are endowed with divinity, to know you are endowed with a greater mind, to know you are brilliant and that you possess genius. Loving yourself means to know that you are, above all, endowed with life. Life! Without it, you are a "no" thing.

You women, for so long you have survived because of your uterus, your vagina, and your breasts. Your body has been your survival. Stop giving your bodies away. It is the hour that you say that you will survive because you are embracing *life*, as an equalness in God. That is loving what you are. When you learn to love yourself, you will not need to grab hold of someone else to make you happy or to take care of you. Then you are free, independent.

And men, you don't have to go out and copulate everything to impregnate the whole world! (In your soul memory, that equates being a man.) You don't have to spill your seed every single day! Every moment you do that, you are *dying*. You have to master the desire to molest your brothers so that you feel you have power over them. When you master those things, that is loving who you are. See women as equals, as brilliant gods, just as you are. That *changes* the

shadow, the destiny; that allows you to go forward in harmony with Nature.

In 1348, when the plague had finished its ravages, a new consciousness appeared. It was a new understanding, a change, a difference. It is the same with this age that you are in. When the decadence that is now upon this plane has left, there will emerge a new consciousness and a new mind. It is called Superconsciousness. The mind will bloom, and the Christus in *all people* will come forth--the realization in all people that they are God. That is the true meaning of the second coming of Christ: "And behold, there came forth a new kingdom and a new Earth. And in that kingdom reigns the Christ, forever and ever and ever."

This is the destiny of your good Earth.

Evolutionary cycles

Dr. Peebles: The evolutionary processes on the planet earth affect not only the human beings, but the plants, animals, and the planet itself. Not only are all the physical and tangible elements affected, but all of the invisible levels as well. The life on the planet, as well as the life in the planet (yes, within the Earth) are affected.

The process of evolution is interconnected totally with all life; therefore, that which affects one human being also affects all life forces, all life elements. There is not *one illness* that manifests that cannot be traced to the growth, the evolution of all species, all minerals, all plants, and all energies upon the planet earth.

Now, let us take a look at that which you call AIDS. This exists, not only on this planet, but on others as well. And it is not new upon this planet or in this era. It can be traced to other times and places; however, it was not known as AIDS because your medical technologies and the scientific evolutionary developments were not capable of adequately defining so many of these viruses and infections. I would say that AIDS is more obvious now and it is being more clearly defined.

It is epidemic of nature; an epidemic which is going to continue for a long period of time. It will be many years before the cure is to be found. By the time the cure is found, the virus itself will have gone through another mutation so it will not be as deadly nor confining. At this point the virus will affect on still another level. The next evolutionary growth of the AIDS virus will not be an epidemic nature as it is in the current era.

This illness coincides with the cycle of evolution that our planet is going through. There is presently a major era shift taking place, from the Piscean Age to the Aquarian Age. People are actually calling upon major configurations so that life will have the *need* to evolve from the Piscean intellectual attitude into the Aquarian spiritual/mental self, the higher self as opposed to the personality, ego/self manifestation.

Also, at this time, there is a major grid alignment occurring within the planet, and it is approaching a major shift of the axis. This vibration has not been on the planet, at this level, for nearly 11,000 years. That calls for a major cleansing process. The appearance of this illness does not mean that humans have failed in the eyes of God. It is because there is need of cleansing. Many souls need it for their fulfillment. Yes, they need it! They *chose* to come into this lifetime for it. They chose bodies that would be exposed to the illness. They chose bodies that would be able to incubate it, that would be able to transfer it, that would be able to manifest it to the degree of illness and even to the transition that you call "death."

Now here is an important point: each and every living human being has the AIDS virus within them. Each and every living being transfers that virus to others on a daily basis. Many of those who have it, in fact the mass majority, never have any symptoms. Many people to whom it is transferred, on a daily basis, will never have symptoms from it. Their natural genetic instincts reject it and counteract it. If your souls chose bodies that would automatically reject it, you do not need it. You will not experience it even if you were to have direct and living contact with an overt carrier of the powerful AIDS virus in its negative manifestation.

I am also suggesting that in this cleansing process, those bodies who have the illness, those bodies who become carriers, those bodies that make the transition, it is for them little more than giving their souls the opportunity for *their* evolutionary process. It is also part of the collective growth of the planet, for it must be cleansed. The planet must lose many of its population and it will be accomplished not only through this illness, but also through many Earth upheavals, through geographical shifts, etc.

I am suggesting that the human being intellect, the human being ego, is overreacting to a natural evolutionary process that they chose to be part of. Many of those who are saying, "Oh, I am frightened. Oh, I'm alone. Oh, I'd better look out for this," are actually counteracting their natural, instinctive immunity system to the virus. And they are calling upon this illness when it isn't even theirs. This activates a stronger element of the intensity of this illness and its manifestation.

Every living human being has the AIDS virus in them, just as they have the cancer virus. And AIDS is little more than a mutation of the existing cancer that each and every one of you have within your bodies. Other life forms, animals, and plants have the AIDS virus. AIDS is transferred, not only through human contact, through the salivas or mucous membranes, but also is transferred through all proteins. Viruses existing within proteins that are actively manifesting the infection's quality are able to transfer cancer, AIDS, etc. You would find this true of protein in red or white flesh, including fish. AIDS and cancer are found to be transferred through the protein in certain vegetables as well. There are minerals, some even that are used in building materials, some that are used as jewelry and adornments, that carry some of these viruses and are able to infect other living beings.

Dear ones, AIDS is *nothing new*. It is an ancient illness that is only more clearly definable and is only more overt at this point because of the shift of energy that you are experiencing on the planet earth. There is no major cure to be found for AIDS *at this point* because it is a soul experience, individually and collectively. It is a natural evolutionary process and so it will not be cured before it has gone about its natural cycle and done what it was designed to accomplish.

I offer these concepts to you to consider, to evaluate. AIDS is not something to fear. It is something to recognize as little more than another opportunity for souls to be fulfilled. If you look back on all of the great plagues or the great wars, you would see that they were elements that led us to evolutional consciousness. The same will be true of AIDS in retrospect.

The gay community - pioneers and mirrors

Dr. Peebles: You are all intensely aware of the homosexual society manifesting AIDS. AIDS is actively transferred and has been around for many generations, though undefined, through those who are *not* homosexual. I would say that already in your Western worlds, including the United States, AIDS was existing in many forms, in many people, before it was considered to be a sexual disease. *It is not a sexual disease.* Sexuality is certainly a way of transmitting it, but it is not a sexual disease. It is not a curse upon the homosexuals, and it is also not that homosexuals are doing a specific "service" to humanity. The illness was there. The illness is going to manifest with or without homosexuality.

The anxieties and the fears of the homosexuals have a more active association on a physical contact level; the mucous membranes, the saliva, the bloods. Combining these elements with their fears, their anxieties, many implanted by parents and society, makes them more susceptible. Your societies have implanted so much anger, guilt, and frustration in homosexual contacts that you have actually made them the vulnerable point.

I do not terribly approve of the term "victim." I am saying they are not victims of other attitudes, for they do not have to take those attitudes as their own. They become victims, if such a thing is possible, of their own willingness to become over-influenced, over-reactive to their own programming and training. Certainly, if you are looking for a common denominator, it is the lack of acceptance, the lack of growth, the lack of willingness to accept the homosexuals as human beings, growing in their own time, space, and way.

And so, if you are looking for a common denominator, it would be the negative programming of people who chose to be exactly what they are. Remember, my friends, that homosexuals *chose* that. It was not designed after they were born. It is the same for them as it is for the saint, the spiritual/religious leader, the prostitute, or the thief. They chose bodies long before they were born. They should be allowed the same.

Dong How Li: It is important for you to understand and to have some sense of an overview about homosexuality, since AIDS appears to be rampant in the gay community. If heterosexuality is the norm, so to speak, then homosexuality and bisexuality are the contraries. Now, what the contrary does is to provide a mirror. The mirror is designed to show the opposite, the reflection, or a different perspective of what is the so-called "norm."

Now, I have a great question about what is the definition of norm, as it usually means statistical. What is different from the numbers, the norm, in this case, is homosexuality or bisexuality. That which is not part of the norm is, by nature, designed to reflect back to the majority that which the majority is *disowning*, what the majority is *not* doing. So, therefore, I am going to define norm as that which is normal and possible in nature. Homosexuality, bisexuality, and all the varieties of sexual expression are possible and indeed natural and normal, regardless of the statistics.

What is happening here has partly to do with the attempt to show so-called "straight" people what they have disowned within themselves. First and foremost, this applies to men, because they are the primary vehicle for AIDS now in this culture, to show men what they have disowned in their relationships with each other. Many straight men, to this day, do not wish to know about brotherhood, do not want to deal with affection between men from fear of it becoming sexual. The fear of it becoming sexual means they disown all of this whole way of being with each other.

This denouncement, this renouncement, this repression, promotes violence, promotes competition, and even promotes a way of relating to women that is unfulfilling to both men and women.

Now, if the statistical norm--straight men--accepted this way of relating with each other, which is fuller and more balanced, the catch is, it need not necessarily be sexual. It might be occasionally sexual but it would not be rampant, and that is what the fear is. But the fear is unjustified. What makes homosexuality rampant is the initial repression that forces it outside of the self into something else.

The norm becomes fixated in heterosexuality, rather righteously, and the opposite, or that which is contrary, does the same. It becomes fixated in *its form of expression*. Neither one is truly appropriate. Both are truly stuck. Neither is capable of experiencing the *full range* of human love and its physical expression.

You now have a disease in the homosexual community that is attacking the immune system. It is as if the homosexual community is saying, "We don't know what to fight, we don't know how to fight. We are open to invasion by something that is weak outside of the body, but inside of the body is most deadly."

The gay people are on the frontier, so to speak. They are outside the statistical norm. They are disrespected, rejected, and disowned. And it is the disowned aspect of the norm which places them on the frontier. This is true about any oppressed group. Because it is contrary and a mirror, it reflects back that which is diseased in the culture. In this culture, however, it is not respected because no one wants to own that which has been disowned.

The appearance of this disease, on this particular frontier, suggests what is already wrong in the male population in this culture. They do not know what they are fighting for anymore. They do not know how to love the softer aspects of their own maleness. Those secrets of being men are gone, lost. Straight men, like gay men, define masculinity for themselves, as well as others, by their cocks. The rest of the male heart is unknown.

The appearance of AIDS in this culture is opening up the possibility for shedding light on the unknown portion of the male heart.

Now, if you doubt what I am saying, just look at what is happening in the families of these gay men with AIDS. In most cases, it is forcing communication which was never possible before. It is forcing people to reconcile their differences in lifestyles, values, and judgments.

The lessons inherent in the disease have first to do with knowing what to fight, when, how, and who. Second has to do with reconnecting and reestablishing communication between the part of the male heart that is known with the part that is unknown. The part that is unknown has to do with brotherhood and cooperation between men. It does not necessarily need to be expressed sexually, although, as I have said

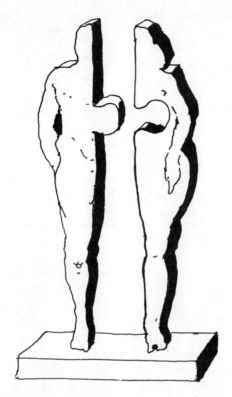

before, occasionally in nature that occurs and it is all right. It is only another aspect of the human psyche.

Any oppressed group exaggerates what is already in the culture.

For instance, those who criticize gay men for being promiscuous ignore the promiscuity among straight men where, in many cases, promiscuity is even honored. You see, that is the mechanism of disowning: "The problem is out there; therefore, I escape responsibility." That is obviously not true. One cannot escape that way because what is out there, *the mirror*, will push it back onto you. Those who are on the frontier get it first, but if the war is not fought on the frontier, it comes in behind the lines, does it not? Those on the frontier, in almost every other culture, are respected. That doesn't mean that you allow them to die for you. It means that you use what they are showing you to own within yourself.

Love is inclusive, not exclusive

Zoosh: AIDS is a cry for help and understanding by certain elements of your community in this country. It is a cry to bring about a greater understanding that loving awareness need not be *exclusive,* but can be *inclusive.*

On this planet, due to your religious and philosophical evolution of thought, there has been a polarity, a separation, a real challenge to be at home within both genders. In other words, there is no understanding that women have both female and male qualities, and that men have both male and female qualities. So, there is a basic separateness that has occurred between them on a physical level.

On many other planets, there is the total understanding that to be of oneself, it is possible to incorporate masculine and feminine traits within one body. This occurs more on an emotional, mental, and soul-light level than on a physical level. AIDS is nothing more than a dramatic sense of drawing attention by a particularly responsible segment of your community on this Earth.

Realize that your *now* experience on this planet is one in which the *squeaky wheel gets the grease*, so to say. It takes a drama in order to draw attention to the idea that something is being overlooked.

Many members of the gay community have gotten together at the soul or unconscious level to say, "Let us draw attention to the idea that love and loving has been very exclusive on this planet, up to now. Let us draw attention to the idea that it need not be so, that it can be much more inclusive, that it can be more simply a sharing of love between individuals who, in that moment, love each other." There need not be this great, almost apocalyptic disease idea.

It is as if a demonstration has been called for on a level at which beings from all sexual persuasions on this planet could come together and say that it is *all right* to love each other. It really comes down to this:

If everyone would care to include in their beliefs that it is all right for people to love each other physically, mentally, emotionally, and spiritually, then it may not be necessary to have any disease.

If it takes a demonstration like AIDS, by a community that is willing to make sacrifices in order to make the point clear, then so be it. But for all of you, including members of that community, demonstrations could be made by simply stating that it is all right to love each other. It is *all right* to love each other. Simply that. Understand that it could, if repeated over and over, become watchwords of inclusivity instead of perpetuating the exclusivity that has gone on.

Our need for experience

Enid: AIDS is an experience to remind us that this is a *finite world*. And at the same time you learn that this is a finite world, you're learning about your own infinity because

human beings are dying. They are just dying here and there and yet all the people associated with them are beginning to get closer to their infinity. In that sense, it reminds us of both ends of the spectrum of the finiteness of the world and the infinity of beingness. Even this world is finite because we don't intend it to last forever. There's a lot of forever, and this is just a spark of forever physically.

I think we can overblow this whole sense of what the meaning of AIDS is. If we could step back a little bit, we could see it as an experience, just as falling from a mountain and breaking your leg is an experience. It is not a greater experience nor is it a deeper experience than many other experiences. For instance, consider the mother whose son has never been found in a foreign war, and who doesn't know for sure whether he's dead or incarcerated somewhere. That mother's experience is just as deep or deeper than if her child had AIDS.

There are so many ways that we go through all of life's deep experiences.

And the experience of mystery and great wonder has been enlivened because of AIDS. We put a man on the moon, we took close-up pictures of Mars, and yet here is this incredible disease that we don't seem to be able to do anything about. That is because people are looking in the wrong direction. The right direction is from Spirit.

If you tell someone who has AIDS that he decided to have the experience, he'll probably hit you in the snoot. He'll say, "I certainly didn't want this." Well, in his awake state, he didn't. If we chose everything from our awake state, our lives would really be totally different. But we don't do that.

We are interacting with our reasons for being here. We are interacting with our own goals of what we expected our life experience to be. It is very important that these things be fulfilled. The surprise is *how* they are to be fulfilled.

For one, it's AIDS and for another it may be falling from a ship into the sea and staying there for three days before being rescued. It can be any manner of ways. It can be being lost in a cave for a week and trying to get out. There can be all kinds of ways in which the end product is achieved. Everything that you're reaching for is a part of your process.

Everything that you experience is a part of your own personal process.

Dr. Peebles: There is no major cure found for AIDS at this point because it is a *soul experience, individually and collectively.* It is a natural evolutionary process and so it will not be cured before it has gone about its natural cycle and done what it was designed to accomplish. So often the human mind says, "Oh well, this is a terrible thing. We're going to find a cure." Rather than becoming encouraged to live up to your soul's choices, you try to cure something that is incurable, something that is a part of the natural evolutionary process. AIDS is not, then, something to fear. AIDS is something to recognize as little more than another opportunity for souls to be fulfilled.

It is no more negative than the wars that have been, and the wars that will be. Many of you look back on all of the great plagues, and on the great wars and say, "Aha, but they were the elements that led us to evolutional consciousness." The same will be true, in retrospect, of AIDS.

My friends, AIDS is here and now. How do we deal with it now? If we want to deal with it, don't be afraid. Don't say, "Oh, my goodness, I must escape!" If you came into this lifetime to have it, you will have it whether or not you live in a cave for the rest of your life or whether or not you go out and carry on with every living human being, male, female, or otherwise. It is an *attitude*, and it is an attitude that must relate to your soul's needs and desires.

Finger-pointing

Dong How Li: When religious leaders point fingers and claim that God is punishing, ask yourself, "Who do they feel is God?" They themselves are God. The people who have AIDS are God. *We are all God.* So who is God?

The part of God they know is punishing. The part of God others know is enlightening and is teaching. The part of God that some AIDS patients are finding is a God of love and allowance.

There is no finger pointing from heaven and saying, "These people are evil." If there was a finger pointing from heaven commenting about who was evil, it would be pointed at those who *pass judgment* despite their very own religion and their very own Godhead, Jesus Christ. But, of course, they do not wish to look at this.

Remember that any sexual disease is called venereal. That means that it is a disease of love, named after the Goddess Venus. Does that make love evil? No. It means, however, that *how you love* needs to be looked at. So the finger here is saying, "Pay attention." It is not saying, "You are evil."

Zoosh: Understand that many of the religious and philosophical leaders have helped to bring about your current situation. They did so lovingly, believing that they were doing what people wanted them to do. In the same way that political leaders will not know what it is you want them to do until you make your opinions known to them, it is necessary for religious people to create somewhat of an outrageous statement, to really fly in the face of their religion. All religions sit on a base of love. If they do not sit on a base of love, they do not sit too long.

Condemnation flies in the face of the basic foundation of any religion. It is important for the world religious leaders to begin to know that their flocks do not wish to hear their fellow beings condemned.

It is no longer necessary to create a lesser class so that people who are insecure have someone who is lower than they are.

So, understand that the issue is not whether you choose to be a homosexual or not a

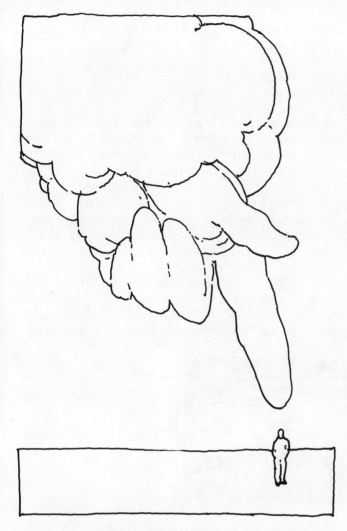

Dr. Peebles: The comments about punishment and God's wrath are another wonderful opportunity for the churches to validate their belief systems, to validate many of their own psychological anxieties, and to validate much of the programing that was imposed upon them. It also is another way to scare people back into the church to build their coffers.

Ramtha: So what about all those entities who are dying of the plague (AIDS) and of the war of nature that is becoming more and more? Well, there are those in religion who proclaim they are spokespersons for God; and they say, in the name of God, that these entities are being punished, that they are condemned.

I will tell you a great truth. These entities who are dying from the plagues are neither good nor bad. They are simply expressing a choice, and they are learning from that experience. It is something they wanted. They chose it and they got it. Is it not enough that these entities are dying a most painful, humiliating, and certain death without your sitting in judgment of them? Is that not *enough*?

These entities are God! And they *will live again* in another place, another time. They are not going anywhere to be tormented. Losing life is torment enough.

Let me ask you this: If the morning to come was your last morning, would you sleep in? Good question? What would you be doing? You would be living *every* moment. And while dawn was not so grand before, you would see it like you never saw it before. What did it take for you to appreciate its splendor? Knowing you would never see it again. Isn't it an irony that it takes disease and death to make you aware of life, the grandest gift of all?

Why do you wait for your *last* moments of life to appreciate it? These entities are counting down their mornings. The reason the disease is slow is that it allows them the painful review of their lives and the opportunity to come to peace and terms with that which is within them.

homosexual. The issue is that some believe the idea of love (physically and emotionally) between people of the same sex is fundamentally wrong. Love between individuals of the same sex or opposite sexes cannot be wrong. *Love is love.* Is love wrong?

The issue is communication. How will we know, as a society, that there are polarized points of view if they do not come to the surface in a dramatic way? This is similar to not putting a stop sign on a corner until after there have been a few accidents. You do not do something about a situation until it comes to the surface. This is the purpose of such apparent polarity.

Isn't it an irony that it takes disease and death to make you aware of life, the grandest gift of all?

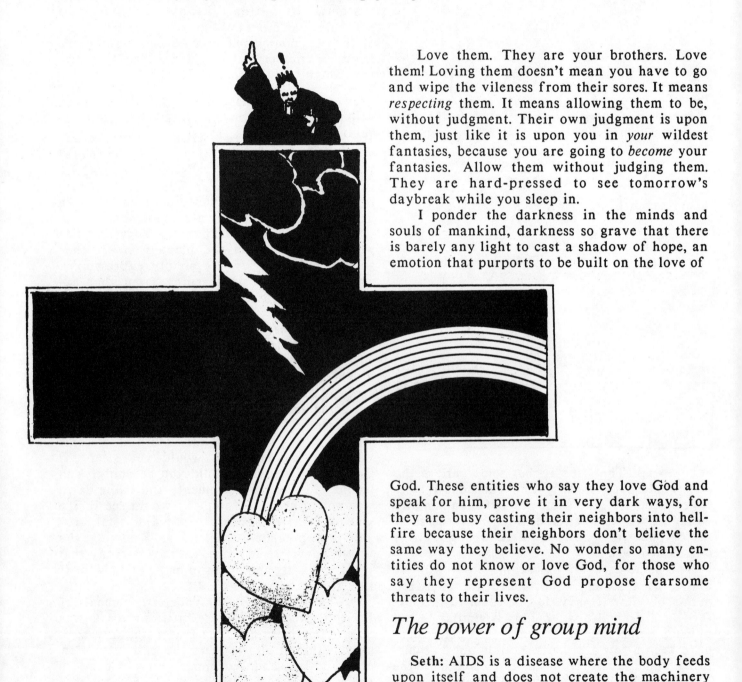

Love them. They are your brothers. Love them! Loving them doesn't mean you have to go and wipe the vileness from their sores. It means *respecting* them. It means allowing them to be, without judgment. Their own judgment is upon them, just like it is upon you in *your* wildest fantasies, because you are going to *become* your fantasies. Allow them without judging them. They are hard-pressed to see tomorrow's daybreak while you sleep in.

I ponder the darkness in the minds and souls of mankind, darkness so grave that there is barely any light to cast a shadow of hope, an emotion that purports to be built on the love of

God. These entities who say they love God and speak for him, prove it in very dark ways, for they are busy casting their neighbors into hell-fire because their neighbors don't believe the same way they believe. No wonder so many entities do not know or love God, for those who say they represent God propose fearsome threats to their lives.

The power of group mind

Seth: AIDS is a disease where the body feeds upon itself and does not create the machinery to fight disease. It is a dramatic manifestation of guilt, of the effects of the conscious mind's ability to affect the physical body with guilty thoughts through judgment. You had, previous to the emergence of AIDS, a so-called liberated time period in your society with free experimentation with sex and with drugs. So you created, through your group mind, a disease which appears to be transmitted sexually as well as in relation to drug use.

In other words, when you have strong group beliefs, strong social taboos, you cannot behaviorally act against them without the mind judging your behavior. We do not say there is any so-called *right* behavior, but your minds do.

It is judgment that is the disease on your planet. It is judgment that creates disease. It is any labelling of, "This is better than that," which creates lack of harmony. We pass no judgment upon sexual practices, upon any practices, but *your* minds do. They judge continually. If the mind were not judging the behavior, the subconscious mind would not believe there had to be punishment for aberrant behavior.

To be "safe" from AIDS in your society, it is necessary to not totally isolate yourselves, for that would be acting from fear. Acting from fear serves more to attract what is feared. Rather, it is necessary to continually process the mind, process the fears, become in touch with the fears, and formulate affirmations to neutralize them.

A great deal of self-forgiveness and forgiveness of others, a great deal of tolerance, and a great deal of lack of judgment is necessary to be safe from AIDS in your society.

AIDS cuts across national and social guidelines. It holds the potential for more and more people to deal with it from the point of view of creative thought, in terms of healing, since you have no known cure for AIDS at present, save the power of the mind. And since it is an international issue, it holds the potential for making avenues for peace possible as nations join together to pool their mental resources in regards to healing AIDS. And since you have a group mind belief that people pull together in crisis, to help to bring your planet together, you create a crisis or a problem to solve.

Now, in order to be safe from AIDS, it is necessary to adopt a high degree of self-love. It is necessary to comb the mind for all the beliefs you hold about others being able to hurt you. It is necessary for you to amplify your belief in self-determination. It is necessary for you to remember that hurt comes from the interpretation of hurt. Remember that you create everything that you bring into your lives. It is important, therefore, not to espouse a victim consciousness, because that can make you prey to AIDS.

The belief that you are a victim opens you up to believing that the source of health or life is outside yourself. Therefore, to be safe from AIDS, it is necessary to believe in your own power of creation of your reality. It is necessary that you believe *totally* in it, so that you do not fear that which is outside yourself. Recognize that your only enemy is the enemy within. By assiduous attention to your bodily responses, and the feelings beneath them, and the thoughts beneath those feelings, you can determine the system upon which your whole reality is based and *re-create it,* rearrange it to allow for health.

As you push beyond limitations, as you let go of a belief in can't and espouse the belief in can, then you go beyond limitation to possibility.

This is not the first time on your planet that group mind has created extinction-threatening disease. Certainly in more recent history, plagues have been manifestations of group mind--group guilt creating illness to create decimation.

Earlier on in the history of the planet, in ancient civilizations lost to history, when man first became aware of his separation from the rest of creation, or when his mind first determined that he was separate, there were time periods when groups of men and women created, from group mind, diseases which threatened their extinction. So, once again you

It is judgment that is the disease on your planet.

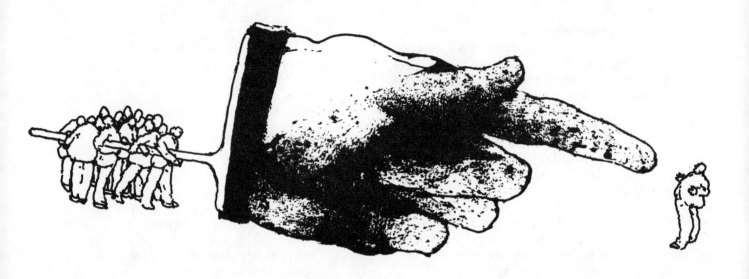

repeat a pattern from the past in order to heal it.

In terms of healing, let us mention the energy of harmonic convergence, which group mind created. In a sense, the solar system partly exists within your minds, and its alignment and its configurations are a reflection of group thought. With the energy of harmonic convergence on the ray of intuition operating upon the planet, and heightened awareness in the power of the mind, in the power of thought, and in the power of belief operating, you have the potential for healing AIDS.

For you see, AIDS is but a manifestation of what is taking place in society, in another sense. You are feeding upon the planet in such a way that it cannot renew itself. You tend to all settle in areas where you deplete the Earth, your mother, where you disturb the balance of nature rather than living in harmony with it.

And so, you have an illness that disturbs the balance of the body so that it cannot live in harmony with itself. It is a metaphor for what man, as a race, is doing on the planet. In order to heal AIDS, it is necessary to heal attitudes toward the Earth, your mother, and to treat her more respectfully (as you have begun to do), but as you have neglected to do for quite a while.

The germ of a possibility exists that things can, in time, shift back to a natural balance, a natural order. And it takes only one mind thinking balanced and orderly thoughts for many minds to begin to think them. This, then, initiates the desire to right the balance of nature, to right the balance of order on the planet, and this pervades group mind, bringing about a healing.

A so-called "cure" for AIDS will be discovered when enough have cured their thoughts about scarcity, about guilt, and about competition. I say competition because the way that you have treated the planet comes from a group belief in there not being enough.

To be healthy, it is important at all times to affirm your innocence, to release guilt, and to affirm being at one with the source of life.

To be healthy, it is important to breathe very consciously, and to take in the source of life in the breath, to allow it to cleanse the body and to be aware of how the planet needs to be aerated.

To be healthy, it is important, most of all, to be innocent and to see others as innocent as well. It is important not to judge good or bad, but to adopt a mind set of neutrality.

Becoming healthy can only be done by releasing all residue of emotions, by righting any un-righted memories and the memories stored in the consciousness which your mind can and does replay, interpreting yourself as victim, not as creator. And so, it is necessary that there be enlightened communities of beings on the planet who devote themselves to clearing their thoughts, clearing emotions out of their bodies, and clearing their energy fields that they may give off rays of harmony and peace to others to electromagnetically ignite their beliefs in harmony, peace, and healing.

Immunity from illness comes far more from what you think than from what you do.

We do not advise that you neglect the state of the art of health practices on your planet. We do advise that you understand you can do all physical practices to be in health and still become diseased if the thoughts are diseased.

We would advise that the *most* important activity is to be learning not to judge, to be learning not to evaluate yourselves or others, but rather, just to be in every moment and to *celebrate* your beingness, moment to moment. That's not so very easy in your society where you are bombarded with judgments. And so, we urge you to adopt an attitude of non-judgment, and an attitude of acceptance of whatever is at any moment, in any area of your life. And that attitude will help you to find the solutions which will lead to better moments.

We have information indicating that group mind, across your planet, is making considerable progress in regard to greater health, harmony, and freedom from disease in regard to a return of paradise on Earth. It may seem otherwise from your perspective, but the seeds of innocence have been planted and are growing among you. And that innocence leads to belief in equality, harmony, and the continuity of all life.

to promote enlightenment, longevity, freedom from disease, and widespread physical immortality.

They know the secrets of the universe. They know about materialization and *being* materialization and hence they think in terms of limitlessness, not in terms of limitation. As you open to their wisdom, and as you take more and more responsibility, each and every one, for the state of your own wellness, and for the state of the planet (not blaming it upon others, but recognizing that you create exactly what you experience), you begin to experience peace and harmony and wellness. And to be with you, others will need to be *in agreement* with your experience of peace, harmony and wellness, and so it may spread.

The prayer for help is being answered. We would urge you, in order to avoid thinking and judging, to make your lives but one continual prayer of praise to divinity and harmony. We would urge you to consider the very potent power of sound and of repeated prayer, like a mantra. Mantras work when they become all encompassing until the whole being resonates with the vibration of the mantra. Throughout time, many societies have had prayer beads as an integral part of dress among the holy ones so that they might focus their minds on a prayerful thought, repeated over and over within, to help them live in total harmony with All That Is.

You might do this same thing by saying, "All are One," over and over within you, or "I surrender," or "Ohm," or "Shanti, peace, peace, peace." The vibrations of repeated words of prayful intention resonate throughout the being, bringing harmony. These are recommendations for training the mind away from judgment into peace, but it may just do (in a planetary sense) what needs to be done.

We bless you, and we send you peace and light, as do all speaking to your mortal minds and coming from this particular realm of consciousness. We give you advice that if you would heal, you want to immortalize your minds and think the limitlessness, non-judgmental thoughts.

We would like to add that there are, what you might call, extraterrestrials among you, enlightened beings who are in bodies, helping

THE ULTIMATE CURE: MAKING THE TRANSITION TO SPIRIT

"You take this 'death' business so seriously when, in reality, it is simply a changing over from one consciousness to another."...John

Li Sung: Your religions often teach that passing into the next world is a thing of joy to be looked forward to. Yet, as we note, no one looks forward to it! It is very curious.

It is because the human mechanism is tuned, is programmed, to protect itself, to live as long as it may, to have an enriched life and to have much influence on others. And it views any curtailment of that life as an infringement on its rights! And so, when people may *say* they look forward to the glorious process of a journey to heaven, in fact they are very reluctant to give up their life on Earth. They are reluctant to give up their power, their love, their influence, and their feeling of being needed by many. Yet, it always happens so. We who have been in spirit a very long time still have acute memories of how it is.

When the spirit comes into our world, it leaves behind the body. It is called death, and the family mourns--or sometimes they are not so nice! We usually stay around for a time to see what people are saying at our funeral, and to hear their expressions of grief and of love and how they plan to take our wisdom into their hearts after our death. We find it sometimes amusing, sometimes deeply upsetting, but always there is a lesson for us.

Well, you might ask, "What advice can we give you? How should you react?" It is the same way that you should react when somebody brings you a present. You should have a certain joy that they have shown you respect and love, and there is anticipation in opening the wrapping to find out what is within. But regardless of the contents of a package, it is the love that has sent it that is the most important thing. And so it is, when the package of the body has been unwrapped, and the body goes into the ground or is burned to ashes, it is the love that has sent that person into being that is the important message.

All persons choose their life on Earth. They also choose their death. It is true, also, that there may be a number of such opportunities from which one may choose, but nonetheless, the manner of death, the time of death, are for many persons already chosen before they are born. It is like closing the chapter of a book. It is to be constructed through the character who has lived in the book. And so it is carefully planned, although to onlookers' eyes, death often appears to be an accident.

You will ultimately understand that birth and life and death are related as parts of expression of an entity's love for a family that has sent the entity into physical life in the first place. This power of love also closes the book. And while you may shed tears and family members may feel grief, there is still a poignant beauty attained in the expression of that life. If persons would regard their lives as more like a book or a painting or a beautiful object, they would begin to see how precious it is!

The process of death itself is very simple. There are thousands upon thousands of ways in which human life can be ended. Indeed, you human beings have shown great ingenuity in helping nature along. You have invented countless poisons and missiles and bombs and explosives--they go on and on and on, the ways in which human beings may be terminated. Therefore, one can conclude the human race has set its heart on something of a suicidal nature.

For many, the possibility of death leaves them frozen in fear. They deny the possibility of death, and fight it to the very last moment! And so, those who fight death, those who fear death, are in for a shock, for when they pass through transition they find that their thoughts beforehand are proved ridiculous, that their religious teachings have proved to be ineffective and, indeed, ignorant.

Many, when they pass into the realm of light, are looking for their punishment! They have had, what they regard, as a wicked life. They are looking for God to be seated on a throne, to judge them, or Saint Peter, to tell them which gate to enter! And so they are very confused when they enter and find nothing of the sort. Indeed, they must then progress through a number of realms into dimensions of light that are closer and closer to the All, to the Godhead.

John: The very first thing that you will see upon passing will be that which you *believe* you will see. If you have conjured up images of a tremendous hell for all the wrong you've done in the world, or the vice-versa of this, a wonderful heaven for all the good you have done, this is what shall occur first. Regardless, you are ever with your friends and loved ones.

More than likely it is that you will see a deified figure, or whatever you wish to call God. This being will come and seek you out. You will never be alone. No one is *ever* alone.

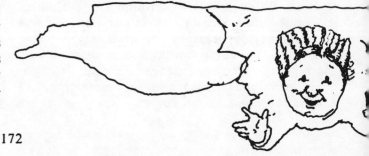

My friends, you take this "death" business so seriously because it is unknown and because it appears as though it is something to be feared. Death is something you should welcome, for, indeed, it is unavoidable. Since it is unavoidable, the next step is to accept it, and if you accept it, then it will be as it is. It is simply a changing over from one consciousness to another.

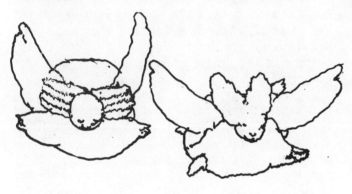

One other thing to say here also. God does not judge. The mind judges. When you pass on, *you* will judge yourself. That is what is meant by the term "judgment day." You don't have to wait until Armageddon.

My friends, realize what you truly are. What you are is beautiful. What you are is spirit in chemical clothing which you call flesh. You know what's funny about this flesh? It's composed of minerals, tissues, muscles, and is 80% water. Am I kidding? You should be flowing all over the floor. So what's the other 20%, what's the glue that holds it all together? The glue is you, the *real* you. And this will never die.

Li Sung: We would remind you that if you understand things from the heart, from the soul--rather than teachings of dogma of ancient religions who have strayed so far from the words of their founders--that you would find, in your own soul, that you can communicate much more clearly the ways of life and death and the ways of spiritual progression after death.

Now, we are not trying to urge upon you that you should dive into this delicious world prematurely, for there are certain *drawbacks* as well. In the physical, material world, you find many obstacles and challenges. Very few persons have charted their courses of life without the great swells and storms.

It is the overcoming of these storms that gives life such sweet meaning.

When you go across into our realm, there are no longer obstacles. You will find that there is only a choice, an understanding that you are capable of swiftly attaining a vibrational rate or a dimensional level to which you will be properly attuned.

We would make a comment here for the living who wish to understand how it is that persons whom they love--especially younger persons, with seemingly long and brilliant futures--can be struck down by death at such a promising age? How these persons can be wrenched from their bosoms? Some would say, "God is cruel!" They believe that it is the will of God.

But let us remind you that God does not create the details of persons' lives! It is each entity, itself, which fixes the point of departure. And so the question should be, "Why might that person have chosen to end their life so abruptly?"

Often that answer will be found in past lifetime experience. They have chosen to cut off their physical life before they have had a chance of failure. Or they may be planning another trip back rather quickly. And so, it is not up to human beings to judge God or even to judge a person who so dies, but rather to accept them, to be delighted that they have *chosen* to exist, to incarnate into their lives at all!

Each moment of life is a precious gift! And one should not put undue emphasis on the ending of that gift.

There are many bright eyes in your world which look into a future that brings promise and prosperity and abundance for many. Yet, many of those soldiers of the spirit will fall. However, the mass of them will go forward and will bring spiritual principles into your lives as you live. More and more souls of enlightened knowledge are coming into incarnation and will bring a transfusion of spiritual ideas into a greater and growing mass consciousness.

And so you might find--perhaps in 30 of your earth years--that there will become a very different attitude toward death. Death will be treated as it is celebrated by the Irish, who have a wake to celebrate the person! There will be celebration for life on a daily basis, and even more so at the time of death.

The grieving process is, in a sense, very selfish. The person who has made it into our world has no grief. There is poignancy that those who loved them are hurt. They may feel disappointed or they may feel anguish--but they feel no grief.

There is a promise--a promise in the soul, in the heart--that brings those who have left the body into light. They become as souls of light. We suggest that you understand this and incorporate, in your hearts, this soul of light. Incorporate, in your hearts, the memory and the living experience of how your friend, your relative, would have lived. You make a living memorial of that person by such actions. It is in such a noble way that, on the physical plane, the ideals and the plans of entities who have passed on continue to be pursued on the physical plane.

There is communication, sometimes, from our side to yours, but mostly only when you invite it. We will not interfere. We come only when asked. If you ask, if you open your heart to entities, to discarnates as you call them, then we can come and whisper in your ear, words of inspiration or words of love. We can stand beside you during your battles. But if you say, "Oh, to hell with them," we do not come. So it is, we hope, that you will say, "Oh, please come into my heart to show me that you are still a being who lives in *my* heart and influences for the good, many of those who are still here on Earth!"

No "body" lives forever, who would want to?

Soli: You cannot live forever. You *do not* wish to live forever. Your higher self has not the slightest interest in living forever within one physical body.

The higher self is already immortal, eternal, universal, and infinite. It hasn't the slightest desire to stay within one physical projection forever upon the earth plane. It decides when there is no further growth to be had within that particular physical vehicle.

The higher self decides when that physical vehicle should decay and end its present projection.

And no healer upon the earth plane will ever stop that happening if the higher self does not feel there is any future growth to be had.

It sometimes happens that if an individual has a strong communication (illness or terminal dis-ease) that it can be turned around. Why? Because the higher self perceives that the individual is learning something new, has made changes within his or her life, has found a way to affect acceptance of that change, acceptance of an understanding of the communication, and is making great changes within their life. Therefore the individual has the possibility of a whole new line of experience, as it were, within this dimension.

So the higher self says, "Well, fine. We will have many more different experiences now than those which we intended to have when we came here. We do not need to leave now. We do not need to leave and come back within another lifetime. The communication has been understood. The illness no longer needs to be there." And so you have, what might appear to be a miraculous cure.

Sometimes the higher self specifically chooses a lifetime that will be cut short by certain illness. Perhaps the individual has a karmic need to experience a particular physical imbalance, for they may have caused just such a physical imbalance for another in a previous lifetime or judged those who had that physical imbalance. You may have an individual who, in one lifetime, constantly judged and made fun of someone with a particular physical disability, and so has decided to have a lifetime where they experience that particular disability.

Once they have understood that, worked with it, and transcended it, then the higher self will decide, "Well, perhaps there is no point in staying here any longer. We can leave now. We've had the experience of that particular kind of disability. We will leave and choose a different lifetime."

And again, you will not stop that happening. You will not stop the higher self deciding to end that life. If you find a physical way of prolonging life, then the higher self will create what is known as an accident.

Exiting life at an early age

Soli: Any child who dies before the age of thirteen is a spirit who has completed all necessary lifetimes upon the earth plane. These children chose to return to the earth plane out of service to the parents who needed the experience of losing a child.

Before the age of thirteen, a child is not fully formed, and is still part of the parent's aura and vibration. After the age of thirteen, all the teaching has been done. The child is fully formed and becomes an adult.

Enid: Outside of a very terrible war experience, there are very few experiences in which people feel quite so helpless as when a child is terminally ill. They see something happening and are not able to do anything about it. They experience this yearning kind of loving, "I wish it were myself instead of this darling child." They feel this great wanting to succor and take care of the child. It elicits all kinds of feelings.

I wouldn't want, for a minute, to sound heartless because I understand the feelings that people have when these things are going on. When experiences are deep and rich, the

All people choose their illness, choose their paths. Many of them have forgotten why. They need to be reminded of their choices. They need to be helped to explore and find out why so they can come into their full selves, confront the illnesses, and learn how to be true warriors for themselves.

rewards are also rich. The more dire an experience is, the heavier it is, the greater the reward.

If you have a child with a great illness, realize that your child has agreed to play a certain part in the family, to help the family grow in their expression of love and compassion in a way they would never grow without the illness. It's almost as if the child is saying, "I'm doing this for you. I'm helping you in your growth and in your loving."

The being himself who has agreed to this kind of experience is exceedingly brave and must be treated as such. All beings are not willing to experience it. Just imagine what a brave individual a child is who is willing to have such a deep experience. This is one of the ways in which we measure our lives here, by the depth of our experiences, our willingness to experience them, and by the grace with which we come out of them.

Dong How Li: I don't think you can deprive children of their pain. That is part of being human and living. But you can share the wisdom of what we are presenting in this book and know that you plant a seed by doing this. Both the parent and child have chosen this. It is important that both the parent and the child begin to realize that they have done so.

If you are helping (as healer, counselor or friend) such people, part of your job is to remind them and to reconnect them to their original purpose, their original soul program and path. If you do that, then they can face their choice as heroes.

Prolonging life artificially

Li Sung: We feel that sometimes your science of medicine is misused, for the choice of death and life should be that of the entity involved, or, in certain cases, of the family or those persons emotionally close to the entity. For medicine to assume that the best good can only come from the prolongation of *every* life is naive. It is certainly not in accordance with God's law.

We are not taking any stand, you understand, for we feel this is your problem and you have to work it out. However, we would suggest that persons, writing their wills or such documents, would have a paragraph about long illness or comas. They would make provisions for such a time when their brain might be dead and their soul yearning to be free of the flesh, but unable to be released. They could determine that, at such time, they would be terminated. We believe it should be the right of each living person to determine such things. We also believe that medicine is getting a bit out of hand when it assumes that everyone wants the same thing.

For those temporarily left behind

Bartholomew: One difficulty with being a human being is that after taking on physical birth, the opening to other realities closes down. You find yourself crammed into a physical body, looking through physical eyes and perceiving the world through the separated awareness of the senses. You are told, from the first to the last day of your life, that all you really

The path to freedom, peace, and harmony lies in the realization that there is something which tells you that you are greater than your physical body.

are is a small person looking through eyes that see chaos. Most often this is how the human sees itself. The path to freedom, peace, and harmony lies in the realization that there is something which tells you that you are greater than the physical body.

The difficulty for those whose loved ones leave the earth plane is clear. Often they believe that the loved one was only a body. They believe themselves as well to be *only* a body. Their spiritual doorways are not opened wide enough to see or sense that the other is all right. The want to know how they can help the departed. They want to know what's happening on the other side of the veil. These are basic questions.

The answer is not simple. I do not know anyone who has not ached and suffered over the death of a loved one. Even the very wise and expanded pass through a time of mourning when a loved one on the physical plane leaves them. We suggest that you mourn boldly, and *claim* your mourning. The least helpful thing is the stoic answer that hides feelings behind a facade and says, "I don't hurt." That kind of pain and suffering turns and goes into the body.

What I am going to say next will not please many of you. But it is my truth, and I offer it for your consideration.

Hidden within the pain of the loss is the antidote to the pain!

By continuing to feel the pain, it one day gives up its treasure. There *will* come a moment when you awaken with the *feeling* that "God's in Its heaven and all is right--with me and with my loved one." And then peace descends. Something has shifted and you will feel better. The sharp pain of sorrow softens and there is more room for it to move around.

Another question that might arise in looking at the situation is, why, if you are masters of your own destiny, would you pick a life that has death in it? This is a very bold question. Part of the answer is that it was not meant for you to run about this earth plane century after century simply enjoying the earth experience.

What you have come here to understand is that you are beyond all those small, limited parameters of being just a body.

You have come to understand that you are vastly more wondrous, more powerful, alive, and compassionate than the human situation shows you to be.

So, death comes and it reminds you that you are more than death. Pain, suffering, illness, and loss all come to remind you there is some greater purpose here.

But it does not help to tell someone who is hurting that everything is happening for their own good. It is not something the heart wants to hear. The heart aches and has to be honored in its aching. And as time passes, the pain lessons and new perceptions and realizations begin to come.

So why did you program death into the Earth experience? The answer is, to keep reminding you that this life is not the All of everything. It is only a very small part of the whole. Compared to the capacity of the human psyche to feel and move into other states of consciousness, it is small.

The more you can remember that death is the experience of *all* mankind, the more you will shift your focus from personal agony and expand your awareness to a greater state of understanding. Man, suffering through his own life, has to know a certain amount of pain. Open the experience up to the greater understanding that this is part of mankind's *total* journey, and the process becomes easier. Know the process of grieving will come to an end.

The process of exiting the physical body

Kyros: Many people on your planet fear the exiting process which you term "death." In fact, many humans, once they become aware that this process exists, begin to fear. Usually, this begins in childhood when a pet or relative *dies*. Adults try to comfort the child by saying, "Tabby or Fido went to heaven," or "Grandma Pearl went to live with God." But because adults oftentimes mourn so and beat themselves up with guilt by saying such things as, "Oh, I wish I had been kinder to Grandma Pearl," or "I wish I had never kicked Fido or left Tabby out in the rain," children receive this as a statement of finality or that maybe *heaven* or *going to live with God* is not really such a positive thing.

Very small children, because they have recently entered from another dimension and still have some dim recollection of it, have less trouble with the process of death. As a child becomes more programmed by the outer adult world, this recollection becomes locked within his subconscious mind and he begins to perceive as the adults in his world do.

The problem of fear exists because most adults, as children, were programmed by other adults. They see death as something inevitable,

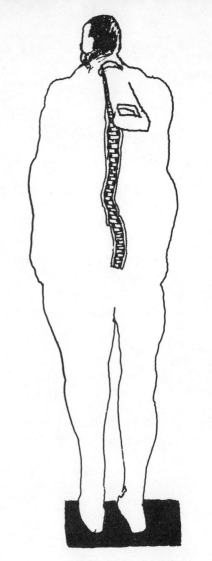

something mysterious, something unknown, something filled with pain, and oftentimes as *something final*. And many go through their lives with this hidden fear inside them. You cannot fully live and experience your physical journey if you fear death.

Many people who fear death do so because they do not understand, at a deep level, that they are *spirit, not form*. Your form (or body) is only a vehicle to carry you through your third dimensional journey. It is like a spacesuit or life-support system for physical life. If you

You cannot fully live and experience your physical journey if you fear death.

178

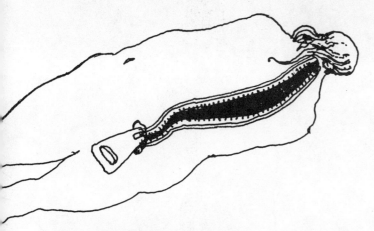

went to the moon, you'd have to wear a protective suit in order to do your work. When you returned to Earth or entered a simulated earth atmosphere, you'd take it off because you'd no longer have need of it. So it is with birth and death. You put on a form when you enter at birth and remove it when you leave at death. It's very important to understand that your vehicle is *not* you.

You are energy which cannot die or be destroyed, but only transformed into a different kind of energy.

You are spirit and spirit contains individual mind with all its levels of consciousness. This is eternal. You were created out of the God essence and God does not die.

Birth and death, in the physical realm, are basically the same process. At birth you enter *from* a higher dimension, and at death you enter *into* a higher dimension. You think of death as an exiting, but the only exiting which occurs is when the spirit exits the physical vehicle. Both birth and death are *processes of entering*.

Many do not fear the actual process of death as much as they fear *how* they will die, or *when* they will die, or the physical pain which sometimes occurs prior to the transcendent experience. Oftentimes, how you will die has been determined by your spirit prior to entering for your own learning, or to teach others, or for some karmic balancing.

There are no accidents, in spite of what you may believe. At higher levels, everything has a purpose and a reason and is designed for growth and unfoldment. *When* an entity dies has

to do with his mission. No one ever leaves his vehicle until his individual mission is completed.

I do not wish to sound insensitive about the fears human entities have concerning the process of death. I do understand your confusions and concerns. On the higher dimensions, we do not use the term "death." We see what you term as death as merely a *transition* from one dimension to another, from one level of awareness to another. You *chose* to enter your dimension to learn and to teach so that you might grow and unfold. When this is completed, you move on. Your great teacher, the Christ, told you about *many mansions* and showed you, through his resurrection, that death is an illusion. If only you would believe.

As for the pain and suffering that sometimes precede the moment of transcending, these are the illusions your mass consciousness has created. You have created pain and disease and brought them into manifestation, and it has become part of the mass belief system which continues with each generation.

You chose to create a world of duality for your growth and unfoldment.

All negative illusions which you perceive are based in fear. The Master Christ was always saying, "Fear not!" Why? Because He knew fear would bind and imprison you, and prevent you from experiencing a full and abundant life. He also knew that fear of anything is ego-based, and the ego's main function (as you know) is to maintain and protect the physical vehicle. The ego knows that once the Spirit is released from the vehicle, it no longer has either purpose or power.

If I were able, I would convince you that there is nothing to fear in the process of transcending. You will be released from fear when you come to the true awareness that the *real* you is *energy* and *Spirit*, not form. You will be released from fear when you reach the awareness that there is no such thing as death in terms of finality. Even form does not die, but merely transforms itself into something

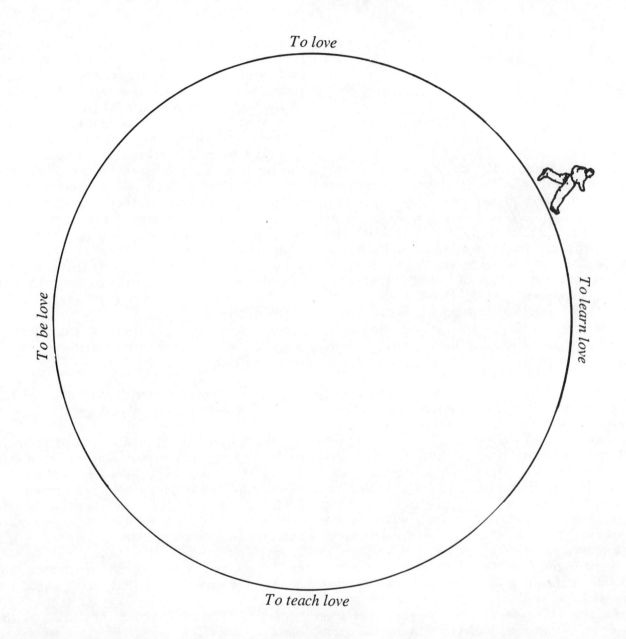

To love

To learn love

To be love

To teach love

new. Ashes and dust return to the Mother Earth and give birth to new life. Nothing dies. All is but transformed. You will be released from fear when you acknowledge who you really are, a Spirit of God, the God Essence. The physical walk is but a short journey in terms of time.

There is so much beauty ahead. And fear is released when you align for your own highest good and growth. Fear is released when you replace it with love, which is the healing and transforming energy of the Cosmos.

This is what your whole purpose is on the Full Circle Journey: *To love, to learn it, to teach it, and to be it.*

180

I would also like to add that sometimes humans fear death because of their attachments to the physical. It is human not to want to leave those people and things which you love and have found joy and pleasure in. Fear will leave if you will remember that those people you've loved and journeyed with are also spiritual beings traveling in physical vehicles and that when you move to another dimension, your spirits are even more connected and attuned to one another. You don't really leave them. As for attachments to physical things, they will no longer have meaning in a higher dimension. Physical illusions belong to the physical realm.

A large part of the learning on the physical plane should be to release from attachments to illusions, to the alignment to spiritual reality. Once you have made this transition, there should be no fear. Joy does not cease at the point of transcending, but increases beyond human comprehension.

So, if you fear death, I would say to begin working on your release from fear. Think of yourself as a caterpillar in a cocoon, preparing to take flight as a beautiful butterfly into a world of sunshine, or as a rosebud preparing to open into bloom. Though, because of current belief systems, you may not think of it as such, it is a *beautiful* and *joyful* experience and not one to fear.

What you can take with you

Li Sung: You take with you what you have sown, what you have reaped. The beauties of all the love that you have sown, and the lives of everyone you have touched--you take all that with you, for it is part of you eternally. You also take with you all the pain that you have sown in the lives of many, and you must endure a process in which you must forgive those who have pained you and forgive yourself for having brought that pain into other people's hearts.

There is a process of learning and forgiveness and spiritual progression in such activities. When persons say, "You can't take it with you," they usually mean you can't take the material wealth with you. After death, entering into the spiritual plane, you have all the abundance you could possibly need. You think and you create. The wonders of the universe are there for your making, for your enjoying.

Those things which you leave behind that are the most important are the legacies of love and respect, of creativity, of leadership, of understanding, of forgiveness, and of true human livin. These are what you leave in the hearts of the many. The more people your life has touched in the physical lifetime, the more bricks you have created in the eternal temple of life.

Question: When the spirit leaves the body, does it incarnate immediately?

Bartholomew: I will ask you to share my view of life for awhile, so you can get a sense of how I see things. Then you will understand my answer. I do not believe in a linear life--like walking down a road. My observation of what I call "deep self" is that you and this moment *together* are a point of amazing beauty and power that is being bombarded on all sides by events, both earthly and other worldly, both past and future, and these things occur outside of what you call "time-space". Together you form an incredibly deep, rich, and *empowered* tapestry. All parts of you are alive. A small part of you is the physical body, which you call your "self." But the tapestry, my friend, is much vaster.

This small part of you is playing out a little drama in one area of this vast tapestry. Then it does what you call "die". In truth, of course, there is no such thing. You ask if the spirit leaves the body? Yes, in actual fact it does, because it goes back the way it came. When you were born, your spirit came and locked into your body, and when you die, it unlocks and departs.

Does the spirit leave the physical body immediately at death? It depends. Sometimes it goes back and forth for awhile. You know how some people can't decide whether they want chocolate cake or vanilla ice cream? It's the same when they are dying. "Should I go? I don't know. Yes. No. Well, maybe." In this case, they don't decide all of a sudden. They go and they return. They do that until they feel comfortable. Then, finally they decide to leave and they are gone. I am trying to make light of death because *it is fun.* You have forgotten that, but in truth you have died thousands upon thousands of times and you are still here and still willing to die again--so it can't be too bad, can it?

The decision to die is made. The body is left and the spirit withdraws. The moment the spirit is no longer encapsulated (in a physical body) it expands. And let me assure you, this is a most

182

wonderful feeling. It is like the genie in the bottle. All of a sudden the top is off and the genie is out and fills the sky. This is what your spirit feels like when you die.

Now, depending on many things, eventually you begin to look around and sift through the events of your recent Earth experience. And with that new view, you may realize you didn't really *get it* that last lifetime. Because you see, what you came to the earth plane to "get" is the knowledge that you *are* Divine. You are the God-Self moving through many experiences, and this *separated world is an illusion.* If you haven't "gotten" that, you realize you can't go past a certain level of awareness until you do!

So you reach the point where you make your decision to again come into incarnation. You decide the time, the place, and the people who would be maximum, and you do it. It's as simple as that. It is simple because you are so vast and have access to the unlimited information you need to make those decisions. It is certainly a much more sophisticated and reliable process than the computers you work with. The variables are infinite and they are all in *your* computer. You simply make the decision based on the data that you have, then return.

Death is a wonderful experience. I tell you this, not so you will run out and do it, but so you will not be so afraid. *Death is a wonderful experience!* Please hear this. Think of that image of the genie getting out of the bottle. In expanded freedom, you are able to see from a *vaster* point of view.

It's rather like the flea that walks through the rug on your living room floor. If there are eighteen colors in the rug, can you imagine what the little flea is thinking as it goes from color to color? It has no conception of what it is passing through. But then, all of a sudden, the flea takes a mighty jump. Up in the air, it looks down and says, "Flowers! That's what all those colors were!" So it is with you. You jump up, out, and look down and say, "I've got it."

Many people have recorded this experience. Carl Jung has a wonderful description of it in his book, *Memories, Dreams, and Reflections.* When he felt himself dying, he experienced it

as a movement up. It was absolutely delightful. He was sitting in a cave, just like in the movies, and there was a wonderful wise man who began to talk with him. Then, all of a sudden, whoosh!

Carl Jung wasn't dying anymore. He was coming back down. And lo and behold, he saw his doctor moving up while he is moving down. He returned to his body, again feeling its pain, and he was definitely angry about it. The first day he put his feet back on the ground, his doctor died.

You worry about death and dying, but Jung loved it. He loved the expansion, the beauty, the wonder, and the experience of it. Please, do not *hasten* your time of dying. But just know, for yourself and for anyone else, that in the end it is a wonderful *release.* And from that expanded place, you will look around and understand what you see. So do not be afraid.

WORDS OF ENCOURAGEMENT

From Master Adalfo: Remember that it is not necessary to rely only on yourself to heal yourself, but that does not mean you could not add to the process. Healing is loving and loving is healing. So, if you are going to heal yourself, you must love yourself. And let there be *much* more of that.

From Soli: The subject of health and wellness is basically very simple. Human beings always want to make the simplest of things more complicated. Your intellects come in and say, "If it is simple, it's obviously wrong. There must be a more complicated answer."

Communicate with your higher self so it does not have to communicate with you through slower vibrations to get your attention while you're so busy with the illusions of the subconscious and the world. You have no need of disease. And yet, disease seems to be the natural state of being in the human body upon the earth plane.

We suggest that you maintain your physical body to the best of your ability. Would you put sugar into the petrol tank of your vehicle? And yet you put it into the physical vehicle that you live in. Ask your body what it needs for proper maintenance--what minerals, what vitamins, and what supplements.

Exercise the body. It was made to exercise. You chose to be within the physical body. Do not deny it now that you are here. Have fun with it. Play with it. Play with others. Be a totally physical being for that was your choice in coming here and that does not negate the spiritual.

Always remember that you are spirit, you are God. You are infinite, immortal, eternal, and universal. You are seeking to go beyond the limiting beliefs of the subconscious mind to understand the universality that you already are. It is as though you had moved into a foreign country and had lost your memory. You are striving to remember *who* you truly are. And as you become more understanding of your beliefs and of your subconscious mind, more of the higher energy, the beauty, and the power of the God force that you are will shine through you and throughout the world.

From Kyros: Please remember that, upon your planet, most entities *are greatly* in need of self-healing, so be gentle with yourself and others. Do not feel that you are alone in the process of self-healing, for there are many human and spiritual entities willing to help you in your progress toward wholeness. As individuals are healed, so also is the planet healed.

From Ting Lao: Appreciate waking up in the morning. Look at the flowers, at the trees. Hear the birds who keep on singing, no matter what.

From Dr. Peebles: I suggest that you make a practice of daily meditation with the white light, cleansing your entire body. When you are eating your foods, or drinking, bless all in light. Visualize your foods and liquids nourishing, not only your physical body, but your etheric body. Visualize that they are bringing you nutrition, balancing, and cleansing. Everything less is released, blessed into the ethers. *Life is delight, enjoy it.* Life was chosen by you. Fear not the experiences of life, for you are the light and you are the power. There is nothing imagined, or in the spirit world, that can harm you. Call upon your higher self and enjoy the challenges, for they are only that. You have free will. Manifest it. Go your way in peace and love and harmony. May the Gods and the kingdoms bless you.

From Li Sung: The first step to excellent health is to know what you are about. There must be a harmony with your soul self. When you are participating in life as your soul chose it, then your energies are high and your life form resonates with well-being. It is only in times of disharmony, when you find yourself doing something that your soul feels is not in your best interests, that there will be precipitated a time of disease.

If each person were to picture, in their mind, everyday, for a few moments, how they are in harmony with themselves, with their fellow men and women and with the universe, this sense of harmony would tend to make the body feel the same way.

And, if you are loving of yourself and loving of others, this too will promote the wonderful feelings that you may have of yourself. Sometimes the feelings of love are most central. Perhaps we should take them backwards and suggest that you find love in your life first and harmony second.

From Hilarion: Striving for personal growth is a labor of love without equal and rewarding beyond description. You take on form in matter simply to learn the wonderful lessons that life has to offer. Your spiritual friends who love you deeply are waiting patiently for an invitation from you to share your life with them. Your greatest blessing to humankind is as close as your prayers. Om Mani Padme Hum.

From Enid: Remember that your body isn't you. It's a *vehicle* for you. It's your own favorite child and you want to treat it that way. Please remember to always love yourselves, no matter what the invitation to do otherwise. And keep yourselves going ever strongly forward.

From Dong How Li: My friends, as we leave you, I hope that you now will have some idea about the importance of all of your being, and especially your heart, as a place of centering in the process of healing. What you are trying to heal is not only your hearts and your bodies and your minds, but indeed your very lives, your relationships to life and to others.

I ask you to sit, please, with your eyes closed and your palms up in a receptive mode. Allow any thoughts that you had to just keep moving. I ask the spirit within each of you, your own higher self, your own soul, to fill you with its blessing, with its love and its presence. May you have and carry, in all of your being, a sense of yourself, your fullness, and the health that you deserve and will have if you *allow* yourself to receive it. In the next few moments of quiet, please enjoy this fullness and this healing.

BIOGRAPHIES/RESOURCES

All contributing channels and spirit teachers who have contributed to this book offer a wide variety of services and related learning tools. Some may be reached through addresses given below. Others wish to be contacted c/o Spirit Speaks Inc., P. O. Box 84304, Los Angeles, CA 90073.

BARTHOLOMEW, as channeled by Mary-Margaret Moore, has been speaking from a vaster field of awareness for over ten years. Although "living" in New Mexico, Bartholomew conducts workshops throughout the country, as well as accompanying seekers to other power places around the world. Information on over 400 informal tapes of meetings may be obtained from Dr. John Aiken, 920 Annette St., Socorro, NM 87801. Two books, *I Come As a Brother* and *From the Heart of a Gentle Brother* are available. For information on the books or Bartholomew's scheduled lectures, travels, etc., write to High Mesa Press, P.O. Box 2267, Taos, NM 87571.

DR. PEEBLES, as channeled by Rev. William Rainen, was last incarnated in Scotland. After years of medical practice in England, he came to the United States to research the philosophy behind illness and accident. The founder of the Universal Life Alliance, William travels extensively, conducting seminars and lectures focused on the study and practice of psychic development, communication with all life, and the practice of spiritual interaction. Dr. Peebles is available for lectures, private or group sessions, and answers written questions with taped responses. Contact c/o Spirit Speaks Inc.

DONG HOW LI was a spiritual counselor and philosopher, last incarnated as a Tibetan monk in the Nepalese Himalayas of 600 BC. From 1982 through 1986, Master Li expressed himself through trance medium Allen Page. Upon completion of their work together, their respective evolutions proceeded independently. Allen presently offers private sessions and classes on facilitating personal growth in North Hollywood, California. He may be reached at (818) 766-6334 or by mail: P. O. Box 5681, Glendale, CA 91201.

EBBAN, as channeled by Randy Spickler, is an off-planet being currently involved with consciousness endeavors pertaining to Jupiter. Randy has been channeling since 1985. He is a composer and pianist, and has scored several films at the American Film Institute. Two albums from his Musical Meditation Series, *Dream Walk* and *Piano Space*, have been released on the Tarnum label. For a free brochure, write: Tarnum Records, 2049 Century Park East, Suite 5020, Los Angeles, CA 90067.

ENID, as channeled by Iris Belhayes, was last incarnated in the 1840's and speaks in an earthy manner with an Irish brogue. Iris and Enid have published a book, *Spirit Guides*, available through ACS Publications in San Diego, or your local bookstore. Iris teaches Yohti Healing techniques which she channeled from the beingness, Octo. Yohti dates back to ancient Tibet and has evolved through three other eras in which it was channeled. Contact c/o Spirit Speaks Inc.

HILARION, as channeled by Bob Helm, has been identified in Theosophical writings as one of the seven masters responsible for various phases of Earth's development. A near-death experience brought Bob into expanded awareness in 1979. He is involved with Peace the 21st, a world-wide thought-image of Peace on the 21st of every March, June, September, and December at 7:00 PM. Bob lives in a Canadian forest retreat and publishes New Open World, a spiritual bi-monthly newsletter. Contact c/o Spirit Speaks.

HILARION, pages 128 through 130, was channeled by Maurice B. Cooke. Working through Maurice, Hilarion serves as the source for a major series of books and other teaching material. For more information, or for the free catalogue, please write to Marcus Books, P.O. Box 327, Queensville, Ontario, Canada L0G 1R0.

JOHN, as channeled by Gerry Bowman, lived in Israel 2,000 years ago. In Los Angeles, John can be heard Sundays at midnight on KIEV Radio, 870 AM. John conducts seminars and workshops nationwide, and offers private sessions by phone and in person. John also has 21 audio cassettes, and two powerful videos taped live on Mt. Shasta. Contact John through the Freewill Foundation, 7210 Jordan Avenue, D-23, Canoga Park, CA 91303. (818) 791-9393.

KYROS, as channeled by Sandra Radhoff, has never been expressed in the physical. Sandra has been channeling for 17 years and is the publisher of the Universalian, a bi-monthly newsletter of channeled material dedicated to expanding conscious awareness. For further information, contact Sandra at P.O. Box 6243, Denver, CO 80206.

LI SUNG, as channeled by Alan Vaughan, lived 1200 years ago in Northern China. Alan is internationally known as an authority on mediumship. His how-to book on channeling will be published by Dodd, Mead. Being reissued are his books called *Dream Telepathy, Incredible Coincidence*, and *The Edge of Tomorrow (Revised)*. For information on readings and tapes, write c/o Spirit Speaks.

MASTER ADALFO, as channeled by Rev. Carol Simpson, was an Atlantean priest. Carol is an ordained Minister of Healing with a private practice in Northridge, CA. She is a staff and faculty member of the Healing Light Center Church in Glendale, CA. She offers private and group trance consultations, mediumship development classes, laying-on-of-hands healing, pastoral counseling, and non-denominational ceremonies. Carol may be reached at P.O. Box 7023, Northridge, CA 91327-7023. (818) 360-3786.

RAMTHA'S teachings, as channeled by J.Z. Knight, have been excerpted from the following publications of Sovereignty: *Ramtha: An Introduction* (copyright 1988), *Ramtha Intensive: Soulmates* (copyright 1987), and *Ramtha Intensive: Change, The Days to Come* (copyright 1987). These works may be purchased from your local bookstore or directly from Sovereignty. For information about books, audio, and video tapes presenting the teachings of Ramtha, write to Sovereignty, P.O. Box 909F, Eastsound, WA 98245 or call toll free, 1-800-654-1407.

ROBBYN AND HIS MERRYE BANDE, as channeled by Karla Spitzer, consist of off-world energies who have helped with social and political change via spiritual enlightenment. Some of the Bande have incarnated most recently in the Sherwood Forest of England. Karla, who describes herself as a cheerfully determined, ordinary mortal, reluctantly psychic since childhood, is a screenwriter now. She has recently completed a comedy script about life "on the other side" called *Conspiracy of Angels*. Robbyn and his Merrye Bande are available for consultations and respond to personal questions by mail. For more information, write to them c/o Spirit Speaks Inc.

SETH, as channeled through astrologer-hypnotist Jean Loomis, describes himself as a "group entity" whose various fragments have lived over 100 lifetimes. Seth and Jean have worked together since 1978 and are available for personal and phone readings, in workshops, and on audio and video cassette through The Aquarian Center, 116 Montowese St., Branford, CT 06405 (203) 481-6091.

SOLI & KAJUBA are channeled by Neville Rowe, a graduate engineer who has been involved in psychic development for over 15 years. Soli is an entity guiding the Earth's evolution and Kajuba speaks as a dolphin collective. Neville specializes in past-life regression (which empowers others to contact their own inner wisdom and guidance) and teaches consciousness-raising classes. He is available for private and group consultations in person or by phone. Tapes are available. Contact at 7985 Santa Monica Blvd., #109/223, West Hollywood, CA 90046. (213) 650-4973.

TING-LAO, as channeled by Kris Topaz, expresses his personality as an Oriental philosopher. Kris is a staff healer at the Healing Light Center Church in Glendale, CA, where she offers consultations with her spirit teacher on physical, emotional, mental, and spiritual levels. Kris lectures, performs pastoral services, and teaches mediumship development. Both she and Ting-Lao are bilingual in Spanish. Contact c/o Spirit Speaks.

ZOOSH, BEAR CLAW, & CLEAR LIGHT FROM THE ONE are channeled by Robert Shapiro. Zoosh, an energy personality from Alpha Centauri, introduces himself as, "I am as you perceive me to be." Clear Light from the One is a direct connection to the One Mind. Bear Claw, a past life of Robert's, was a Native American mystical man. Robert provides workshops, experiential classes, and private sessions. He allows energies to pass through him into others to activate them toward their purpose, their reason for living this life. His spirit teachers are available for consultation via the telephone. Contact c/o Spirit Speaks Inc.

Some of the material in the book has been excerpted from:

DISEASE: Your Choice, Issue #4 of *Spirit Speaks* magazine.

HEALING, Issue #8 of *Spirit Speaks* magazine.

AIDS: From Fear to Hope, published by New Age Publishing Company, P.O. Box 01-1549, Dept. M, Miami, FL 33101.

Companion Publications from Spirit Speaks

The helpful guidance and wisdom from *Healing the Whole Person, the Whole Planet* is also available in *SPIRIT SPEAKS* magazine. Published bi-monthly, and fully illustrated by Gary Lund, each 80-page issue focuses on a specific topic as addressed by many of the same spirit teachers who have contributed to this book. They share diverse points of view on such topics as health, relationships, money, sex, etc.

Reading *SPIRIT SPEAKS* will assist you in understanding more about yourself and how to create a life filled with joy, excitement, and success. Yes success! Despite occasional evidence to the contrary, life is meant to be fun and succcess-ful.

Start your library today by ordering a subscription.

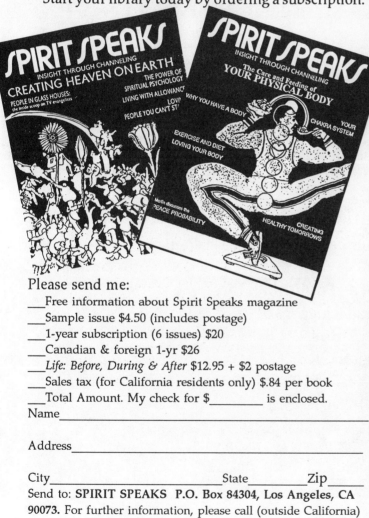

Please send me:

___Free information about Spirit Speaks magazine

___Sample issue $4.50 (includes postage)

___1-year subscription (6 issues) $20

___Canadian & foreign 1-yr $26

___*Life: Before, During & After* $12.95 + $2 postage

___Sales tax (for California residents only) $.84 per book

___Total Amount. My check for $_____ is enclosed.

Name_____

Address_____

City_____State_____Zip_____

Send to: **SPIRIT SPEAKS P.O. Box 84304, Los Angeles, CA 90073.** For further information, please call (outside California) 1-800-356-9104. California residents, call (213) 826-9197.

ALSO AVAILABLE, Volume II

20 spirit teachers share wisdom and techniques for playing and winning at the game of life. You'll learn about the process of creating your specific life experience, and why you have made certain choices. This book will help expand your understanding about many aspects of life, some of which you have not considered before. This knowledge will enable you to win the grandest prizes available on this planet: peace of mind, abundant health, bountiful friendships, lasting prosperity, and a zest for the living of every moment of life. 192 pages, fully illustrated, $12.95. Available at major bookstores. Or, you may order directly from SPIRIT SPEAKS.

AVAILABLE IN SPRING, 1989, volume III in this book series:

RELATIONSHIPS:
Mine, Yours, Ours, and Theirs

New from BEYOND WORDS

Children's Books, Coffee Table Gift Books, Self-Help Books, New Age Books, Psychology Books, Audio Tapes, Calendars . . .

Books of uncompromising standards and integrity.
Books that invite us to step beyond the limits of our experience
to discover what lies within, beyond words.

For a free catalog of our newest titles please contact:

Beyond Words Publishing, Inc.
Pumpkin Ridge Road
Route 3, Box 492 B
Hillsboro, OR 97123
503-647-5109
800-284-9673

A celebration of life through publishing.